[redacted]

Babatunde, Emmanuel D.

A critical study of Bini and
Yoruba value systems of

[redacted]

A CRITICAL STUDY OF BINI AND YORUBA VALUE SYSTEMS OF NIGERIA IN CHANGE

Culture, Religion, and the Self

Emmanuel D. Babatunde

The Edwin Mellen Press
Lewiston/Queenston/Lampeter

[redacted]

Library of Congress Cataloging-in-Publication Data

Babatunde, Emmanuel D.
A critical study of Bini and Yoruba value systems of Nigeria in change : culture, religion, and the self / Emmanuel D. Babatunde.
p. cm.
Includes bibliographical references and index.
ISBN 0-7734-9501-0
1. Bini (African people)--Social life and customs. 2. Yoruba (African people)--Social life and customs. 3. Values--Nigeria. 4. Bini (African people)--Psychology. 5. Yoruba (African people)--Psychology. I. Title.
DT515.45.B56B33 1992
305.896'3330669--dc20 92-12477
CIP

A CIP catalog record for this book
is available from the British Library.

The Edwin Mellen Press
Box 450
Lewiston, New York
USA 14092

The Edwin Mellen Press
Box 67
Queenston, Ontario
CANADA L0S 1L0

The Edwin Mellen Press, Ltd.
Lampeter, Dyfed, Wales
UNITED KINGDOM SA48 7DY

Printed in the United States of America

DEDICATION

In gratitude to God, this book is dedicated to two very special people in my life; the Late Augustine Akanbi Babatunde, *Ọmọ oloofínja, Ọmọ atìtí olú, Ọmọ Asorooko bi àlùsì*, my father and The Reverend George Hilary Ọmọwále Clements, my spiritual father, for the lessons in hardwork, faith and the ability for understanding that is uncommon. Ẹṣeun pupọ̀, Ẹyin ọkùnrin nla, ẹ̀nìyàn pàtàkì, akínkanjú ọ̀ṣìṣẹ́.

Part 2

TABLE OF CONTENTS SUMMARY

Chapter One

It is a brief introduction to who the Bini and the Yoruba are and what are their patterns of Ideal Relationship. As indices of Traditional Value exposition and value change, essays written by adult-student teachers, reflecting views on tradition and modernity are presented. Then comments on more public qualities and the changes in that field are discussed. It ends on the question, "So what in these societies is the traditional view of a 'proper' human being?"

Chapter Two

In order to provide an insight into the metaphysical beliefs and symbolic notions that generate, at the surface level of human interaction, the peculiar social expectations that qualify and certify persons as both "successful" and "good", a critical analysis of Bini and Yoruba religious belief systems is made with a view to showing their cognitive purpose and social significance.

Chapter Three

In this chapter, qualities of the "good" person are discussed, in terms of the traditional cultural expectations. Hardwork, truthfulness, kindness, dissembling or traditional diplomacy in private, and public relations are discussed in a tripartite paradigm of the two extremes and a middle way. These qualities serve as indices that allow for demonstrating, through comparison with the existing patterns of behaviour, the change in social expectations.

Chapter Four

This chapter explores the notions of human personality among the Bini and the Yoruba. It examines the different cultural distinctions between the physical and the non-physical aspects of human personality, showing the special meaning attached to specific areas of the human person.

Chapter Five

This is a case-study of the life of Papa David Adepoju Adeniyi an 81-year-old man whose life demonstrates the changes both in fortune and social values both during the period of colonialism and "Independence".

Chapter Six

Since the Bini and the Yoruba are strongly patrilineal (with some bilateral variations) most of the discussion on these qualities and on the aspects of the cultures are in terms of what constitutes a proper man. This chapter makes up for that imbalance between the sexes by devoting discussion to female roles as perceived by females. It is therefore written from a matrifocal point of view.

Chapter Seven

This chapter throws the changes in value transformation in perspective by showing the impact on contemporary practice of the Bini and the Yoruba. It explores the conflict arising out of the creation of the two publics, the kinship group and the national group. It emphasizes that so long as the demands of one are to be met at the expense of another, ethical and realistic problems will undermine the efforts towards a more integrated and stable society. It ends on the note of cultural comparison of the archetypal symbols of the good person among the major sociolinguistic groups that make up the bulk of the population of modern day Nigeria; the Yoruba, the Igbo, the Hausa and the Bini. Thus the value components of these representative linguistic and social symbols which stand for the "good person"; *Omoluwabi*, the owner of the *Ikenga*, *Mutumin Kirki*, *ovbunoma* respectively are compared. The similarities in the value components are suggested as constituting the basis for a natural process of social engineering exercise based on shared cultural values which can be mobilized as counteracting forces to combat fears against people of other groups. Such fears are transformed into a behavioral pattern of exclusion - tribalism - a formidable barrier to the evolution of the nation state into a stable entity.

Dr. Emmanuel Babatunde
Department of Sociology
University of Lagos
Akoka, Lagos, Nigeria

ABBREVIATIONS

A.A.	African Arts
Am. A.	American Anthropologist
A.C.	African currents
A.J.S.	American Journal of Sociology
A.N.A.M.	American Anthropological Association Memoirs
A.S.Q.J.	African Studies Quarterly Journal
C.U.P.	Cambridge University Press
I.U.P.	Ibadan University Press
J.A.H.	Journal of African History
J.A.S.	Journal of African Studies
J.A.S.O.	Journal of Anthropological Society of Oxford
J.B.S.S.	Journal of Business and Social Studies
J.D.S.	Journal of Development Studies
J.H.S.N.	Journal of Historical Society of Nigeria
N.J.E.S.S.	Nigerian Journal of Economic and Social Studies
O.U.P.	Oxford University Press
P.A.	Presence Africaine
R.A.L.	Research in African Literature
S.N.R.	Sudan Notes and Records
S.S.	Sudan Society
U.A.C.	United African Company

LIST OF PHOTOGRAPHS

FOREWORD

The time is long past when the anthropologist was, almost by definition, a stranger describing an alien culture he or she had come to know in the course of a necessarily limited fieldwork visit. Increasingly, anthorpologically-trained observers work "from the inside": describing what they have perhaps known all their lives, but in terms that will be understandable "outside"–both in the academic world, and (with luck) in wider society. The task of the "inside" anthropologist–the person closely involved in the society he is describing–is, I suggest different in kind from the traditional ethnography and interpretation: equally valuable, equally difficult, but with its own peculiar problems and rewards. He (or she) may well be their own best informant; but if the result is to be more than a mass of interesting but disorganized new material, a formidable task of interpretation must be faced.

In analyzing and comparing Yoruba and Bini notions of the human person, Dr. Babatunde has courageously tackled both approaches. As regards Yoruba culture, he is a participant member (albeit, as both a Christian minister and an anthropologist, a somewhat distanced one); when it comes to Bini culture, he is a stranger (albeit, as a member of a neighbouring culture, closer to what he is describing than a European or an American would be).

The result casts a totally new light on what used to be called "culture and personality" studies. Babatunde approaches both Yoruba and Bini cultural expectations, the notions of the "good" and "socially successful" person, initially through the practices and beliefs surrounding death in each of these societies – the process whereby the dead person may become an honoured ancestor, the conditions for reincarnation, the differences generated by different descent-group structures. Then, against this background, he considers the unseen world of gods and spirits.

Both Yoruba and Bini have a rich pantheon; that of the Yoruba has often been compared to the classical Greek array of deities. The comparison is illuminating as regards the sheer wealth of myths, the complex loves and wars of these unseen, powerful beings; but also, more subtly, in the very human foibles displayed by them. Jove nods; and for the Yoruba, the demiurge Obatala forms the child in the womb, the pure, gentle, patient artificer and "father of laughter", gets drunk so that his hand slips in his craft, producing malformed children who will then become his special devotees and priesthood. (But when Obatala is imprisoned for his transgression by the bloodthirsty war-god Ògún, women everywhere die in childbirth: there are worse things than bearing a defective child.) Gods, like human beings, ar imperfect: wisdom lies in acceptance, in moderation, in a golden mean which – as Babatunde points out – is similar to that advocated in Aristotelian ethics. The similarity is not accidental: both bodies of thought grew out of comparable mythical backgrounds.

Bini deities, as described by Babatunde, bear a certain family resemblance to those of the Yoruba. The figure of Ògún, the god of iron as well as war, is indeed common to both pantheons; but with interesting differences. The Bini Ògún, though fierce, is also creative: the metal he wields makes farms as well as war. But his junior in the divine genealogy to Olókun, god of wealth and the sea, the creator deity's eldest son (a role structurally crucial for Bini status transmission).

For the Bini, admired attitudes have a socially vertical dimension modelled on the ideal father-son relationship: kindness travels downwards from superior to inferior, dutiful respect upwards. Yoruba virtues, on the other hand, are organized around the twin poles of Obatala and Ògún: to the latter pertain the "hard" virtues of bravery and truth (which carry the danger of toppling over into violence), while Obatala is the patron of the peaceful virtues, and of that kindness which may, however, degenerate into imprudent folly. But in the last resort, as the story of Obatala's imprisonment has shown, it is the gentler virtues that prevail if community is to be maintained; which accounts for the central place accorded in this ethical system to prudent diplomacy: as in the French proverb, not all truths are good for telling.

Even in so carefully balanced a system, real life will offer puzzling conflicts between incompatible expectations. For both Bini and Yoruba, albeit in somewhat different ways, these are resolved by a subtle metaphysic involving separate components of the human personality and the ideas of a destiny individually chosen before birth. A Yoruba will pray, "May my inner self not frustrate the efforts of my outer self": the inner self, so close to the modern Western concept of the unconscious, being that part which has already "chosen" a destiny that may be at variance with both individual and social expectations. We are here no longer in the world of Aristotle, but in that of Freud. And wisdom, naturally, resides in awareness of the pre-natal choice; expert diviners are there to help "drag" this awareness (in Babatunde's vivid phrase) from the unconscious into the conscious mind.

The divination system used, Ifa, has been well describe elsewhere, and is familiar to Western scholarship. But Babatunde is illuminating on the subject of its patron divinity, Òrúnmìlà, who may be said to stand for divine omniscience, and his relationship both with his complementary deity Eshu (god of chance and change) and with his own consort, Iwa.

For not even Òrúnmìlà is a perfect model for human beings. In a fascinating chapter on women's roles – necessarily backgrounded in the ideology of these staunchly patrilineal societies – Babatunde, after duly discussing social expectations as bodied forth in marriage customs and their necessary transcendence through the politically safe reversals afforded by ritual, gives us another story of a fallible god: Òrúnmìlà himself is prone to bad temper, and makes life impossible for his wife Iwa (whose name means "good character"). Iwa leaves him to return to her father's house, not even when tricked into re-appearing by the Hermes-like Eshu will she live with Òrúnmìlà as his wife again. But she will remain with him as invisible helper and counsellor, to remind him of those traits of "good character", kindness, consideration, that the Yoruba see both as essentially feminine and as an indispensable complement even to omniscient wisdom.

All these ideas and values – Bini as much as Yoruba – assume a certain social and economic fabric of society: one in which both the descent group and the closer relationships that vest within it remain crucially important to the individual. It is this fabric that has broken down over the last 50 years: first, during the colonial and early post-colonial period (when, however, some skeleton of the fabric could be sustained by the familiar devise of using one's public role, at whatever cost, to meet the primary obligations of kinship); and then, far more devastatingly, during the recent years of oil boom and ethnic conflict.. But, as Babatunde shows by means of contemporary texts, Bini and Yoruba values are still alive in individual memory; moreover, ideas of what constitutes a good person, a successful human life, show a very considerable overlap – not only as between Yoruba and Bini, but also with Ibo and Hausa ideas on the same cluster of values. He expresses the hope that his comparative study of these values and ideas, limited to two of Nigeria's main ethnic cultures, might be extended to the others in such a way as to help his fellow-citizens, while each taking a pride in his or her own culture, to understand how large and solid is the common moral heritage that unites them. Alas, perception of a common moral and spiritual heritage, as between Catholics, Protestants and the Orthodox Christians, does not seem to have done much for either Northern Ireland or Yugoslavia; but they may yet order things better in Nigeria. If so, this new approach to "culture and personality studies", written by someone closely involved in what he describes, will have made a praiseworthy contribution. In any case, the book adds a great deal to our knowledge of two fascinatingly complex cultures, and it has been a privilege to write this foreword to introduce it to the general public.

Eva Gillies, B.Litt., M.A., D.Phil. (Oxon).

PREFACE

PROPOSAL ON THE MANUSCRIPT:

CULTURE, RELIGION AND THE SELF:

A CRITICAL STUDY OF BINI AND YORUBA VALUE SYSTEMS IN CHANGE

Background Information: This work is a revision of a doctoral thesis in Social Anthropology at Oxford University (1982). The revision has tried to study the impact of social change on values, using the cultural notions of human personality as the key to identifying changing expectations in both the Bini and Yoruba societies in modern day Nigeria. Precisely because human societies are made up of people who live in dynamic interaction with one another, change was an inherent factor to the scheme of things, even in traditional, non-industrialized societies. The force of social change intensified with contact with the West through the colonial, commercial and religious agents. The combined effort of these agents produced the local elite at "Independence". With particular reference to "Independent" Nigeria, the change prone-events with significant impact on the value system were the Nigerian civil war (1967-70) and the subsequent peak of resources from petroleum (1970-1980). The vast petroleum resources available during this peak period was christened "oil boom".

The civil war re-emphasized the use of force as a legitimate means of survival. It also sanctioned the business of killing as a respectable profession even when the evolved social values reiterate the sacredness of human life and harmonious existence. Civil war also moved the soldiers from the margin, the precincts to the center as the custodians of a new order; the functionaries of government. "Oil boom" shifted, for the majority of the people, attention from farming in cooperative groups mobilized either on the principle of kinship or age-grade associations. It replaced cooperation with negative and individualistic competition for what amount of the petroleum resources that central control allows to trickle down. In the unplanned but aggressive attempt to industrialize, made possible by the resources from the oil boom, the traditional standards of success whose indices were hardwork, fairness and accountability were thrown over-board. Traditional measurement of success specified that the end does not justify the means, the propriety of means was essential to the societal approval of enterprise as successful. Oil boom measurements established on the contrary the fact that the end justified the means. It did not matter how wealth was accumulated, over what period and through what means. Wealth justified itself and found approval in selective acts of largesse and flamboyance.

This situation created manifest problems in the social-action based areas of political stability, marital stability, accountability for the management of resources, and the principle of trust as the foundation of patterns of interaction in the society. The concept of the "successful" and the "good" person in the society became transformed. This work on *Culture, Religion and the Self: A critical Study of Bini and Yoruba Value Systems In Change*, studies the change and some of their consequences.

ACKNOWLEDGEMENTS

The constant encouragement of Dr. Godfrey Lienhardt, my mentor and former supervisor, Drs. Sally Chilver and Eva-Gilles, has spurred me on to work on this manuscript for publication. I am indebted to them. I am grateful to the MISSIO of Aachen, Germany, for the scholarship to study at Oxford and carry out a year long fieldwork research in Nigeria. I am also grateful to Archbishop Anthony Okogie for the opportunity. Revd. Paul Edwards, S.J., the former Master of Campion Hall, Oxford, read this manuscript in the thesis form and advised me on style. I am eternally grateful to him. The benefit of the refreshing friendship of Dr. Peter Lienhardt (of happy memory), Revds. Edward Yarnold, S.J., Ezekiel Gwembe, S.J.; Drs. Wambui Karanja-Diejomao and Martin Uhuomoibhi, was a constant source of creative stimulation.

During the fieldwork experience, I was granted the privilege, by Oba Samuel Akinsanya, the Odemo of Ishara, Oba Uku Akpolokpolo, Omo N'Oba Erediauwa, the Oba of Bini (Himself an Oxbridge product) and Oba Lamidi Adeyemi, the Alaafin of Ọ̀yọ́, of interviews with their revered personalities in their palaces as well as the permission to observe some of the rituals. I am grateful to Prince Edun Akenzua, to the Revd. Albert Fashina (now Bishop of Ijebu-Ode) and Revd. Emmanuel Yakubu for arranging the contact with the palaces.

During the period of revision and further fieldwork, I had stimulating discussions with senior colleagues at the University of Lagos on various aspects of this manuscript. Professor Ebun Clark, Director of the Cultural Center, University of Lagos, offered me the benefit of the Tuesday lunch-hour seminars to present paper and lead discussions on the Nigerian Ethical Revolution theme. Professors Moibi Amoda, Anthony Asiwaju and Dr. Taide Aina have been most kind in engaging me in critical discussions on the theme of value systems in change. I appreciate their clear thoughts, freely given.

Writing up the revised material proved impossible for three years in Nigeria and would have remained, perhaps so, but for the timely invitation to teach and do research, as a Visiting Professor, to the School of Social Work, University of Maryland. I am indebted to Professor Cyprian Rowe for establishing the contact, and to Deans Ralph Dolgoff, Howard Alstein and Jessie Harris and Associate Deans T. Vassil and Lily Gold for providing me with the conditions agreeable to productivity. Ms. Diane Harris typed the manuscript entirely, and sections, again and again without complaint. I am appreciative.

If the process that has led to the publication of this manuscript is understood in dialectical terms, some people have served, at various stages, as the thesis or the antithesis of the synthesis of publication. Some have even provided the two, now thesis, now antithesis. I am immensely grateful to them for without the thesis or the antithesis, there never would have been this manuscript, which if true to all the characteristics of a synthesis, must have within it the conflictual categories which provide the basis for the dialectical dynamics.

CHAPTER ONE

PART 1

INTRODUCTION

THE BINI AND THE YORUBA

The Bini, referred to as the Edo proper (Bradbury 1957; 13) live in the ancient Bini Kingdom[1] located in the rain-forest vegetation zone of southern Nigeria, between latitude 6° and 6° 31' north and longitudes 5° 10' east. This ancient kingdom, which became transformed into the Benin division of the defunct Western Region of Nigeria covers an area of some 4,000 square miles and had a population of 292,000 (1952 census figures). Renowned for their sophisticated artistic tradition (Beier 1957; Dark and Forman 1960; Fagg 1963; Ben Amos 1980) complex politically articulated organization (Bacon 1897; Cordwell 1952; Egharevba 1960; Bradbury 1964, 1967), the Bini had a prosperous commercial enterprise with Europe (Ryder 1977) that dated back to the end of the fifteenth century.

Although the name "Bini" refers to the kingdom itself, it is used also to refer to the capital city of the kingdom as well as the empire, that resulted from the military ventures of Ewuare, Ozolua, Esigie, Orhogbua and Ehengbuda, the Bini warrior kings of the fifteen and sixteenth centuries. When "Bini" refers to the capital of the kingdom, it concerns, in particular, the King and his complex palace administrative machinery and then, the subjects of the king divided into some fifty wards, each of which performs some special duty for the King. The chief ranks of the seven Uzama,[2] Oliha, Edohen, Ezomo, Ero, Eholo n'Ire, Oloton and Edaiken (about whom more will be observed later) together with the Bini town chiefs under Iyase referred to as Bini Prime Minister, come under the total polity of the capital. When Bini refers to the kingdom, it embraces not only the capital but also Bini villages, east and west of the capital all of which share a common language, a uniform culture, similar patterns of social organization and a strong sense of awe and reverence for the Ọba (king) of Benin which enables them to accept gladly the appellation "Ovbioba", the king's children. In historical times, the power of the King was effective within this polity and his word was law.

When "Bini" refers to the empire it embraces in addition to the capital and the kingdom, three other groups; the Esan of the defunct Ishan Division to the north-east, the Urhobo and the Isoko of the Niger Delta to the south and the subgroups referred to as the Northern Edo. These subgroups of Northern Edo include the Ivbiosakan in the southwestern area of the Kukuruku Division with a population of 93,000[3] and the Etsako (Afemai) of the defunct Kukuruku division with a population of 88,000. Other subgroups of Northern Edo are the North-west Edo (Akoko Edo) with a population of 46,000 and the Ineme who live in Etsako villages.[4]

Although the specific interest of this work is on the kingdom of Bini itself, it is relevant to note that the subgroups of the Bini Empire share some distinctive cultural features with the Bini kingdom. Cordwell (1952) and Bradbury (1957) summarize these common cultural traits in terms of descent and political organization. Firstly, the village constitutes the basic political organization. Secondly, each male member of the village belongs to one of three age-grade associations. Thirdly, the kinship and lineage organization shows a strong patrilineal bias as well as a preference for primogeniture. These common features, not withstanding, it is possible, on the bases of subtle variations in language and some cultural institutions, to distinguish between them and the people referred to as the Bini proper. It could be said with some justification that after the military conquests of the warrior kings of Bini, in the fifteenth and sixteenth centuries, the Bini King's authority was felt in different areas of the empire. Of the many practices manifesting the presence of the king in the periphery of the empire, three stand out. The first was the king's representative, *Onogie.* The second was the official appointed as the representative of a group of villages at the court. He:

> ....visited his villages once or twice in the year chiefly for the collection of tribute or to organize its collection, while for the rest of the year he resided at the "equaoba" the Court of the Oba (Simpson 1937:56).

The third practice enforced all hunters in the Bini areas of influence, who killed a leopard, to carry their game to the palace of the King of Bini. The Bini who divided the earth into the waters - ruled by Olokun also subdivided the land into the parts inhabited by human beings and the bush (forest). The king administered the villages, hamlets and the capital. The leopard controlled the forest. As a demonstration of the supremacy of the king of human beings over that of the forest, a leopard was sacrificed annually to the head of the king. The king alone had the right to kill leopards. Anyone who did was forced to make a journey of no return to the palace of the Ọba of Bini.[5]

The location of the Bini Kingdom in the rain forest vegetational zone determined the occupation of most Bini. Farming was, and still is, the major occupation of the majority of Bini. The Bini area, like most of Southern Nigeria, has two main seasons, the rainy season lasts from April to October while the dry season lasts from November to March. The copious amount of rainfall which gives the vegetational zone its nomenclature enables farming of food crops on a large scale. Yam was the most prized food crop and the bigger the size of a man's yam barn, the more successful he was considered in the community. Fishing is done in the delta areas of the kingdom. In addition to these occupations, the Bini have a tradition of artistic works. While special wards in the capital have a monopoly of the production of certain art forms, for example, bronze-casting, there is little guild control in the periphery with the result that many people were engaged in certain craft works that were restricted to a group in the capital. Hunting is generally practiced although the hunting of certain types of quarry such as elephant (Erin) and leopard (Atalakpa) are restricted, for purposes of commerce or ritual, to a few representatives of the Ọba.

The Yoruba of south-western Nigeria form one of the four major sociolinguistic groups of the modern day Nigeria. The other three are the Fulani, the Hausa and the Igbo. The subgroups of the Yoruba in Nigeria include the Awori, the Ijesha and Ọ̀yọ́, the Ife, the Egba, the Egbado, the Ketu, the Ijebu, the Ondo, the Ekiti, the Yagba and the Igbomina. Their populations was estimated in the 1952 census as between six to twelve millions. On account of such binding cultural factors as a generally intelligible language, common tradition of origin and basically similar political structures, all these subgroups have been described as belonging to a cultural category of their own, known since at least the early nineteenth century as the Yoruba (Koelle 1854:6). All the Yoruba have an emotional attachment to the story that Ile-Ife, the cradle of Yoruba civilization, as their common ancestral home (Idowu 1962, Asiwaju 1976:9). With the exception of Igbomina and Yagba, all the sub-groups formed the administrative area of the defunct Western Region of Nigeria. This area has been subdivided, in the last ten years, into four administrative states - Ogun, Ọ̀yọ́ Ondo, and Oshun.

Beside the Yoruba in Nigeria, the country with the largest concentration of them, other subgroups of Yoruba descent exist in other areas of the world as a result of various historical factors. The latter include the protracted Ọ̀yọ́-Dahomey wars which lasted from the last quarter of the seventeenth century to the last decade of the nineteenth century; the inter subgroup hostilities which originated from the political vacuum created by the demise of Ọ̀yọ́ military power (Ajayi and Smith, 1964); the Atlantic slave trade, which gave the neighboring coast the name of the Slave Coast; and the 1889 boundary settlement (Newbury 1961). As a result of these factors, there are a considerable number of Yoruba in the Republic of Benin (Dahomey), in Sierra Leone and in Brazil.[6] Among the Yoruba in Nigeria, a broad cultural unity is combined with local variety in detail such that in an area like social organization where one might expect close similarity, there is sometimes a surprising degree of variation. In myths of origin, there is a similarity. Although patriliny was alleged to be the common kinship and descent practice (Bascom 1969, Fadipe 1970, Schwab 1955, Lloyd 1955) controversy surrounds the claim that it prevails all over Yorubaland (Lloyd 1962; Eades 1980).

These slight modifications and diversities caution the researcher among the Yoruba to resist any temptation to generalize, except in certain very obvious areas of concurrence (Peel 1968; 19) such as views on human personality and characteristics. There is surprising uniformity in what goes into the evaluation of the person in the different Yoruba subgroups. This uniformity reinforces the approach of looking at the qualities of man and the characteristics associated with the successful person in Yoruba society. Perhaps this uniformity of opinion was strengthened by the military conquests of the Ọ̀yọ́ Yoruba kingdom.

At the beginning of the eighteenth century, the Ọ̀yọ́ kingdom had extended its military hegemony to most parts of Yorubaland and even beyond (Peel 1968:19; Smith 1969:71; Law 1977:50-53). By 1790 it had representatives in Abomey, the capital of the then slowly emerging Dahomey kingdom. The extensive military power of Ọ̀yọ́ often led some observers of, and researchers among, the Yoruba to the error of thinking that the whole of Yorubaland was formerly one vast kingdom under the leadership of the King (Alafin) of Ọ̀yọ́ (Morrel 1911:87). J. S. Johnson, the Ọ̀yọ́ Yoruba historian in his work *History of the Yoruba* (1921) supported the myth of a formerly united Yorubaland under the awesome direction of the Alafin of Ọ̀yọ́. Niven, writing in 1937 stated that with "Abiodun (a king of Ọ̀yọ́) came to an end the unity of the Yorubas. He was the last Alafin of an undivided country" (1937:70-71). In actual fact the Yoruba[7] sociolinguistic group was never under one single political control. Although the Yoruba were not under a vast kingdom of Ọ̀yọ́, Ọ̀yọ́ military conquests and the subsequent need to maintain some presence in the conquered areas ensured the spread of what would have been regarded as distinctly Ọ̀yọ́ Yoruba cultural traits (Atanda 1973).

The effect of human environment on human activity is exemplified by the nature of Yoruba occupation. Yorubaland like Biniland, has two major seasons, the rainy and the dry. Unlike the Bini area, with a homogeneous vegetation, vegetation in Yorubaland ranges from the swamp forest at the coast to rainforest, to dry forest and the savanna grasslands. The variations in vegetation affect the main occupations of the Yoruba in these zones. At the coast, little farming is combined with fishing. Inland, farming is the main occupation although the crops planted vary according to the amount of rainfall and the type of soil. The rainy season from April to October is the planting season and it demands intensive work of weeding on the farms. The Yoruba agricultural methods being unmechanized, such work as cleaning the ground for planting, making mounds, and weeding are done with rudimentary implements like hoes and cutlasses by farming groups.

As among the Bini, yam was the most prized product before the introduction of cash crops transformed farming from solely a pre-occupation with subsistence needs to a concentration on market economy. Thirty varieties of yam were recorded in Yorubaland (Bascom 1951:47-53). Other varieties of farm products the Yoruba have in common with the Bini include cassava (Manihot utilissima), cocoyam (Colocasia *esculenta*), oil palm (*Elaeis gaineensis*), maize (*Zea mays*), cow pea (*Vigna unguiculata*). Other food crops such as pap pawpaw (*Carica papaya*), banana (*Musa sapientum*), mango (*Magnifera indica*) and mushrooms (*Agarious campestis*) were originally not cultivated. Different kinds of pepper are grown.

The introduction of cash crops such as cocoa and cotton affected the Yoruba and Bini evaluation of human personality. Before the introduction of cash crops, rank and status especially among the Yoruba, were built on the surplus food products. This was a reasonable way of disposing of surpluses in the absence of means of storage and preservation. With the introduction of cash crops and money economy, food-crop surpluses no longer conferred status which was now measured in terms of the amount of liquid cash one could command and display. The successful man was no longer measured in terms of the huge barns of yam that he possessed but in terms of items introduced along with money economy. The conspicuous manifestations of money were in the possession of lorries for commercial transportation and the erection of buildings made of cement and roofed with corrugated iron sheets.

The dry season is given over to harvesting. Besides harvesting, some hunting is done as the dry grasses are fired. The abundance of game provides for feasting. Since there is little to be done on the farms, the gregarious and urban instincts of the Yoruba noted by Simpson (1937:6) have full scope. This is the season for important ritual dances such as the *Gẹ̀lẹ̀dẹ́* in Western Yorubaland and the Egúngún. The *Gẹ̀lẹ̀dẹ́* ritual masked dance is performed by men dressed as women in order to placate women who are said to be witches to induce them to employ their mystical powers for the service of society. The Egúngún festival expresses the return of the ancestors to their progeny.

Patterns of Ideal Relationship Among Bini and Yoruba Kinsmen

The ideal relationships between kinsmen rather than "the kinship system" in the abstract provide an insight into the ideas of personality which is the central concern of this work. In both societies, children are taught the "proper" way of relating to their elders and people of the same age group. Parents of children who behave in approved ways are looked upon as successful. Parents of children who misbehave are treated with disdain and they are gently told to "put their houses in order", an allusion to their failure as responsible parents.

Among the Bini, the father/son relationship, particularly the *Omokpia Odion*, "first son" is formal. Although the father, as the head of his family has considerable control over the activities of members of his family, his power is limited by the presence of *Odafen Noyanwa*, or *Edionwan*, that is the eldest member of the extended family. The power of the Edionwan within his family is considerable and an insight into it was provided in an observation about his position.

> He (Edionwan) must be obeyed and honored by all living in the compound, and in his turn is responsible for their protection and is answerable to the authorities for their good behavior. Any trouble in the compound can be reported to him by any member of the family. The *Odafen* has the power to settle minor palavers not worth the interference of an outside authority and he can punish by fines, or if the culprit is young, by flogging, whipping, binding or chaining according to the nature of the offence (Egharevba, 1964:13-14).

It is important to note that the Edionwan may be seen as the representative of two types of powers which form the basis for his own power. He represents central authority, His activities within the family group were seen as having ancestral approval and to disobey him was to disobey the ancestors. Thus, seniority as a principle of social ordering helped to maintain order within the Bini family group. Children in the same age-association played with and helped each other. They were under strict obligation to respect members of the next age association. Thus, while familiarity dominated the interpersonal relationship of members within an age association such as the *Iroghae*, (Youth) some formality and respect informed the relationship of those members within those of the *Ighele* (Adult) age association.

The *Ov'biye* "Mother's children" social group within the extended family, enjoyed the warmest relationship of closeness. The Bini were unequivocal about the love that ought to inform the relationship of full siblings. The Bini who said in their proverb, "the feeling of a brother or sister for another of the same mother cannot permit indifference" (*Ekhoe ovbiye igia zin*) also insisted that "there is no relationship like that between children of the same mother" (*A imien ere ovbiye*). The bond between children of the same mother was rated higher than that between parents and their children. Thus, the Bini adage stated that "One can get a child to bear but not a brother or sister" (*A imien Omo bie, a imien ovbiye bie*).

The relationship between half-siblings was less cordial and warm. The strains between *ivbierha* "father's children" were exercebated by primogeniture, which made the *ovbiye* group with the first son a more privileged social group within the extended family. The *ivbierha* had no choice but to pay respect and obeisance to the Omokpia Odion, the first son, who was their spiritual representative. The relationship was not close. The Bini stressed the distance and lack of warmth which characterized relationships between "father's children" when they say in one of their proverbs:

> A half brother or sister of the same father says "Let us wait till the day breaks" but one's brother or sister of the same mother says "your destination shall be my destination" (*Ovbierha we gie ede gbe; ovbiye we ehe no rhirhi se iren lelie se*).[8]

In the extended family, the relationship between wives was regulated by the principle of seniority in terms of the time of incorporation into the group. All wives were under the direction of the most senior wife *Okhuo dien*. She arbitrated in female affairs in the lineage. She was consulted by the *Edionwan* on matters which pertained to female affairs within the extended family group.

Among the Yoruba, deference for old age and the recognition of seniority are two important aspects of etiquette. A common Yoruba adage states that "no matter how rich a child is in beautiful clothes, he cannot have more used clothes than his parents" (*Kosi bi omode se le ni aso to ti yio ni akisa to obi re*).[9] Elders ought to be given respect on account of their age and the experience that it entails. Yoruba tradition stresses that the parents are the first teachers of their children, and the father especially, does not make light of this task, since any faults noticed in the child are blamed on the parents. The strong tendency of the father not to spare the rod and spoil the child is borne out in another proverb. "The child behaves foolishly and instead of reprimanding it, we pray that it may not die what kills more quickly than foolishness?" (*Omo kogbon aniki omaku, kini npa omo bi aigbon*). The father/child relationship is very cool and formal.

This image of the father as a keen disciplinarian, is complemented by that of the mother who is a refuge, a kind of "human shock-absorber". She is in the Yoruba image of parenthood, the "gentle side". The father is the right arm of firm discipline which scares the child. The mother's side represents that of gentleness which brings back the child and consoles it. The proverb "when we use the right hand to flog the child, we use the left hand to draw him back to ourselves" (*Ti aba fi owo otun na omo afi osin fa a mora*) makes the point clearly. The mother proves the reconciliatory medium, and hence again, the Yoruba child make no mistakes about whom among both parents is higher in his affection.

It is a common Yoruba saying that, "The mother is gold, the father is glass" (Iya ni wura, *Baba ni digi*). The symbolism of this saying brings out the valuation of the parents. The affection of the father for his child is fragile and is hard to come by (glass was both foreign and scarce to Yorubaland).

So, when the child has misbehaved, that affection is quickly broken. Mother-love is as durable and as fine as gold. She is the mainstay of the life of the child. The affection of the father-like a piece of glass, can, by the misbehavior of the child, be splintered never to be restored. He may disown the child, the mother will never do so. Referring to the unending love of the mother, the Yoruba say "No matter how terrible the mouth is, the owner will always lick it" (*Ti enu koba sunwon ẹlenu a ponla*). While the mother is most likely to be blamed for every fault in the child, she does not receive the credit for the child's good qualities. This point is made unequivocally in the adage "when the child is good it belongs to the father; if it is bad, it is the mother's (*Ti omo ba dara ti baba re, ti oba baje, ti iye re*). This saying clearly reflects the patrilineal ideology to some extent. The well behaved child is regarded as the normal child and naturally in the male-oriented Yoruba society, he belongs to the father. A poorly-behaved child was not normal and, therefore, belonged to the mother.

The relationship of the child and its grandparents is one of over-pampering. It is traditional that Yoruba grandparents bring up some of their grandchildren. The paradox of a disciplinarian tradition like that of the Yoruba, is that, while it insists on the discipline of the children, it allows them to enter into the care of their paternal grandparents, even though experiences have confirmed that grandparents do not have much corrective influence on their grandchildren. A Yoruba adage makes this point when it states that "The child of the elderly one is as spoiled as the left hand" (*Omo aru gbo baje bi owo osin*). Yet they will not hesitate to allow their children to be brought up by their grandmother.

The father's sister (FZ) and the mother's brother (MB) regard the children of their brothers and sisters as their own. The mother's brother (in the case of his sister's children) even though the rule of patriliny has established his sister's children in another patriclan, treats them with great affection, as they symbolize the fertility and the creative power of his own lineage. The brother always makes his sister's children welcome and cases abound of children who have broken off or have been expelled from their patrilineage, going off to settle with their mother's patriclan, *Iyèkan*.

Since seniority is one way of regulating social relations (Bascom 1942), relative age affects a lineage member's behavior. While he is expected to treat those members of his generation who are older than himself with respect, he treats any member of his parent's generation, who is his junior, as his inferior, the emphasis being placed on seniority rather than generational difference.

CHAPTER ONE

PART 2

VIEWS OF BINI AND YORUBA YOUTHS ON HUMAN PERSONALITY:

ESSAYS ON THE "IDEAL HUSBAND" AND THE "IDEAL WIFE"

To show the persistence of traditional expectations and the influence of new patterns of living on views about the characteristics of human personality five selected essays written by adult student-teachers in training on the topics of the "Ideal Husband" and the "Ideal Wife" are presented. They show how the new standards and patterns of living have caused a shift in the emphasis and a change in the qualities which are admired in the respectable, responsible person. Essays I and II present traditional views on the proper man. Essay III provides modern expectations on the "enlightened man who is a product of social change. Social change itself is conceived as "enlightenment" (*Ọ̀làjú*). Essays IV and V will provide traditional and modern views on the proper woman.

Essay I

Writer:	Miss Adewunmi A. Balogun
Age:	Twenty-one years
Place of Birth:	Oro, Igbomina

I would like to marry a proper, responsible man. Although there are many who pretend to be responsible and proper, in actual fact, nowadays, they are only few. My proper man must be one who has respect for elders and who can be relied upon.

I make a distinction between a proper man of earlier times and one today. This distinction touches upon the difference between what was considered "enlightenment" (*Ọ̀làjú*) then, and what is taken as enlightenment today. In earlier times, enlightenment was to live in peace with others. Then, wealth did not guarantee a wife. A man who eventually gets married must have proved himself to be respectful to his elders, law-abiding, sensible and responsible. It was only on account of this that he was given a wife.

Nowadays, young wealthy men think that their wealth confirms their maturity. They plunge into marriage. Such marriages break down due to problems caused within the family on account of maturity. These considerations aside, the present type of enlightenment (*Ọ̀làjú*) has introduced confusion into things related to marriage, and it is on the account of this confusion that I think that I must exercise care in choosing a marriage partner. I do not want a man because our society of today pronounces him a great man. All it costs to be great today is money. No one gives a thought to the way in which an individual becomes a rich man. People do not concern themselves as to whether a rich man has a good character. All they care about is to get some share of his money and then they will pronounce him a great man. I do not want such great men. I want a man of good character.

Some of my friends have, in discussions, expressed the view that their ideal husband must be a man of considerable means and that he must possess a big car with air-conditioning facilities (ọkọ ayọ́kẹ́lẹ́ ọlọ́yẹ́), a television set (*ẹ̀rọ amọ́hùn máworán wá*), a radiogram (*ẹ̀rọ afọrin mú `ilúdùn*) and a big refrigerator stocked with different types of drinks. The question I ask them is, "How does the possession of these luxury items guarantee marital happiness? Besides, how would men be able to acquire all these expensive items from their modest salaries and still be able to take care of their family needs. These demands on our men oblige them to take bribes and suppress their principles in order to appear wealthy in the society. I will not have any part to do with this. My own husband must be a man of principles who can provide for the basic needs of the family without compromising his good character. This is the man I want, not a "successful businessman" (A translation).

Essay II

Writer:	Miss Osaro Ikopnmwenhi
Age:	Twenty-three years
Place of Birth:	Benin City, Bendel State

In my place of birth, custom has set out the conditions that must be fulfilled before a man or a woman is looked upon as a responsible and properly matured person. I will set these conditions out, step by step, so that when I insist that I want my husband to be a mature person, you may understand all that is required of him. A mature person must have respect (*Uyi*) for elders and must be at the service of the community. He should not think it below him to perform such civic duties as clearing the village or ward of bushes and cleaning up its surroundings. He should help in the thatching of roofs and in giving assistance to the elderly. A mature person must also have the means to take care of his family.

I expect my ideal man to provide me with some comfort in the house. He ought to buy clothes for me and the children at regular intervals and feed us well without difficulty. In my place, the more wives a man has, the greater his prestige in the society. If my husband can stand up to the strain and provide for the needs of as many as seven wives and their children, I do not mind. However, I would prefer my own man to be my own man and be satisfied with me. Over and above these expectations, I hope that my own man has good parents because one needs understanding parents-in-law to make a marriage successful. If in addition to all these requirements he is able to own a television, a car and have some money, I will be happy. If not, we will manage on what we have.

Essay III

Writer:	Musili Alimi
Age:	Twenty-three and one half years
Place of Birth:	Sango-Ota

The world has changed and I think I would like to change as well. I know the pleasure of having what you want and the strains that come with being forced to accept what you do not want. I would like to be a business woman who is wealthy. On this account, only a man with my interests would be able to satisfy my expectations. I would, therefore like to marry a businessman who is of considerable means. I do not want to marry a farmer. Farmers are the poorest people in the area. They cannot provide for the needs of their children and their wives. Their children often look wretched. I do not want to marry a teacher either. His poor salary cannot afford him to meet his financial obligations. My businessman husband and I would co-operate to build a big beautiful house and buy air-conditioned cars and, above all, to travel to wherever we want.

My ideal husband would understand that I would not submit to the treatment and expectations of other women. He will not expect me to kneel down for every little boy that is his relative as is customary. He will not expect me to cook for him every time because he should realize that I have to look after my business. As for the number of children that I would like to have, I think that three will be fine with me. I have seen many women who give birth to many children only to become worn out like dried fish (*panla*). I disagree with this. My husband would understand my own needs too. After all, one only lives but once and one has to make the best of it (A translation).

Essay IV

Writer:	David Osarunwese
Age:	Twenty-seven years
Place of Birth:	Iyowe, near Benin

I would like to get married to a well-brought up girl. There are many things that go into the making of a girl considered to be well brought up. She must be one who is able to keep the compound clean, take care of the needs of the elderly people, look after her husband properly by providing him with meals at the appropriate time, washing his clothes and behaving respectfully towards him. My girl would not find it too much to kneel down to greet the elders in our compound. She would not be the type who complains everyday about everything. Above all, the girl of my dreams would be one who can bear as many children as possible, because in my place, a man will not be considered a mature and proper person if he has not got many children. In fact, if she has all these qualities but she is unable to bear children, she would not be looked upon as a mature woman. She would always be treated as a junior of other wives who have borne children. I do not like the modern woman of today. They lack respect for their elders and are not content to stay in their marital place. They move from one husband to another. My wife would be a woman from my village who has been trained in the art of pleasing her husband and who will stay with me.

Essay V

Writer:	Uyi Omorodion
Age:	Twenty-two and one half years
Place of Birth:	Benin, but lives in Lagos

My own ideal wife will be a woman who loves me and whom I love and trust. In my place of birth, arranged marriages are common. I do not want to submit to that kind of marriage because it means taking a woman that your parents give you. I love and respect my parents and I know that when they arranged marriages for their other children, they thought it was the best thing to do. Love is what matters in a marriage, not just obedience to parent's wishes. Judging by the amount of sorrow that exists in marriages of my own close relatives, I do not want to go through the same experience. My own wife would be a swinger sophisticated lady who can enjoy life. She must have a good job so as to be able to contribute to the smooth running of our family. Through her cooperation, we shall be able to provide for our children some of the things we did not have when we were growing up. We would have a television set, good car and a beautiful house. When one has all these things in one's house, one's wife will not be enticed outside and one's children will not feel deprived in the company of their mates. So, my ideal wife must be one who has a good qualification and can co-operate with me to have all these things which make life comfortable.

Indices of social change noticeable in changing expectations of the "proper" person from the traditional standards to the modern were confirmed in the statement of King of Ishara, Ọba Samuel Akinsanya (photo page 20a). He gained national reputation in Nigeria as the king who could not be corrupted by partisan politicians at "Independence". In 1965, in the heat of the manoeuvre for political supremacy in Western Nigeria between the Nigerian National Democratic Party and the Action Group, manoeuvre which ultimately culminated in the breakdown of law and order in 1966, Ọba Akinsanya rebuffed the advances of the members of the then dominant political party on the conditions that he as the father of all his subjects could not align himself to any political party. It was alleged that, subsequently, members of the dominant party tried to make life impossible for him since he did not capitulate as the other kings. One of the dominant allegations of persecuting him was said to be a reduction of his annual salary from 1440 to one penny (he informed me that particular information about salary was false, that a prominent politician of the day had derisively referred to him as a penniless king). Ọba Akinsanya who was born in 1898, enthroned in July 1941 and died in 1983 became, on this account, the national symbol of resistance against manipulating modern politicians.

Commenting on the changing expectations in the ways of doing things and measuring success, Ọba Akinsanya noted, and I quote at length:

> the manner in which the world [ways of doing things] has changed so rapidly is frightening. Before now, it was normal for parents to expect obedience from their children.

Nowadays, you dare not take it for granted. We were brought up on the importance of truthfulness and honesty and particularly, in the honour of not bending on matters of principle. But who cares about principle anymore? Before now, if a man bends his principles on account of financial gain, he loses his prestige and good name in society. Nowadays, your status improves the more you cheat and exploit people and the more money you have to keep people merry.

You talk about the fact that people claim that I try to stand on principles. Yes, I do, but there is a price for every stand and nowadays, the cost is even higher but the end result is peace within yourself. An Ọba has a greater responsibility to honesty and fairness. I am the father of my people and their peace is my well-being. Why then should I align myself to any one group? The position of kingship does not enrich one. It is a service to my people and a life that has pledged service to all but gives to a few is useless. I was by the standards of that time, a successful businessman in Lagos with considerable prospects for the future. Suddenly the town delegation called me to service. I knew what I was going into but I dare not disobey the wishes of the elders. I knew that unlike Lagos, the town was neither as modern nor did it offer the same opportunities. Yet I had to come because a man must stand up to challenges and conquer them. I was subsequently enthroned on the fifteenth of July 1941. I have since stood on the principles on which I was bred.

The position of the king is demanding financially, and although I was succeeding in business, I would not say that I was a rich king. No sooner did the Europeans hand over that the Nigerians who took over the reins of power made attempts to exploit the week financial situations of us, the kings. Some politicians dangled powerful salaried positions in front of us. Some us went for it but I knew then that such attractions were not for me. When you take sides with money against the truth today, you will have to stand up to shame tomorrow, because in the end, the truth will prevail. Some of my own people were incited against me. Even my palace was burnt. But in the end, the truth has prevailed.

Where is honesty today among our young men? They make money suddenly and dubiously (*owó òjijì ati owó àbùsí*). Most young men are contractors of one sort or another. As they come into money quickly so they spend it quickly. Yet we hear that our country Nigeria is very rich. We in this town find that claim difficult to believe because there is so much poverty. The distressing thing is that money has become the end of everything. People perjure themselves to make money. Brothers deceive brothers to make money. Children deceive parents to make money. When people know the dubious basis on which the wealth that a man displays is built, nobody cares

> except they get a share of it. Subsequently, they sing the praises of people who would have, in normal times (olden days when traditional values held), merited the sharpest condemnation. This is the new world in which we live. To be a respected man, therefore, you had to live up to good principles. To be a man today, ignore them (good principles) but have money. This is the new order of things" (translated from a recorded interview).

The Essays quoted and the abbreviated case study of Ọba Akinsanya transform the treatment of qualities and characteristics of the human from the merely abstract set of categories to a level where they become the practical principles which regulate the lives of the individuals. As people respond to important challenges in the course of their lives and as the young look forward to meeting others who possess the qualities they admire, an insight is provided into the extent to which the actions of a people are affected at different periods, by the values which have been imbued in them. But in a situation of change, the flux which implies that the old values no longer enjoy dominance as guides for the behaviors of people also ensures that the new values that are emerging have not taken hold. This creates a confusion in the young people in terms of which standards of measurement or preferred rules of behavior they should adhere to. Besides, the perception of social change itself can be confusing as it has both negative and positive aspects and as it takes different connotations at different periods.

Obe Samuel Akinsanya, Odemo of Ishara, in Ijebu Remo Division of Ogun State of Nigeria. Oba Akinsanya became, in the 1960's the national symbol of resistance against the manipulative and divisive tendencies of modern Nigerian politicians.

CHAPTER ONE

REFERENCES

1. Chief Jacob U. Egharevba, the Bini traditional historian and Prince Edun Akenzua, confirmed the view in interviews that the name "Bini" derived from the Yoruba words *Ilu Ibinu* which literally translates "the town of vexation". This was alleged to have been the manner in which the founder of the second Bini dynasty, Oranmiyan, characterized the hostile reaction of traditional Chiefs to him.

2. The first five of the seven Uzama were the original members of this exalted chiefly group. They are alleged by informants to be the descendants of the autochthonous chiefs, otherwise known as *ovbioto* "sons of the soil", who asked the Oba of Ife in Yorubaland to send a ruler to Benin, Oloton and Edaiken were, later, added to the Uzama.

3. These population figures are provided by the 1952 census. It recorded the population of Nigeria as 31,152,027. Although its figures were regarded as an understatement, they have served as the basis upon which further population projections were made for the purpose of economic planning. Subsequent Censuses have been alleged to be inflated for political purposes.

4. Bradbury, (Bradbury 1957:13) who referred to the subgroups within the Bini Empire as the Edo-speaking peoples' included the Itsekiri who speak a Yoruba dialect and claim descent from an early king of Bini. Their culture has been influenced strongly by Bini, Urhobo and the Ijaw of what is now The Bendel and Delta States of Nigeria.

5. Evidence pointing to the prevalence of this practice among Northern-Eastern Yoruba of Akure who came under the influence of the warrior kings of Bini include the change of the title of the king of Akure from Ajapada, for "killer of the leopard" (Udezi), called Deji in Yoruba (Akintoye 1969:542) and secondly the proverb originating from this area: Anyone who kills a leopard sends himself on a journey of no return to Bini" (*Eniti opaja ran arare lo silu Ọba Ado*).

6. In these places of the diaspora, the Yoruba have acquired different appellations. Those in French Dahomey are known as "Nago" (Dalzel 1973:20). In Cuba they are known as the "Lucumi" (derived from the common Yoruba greeting *Oloku mi* "my friend") (Bascom 1969). In Sierra Leone, the Yoruba are referred to as the Aku, possibly from the common prefix to most Yoruba greetings - *Eku*.

7. The word "Yoruba" was exclusively used to refer to the Ọ̀yọ́ Yoruba. Its terms was alleged to have been extended to cover all other subgroups, sharing the common cultural and linguistic traits by the missionaries in the nineteenth century (Koelle 1854:6).

8. This proverb shows that while a half-sibling delays acting on behalf of his half-sibling on the point of death, the sick-man's full sibling decides on prompt action that ignores all hazards.

9. Most Yoruba in the rural traditional societies have a habit of getting new clothes to commemorate important occasions at which time they dance around the town in groups of identically clad members. These occasions are usually not more than three in the year. Thus, numbers of clothes represent seniority.

The late King, Oba Akenzua (dressed in white) posed with a tame leopard. The Bini divide the earth into the forest ruled by the leopard and the villages and towns ruled by the Oba. Each year the king ritually kills a leopard as a symbol of his supremacy over all the earth.

CHAPTER TWO

PART 1

BINI AND YORUBA METAPHYSICAL BELIEFS

Bini and Yoruba belief systems are complicated (Bascom 1969:103; Ben-Amos 1980:11; Cordwell 1952:56-7) as attempts to analyze them have shown (Ellis 1894; Frobenius 1913; Johnson 1931; Farrow 1926; Idowu 1962; Morton-Williams 1960; Soyinka 1976; Bradbury 1957; Hamlyn 1960). It is this complexity that the Bini convey in their proverb, the closer one gets to Benin, the farther away it is.[1] The essential tenets of both world-views have become institutionalized into customary systems in which the new generations are socialized to conform to each society's idea of the person.

A treatment of both the Bini and Yoruba ideas about the world and the metaphysical beings that sustain it is vital to an understanding of the way in which these ideas influence expectations of the self in society. An analysis of the perception of self (the human) in societies that are religiously oriented ought to begin with a treatment of the people's ideas of God. Such traditional views or theologies will show the extent to which the relationship assumed between man and the metaphysical beings, influences that between men in the society. Professor Swanston, a theologian, has drawn attention to the link and relevance of such views to anthropology when he noted that:

> ...theology is nothing if it is not anthropology. He who undergoes the discipline of theology must be content to talk not of the divine but what human beings have said about their

> experience of the divine. We have to pay deliberate attention to the stutterings of Moses, the fantasies of Apuleius, the grandiloquence of the fourth Evangelist, the schizophrenics of the Shaman (1981:1).

This preoccupation with the world-view would go beyond a mere presentation of Yoruba and Bini views on their spiritual universe to show that these conceptions of powers represent the peoples' reaction to their environment and the need to order and explain phenomena by classifying known realities and apportioning them to unknown powers. It will involve the application of Dr. Lienhardt's approach to the Dinka world. As he noted:

> Dinka Powers be representations, what is it that they represent? I have described them for the most part as the Dinka themselves understand and account for them, not now as ultra-human beings which might form the subject matter of a Dinka theology, but as representations (or as I prefer to call them, images) evoked by certain configurations of experience contingent upon the Dinkas' reaction to their particular physical and social environment, of which a foreigner can also have direct knowledge (1961:147).

The Bini and Yoruba spiritual universes are populated by beings whose images appear to be closely linked to the human conditions which gave rise to them. The Yoruba and Bini to a large extent predicated the effectiveness of an *eboh* or *orisa* (divinity) respectively, of the effectiveness of its devotees. The Yoruba give their king (Ọba) the title of the companion of the gods (*èkéjì òrìsà*). Yet they point out that like the divinity's, the Ọba's presence is ubiquitous because of the efficiency of his subjects (informants). Thus, they say the ear of the king hears both in the farm and in the town; it is human beings that make it possible (*etí ọba ní'lé etí ọba L'óko èniyàn ni nję bẹ́ẹ̀*). They also manifest their willingness to abandon a divinity that is not proving its effectiveness when they say in their proverb, such and such a divinity, if you will not improve my condition, leave me as you met me (*òrìsà bi o o lè gbè mi, ṣe mí bí o ṣe bá mi*).

The Bini, whose cultural institutions show a more rigid adherence to traditional mores with their mystical sanctions, are also unequivocal in pointing out the importance of the effectiveness of an *eboh* to his survival as an effective spiritual medium. Thus, a soothsayer - a medium between the people and the divinity - who consistently defies the will of the people, will lose his reputation. This attitude is insitutionalized in such Bini proverbs as A soothsayer who refuses the people will not display his divining instruments' (*Obo no semwen evbo iwa iha*); and, when a god is too mild, grass will cover its face' (*Ebo gha fu gbe irunmwun ghi son ere aro*). Such statements show that the relationships of men to the spiritual beings is not characterized by a feeling of helpless submission. This attitude is different from that described to characterize the relationship between living human beings and the gods by Shakespeare, who noted: "As, flies to wanton boys, are we to the gods: they kill us for their sport" (*King Lear*).

The world-views of these two peoples are approached through the idea, shared by both, of reincarnation. This is the link between the world of the dead and the spirits, and that of living human beings. Similarities between Yoruba and Bini beliefs and institutions are so close that the two peoples, in these matters, may appear to be identical (Talbot 1926; Cordwell 1952). Field-work data does not support this claim (Bradbury 1964:147-59) as the cultural system of each group is unique and traits and institutions which occur in each have their functions determined in relation to the other institutions in the cultural whole of which it is a part. Thus, Cordwell's observation that Benin shares with Yoruba the main focal aspects of religion and the hierarchical structuring of the supernatural and society' (1952:55) ought to be qualified. The similar traits in both structures develop along different lines. Although they appear identical, in fact the position of the Yoruba King (*Ọba*) and the meaning attached to it and to the ideas about reincarnation, differ considerably from those of the Bini to reinforce the notion that teach cultural trait ought to be seen as unique to the cultural complex in which it operates.

Cosmologies Compared

Yoruba cosmology has been accurately outlined in Morton-Williams' work (1964). The Yoruba universe is made up of three domains the heavens or the sky' (*Ọ̀run*), the visible and tangible world' (*Aiyé*) and, what is in the earth itself (*Ilẹ*). Each domain supports a mode of being which is peculiar to it, but in which those who have died properly (as I later describe) will participate. *Ọ̀run* is the abode of the Supreme Being, *Olódùmarè*, the divinities who are assimilated to him in thought, but to whom their devotees often attribute independent existence.

In other words, Evans-Pritchard's observation that the divinities are refractions of the numinosity of the God-Head (1940:316) is useful here if understood in line with Max Muller's evolutionary psychological intellectualist approach to the origin of religions and the making of the divinities. Although the divinities ought to be seen as traditional theology depicted them to be - refractions of the Supreme Being - the enthusiasm of their Bini and Yoruba devotees as well as the promptings of priestcraft have led to the tranformation of the *Nomina* into the *numina*.

These divinities are graded into major and minor divinities. An extract from a verse of the corpus of Yoruba divination, *Ifá*, given by Babaláwo Ifatogun, an informant, provides an insight to the uncertainty that surrounds their exact number:

> The Head should be accorded his due respect
> This is the oracle's charge to the one thousand
> and seven hundred divinities
> Who were taking horses as annual tributes to
> the Supreme Being.
> *Olori la fori fun*
> *L'o d'ifa fun erunlójò òrìsà*
> *Nigbati won nko ẹṣin ọdun re ọ̀dọ̀ Olódùmarè*

The one thousand and seven hundred gods or divinities enact the main outline of the protocol between a king and his vassals by taking annual tribute of horses to the Supreme Being, *Olódùmarè*. The ancestors (*Baba ọrun; Ara ọrun*) are also in the sky or heavenly abode.

The abode of the living, *Ile-aiye*, is under the authority of the king (*Ọba*) in council with his chiefs. It has been said that the ordering of this domain and the manner of exerting control on the subjects in society is a direct reflection of the way in which *Ọlọ́run* is understood to rule over divinities in the spirit world (*Ọ̀run*) (Morton-Williams 1964:245; Idowu 1962:49; Babayemi 1979:2; Eades 1980:119). W. Abimbola, who claimed that Yoruba cosmology provided the framework on which Yoruba political organization is based, made a series of equations between the roles of the gods' in the spirit-world and those of functionaries in Yoruba society. He equated the roles of the Supreme Being (*Ọlọ́run*) and the King (Ọba); *balẹ*, village heads and gods' (*òrìṣà*); the dreaded messengers of the Supreme Being (*Alájogun*) and those of the King (*Ìlàrí*) (1972:73-83).

The suggestion made in this work is that rather than see the cosmology as providing the framework on which the principles of Yoruba political organization were built, the Yoruba built their cosmology from their ideas of political organization. The projection of the origin of the universe and the mundane plan of social organization onto a celestial or metaphysical source accords it sanctity and credibility in the eyes of a religious-minded people and supports its customary rules and expectations with the buttress of divine sanction.

The earth (*Ilẹ̀*) is said to be the domain of the earth goddess, variously called the owner of the earth' (*onílẹ̀*), the great mother (*Iyá-nla*), who is taken in some areas of Yorubaland to be the co-eval counterpart of the Deity (*Olódùmarè*) (Verger 1976; Odugbesan 1966:99; Harper 1970:67). The main outline of Yoruba myths of creation specify that the earth came into being when *Obàtálá*, the Yoruba arch-divinity, or *Oduduwa*, the alleged progenitor of the Yoruba (depending on the variants) carried out the instruction of the Supreme Being. An early version of the myth of creation states that the earth goddess was the wife of *Obàtálá* and not *Olódùmaré* (Baudin 1885:63). But those I questioned about the idea that *Olódùmaré* had a co-eval counterpart were unanimous in stating, independently of one another, that the Supreme Being has no equal. An informant, Sanni Ojẹdeji, the Baale of Tewure,[2] agreed that there is no equal to *Ọlọ́run*, but that the farming Yoruba population, who depend entirely on the proceeds of the earth for survival, would normally have thought of the earth as having an importance which brings it closer to that of the Supreme Being.

This explanation was revealing because, unlike the Yoruba King, (*Ọba*), who is dependent on the labour and gifts of his subjects, a dependence sanctioned by his pedigree and the authority of ancestors, his subjects - the farmers - depend on the earth for survival. Thus, while the king would hold as important the things deriving from his ancestors who represent the will of the Supreme Being, the farmers on the other hand would put emphasis on the importance of the earth, the source of their sustenance and raise it to the level of counterpart to the Deity.

The earth-goddess has different cults in different areas of Yorubaland. In the Ọ̀yọ̀, Ife and Egba areas, the cult of Ogbóni is predominant. As Morton-Williams wrote the Ogbóni, "the cult association for Earth, which had judicial and political functions, sanctioned bloodshed, for to shed human blood on the ground was a grave sin against the Earth" (1964:252). In Abeokuta where the Ogbóni cult association reached perhaps its highest level of development as an instrument of political control, it appeared to have shed part of its natural functions in connection with the earth goddess and taken up the political role of the *Ọ̀yọ̀-Mesi* and the Ogbóni of Ọ̀yọ̀. This particular role is described by S. Biobaku in relation to the Ogbóni among the Yoruba Egba:

> ...the Ogbóni constituted at once the civic court, the town council and the electoral college for the selection of the Oba from candidates nominated by the ruling houses. By keeping their proceedings secret and binding their members by blood oaths, the Ogbóni ensured solidarity for their decisions. They used the *Oro*, an ancestral cult organization, whose symbol is the Bullroarer, to proclaim curfews when riots were expected, in apprehending criminals and to execute the guilty ones in secret recesses of the *Oro* grove. In principle, the Ogbóni stood between the Ọba and his subjects preventing the one from becoming despotic and ensuring the proper subordination of the other (1957:6).[3]

In the Ketu Yoruba area, with the possible exception of Imèko,[4] of the ancient Kingdom of Ketu, the Ogbóni cult is conspicuously absent. In its place, the Ketu have the *Gẹ̀lẹ̀dẹ́* cult of the Earth mother *Iya-nla*)[5] which performs the *Gẹ̀lẹ̀dẹ́* ritual masked dance to propitiate the earth-goddess and persuade her devotees, women associated with mystical powers, to employ these powers in the service of the community. Members who look for the blessings of fertility for their wives and farms would enrol as members. *Ilè* is also the gateway to the spirit world. The tripartite Yoruba cosmological division of the heavens (*Ọ̀run*), the abode of the living (*Ile- aye*) and the earth (*Ilẹ*) can be reduced to a two-fold division, the Ọ̀run/aye polarity. The *Ọ̀run* stands for all it covers in the tripartite division. The *aye* embraces the physical earth with its divisions of the abode of the living built on the earth and its outlying environments, including the rivers.

Variants of Yoruba myths of creation occur which explain the Yoruba idea of how the physical world came into being. The verse of the authoritative voice of *Iwòrì Meji*, one of the sixteen principal texts (*Odù*) of Ifá divination collected in Abeokuta records the story:

> Matters that ought to be resolved in the morning
> Ought not to be left until the evening.
> The oracle was made on behalf of kòkòniyèlè
> Who will help us to repair the house,
> What will help us to repair the ground?
> kòkòniyèlè
> *Ifá* will help us to repair the ground.
> When the people first came into the abode of the living
> They could not find any place to live
> Because the place was covered with water.
> Then Òrúnmìlà (the divinity of divination)
>   consulted Olódùmaré.
> Olódùmaré gave Òrúnmìlà four pigeons and one cock
> It was (4 pigeons and 1 cock) that spread the
>   sand in the basket.
> That Olódùmaré used to let down sand from the heavens
> That the earth became a mixture of forest and grassland.
> It was the Ifá divination verse of Iwori Meji that
>   was divined for them.
> That is why hens and cocks repeat when they scatter the earth
>   to find food;
> wòrì yèlè
> wòrì yèlè (onomatopoeic words for the noise made by hens)[6]

The three domains of the Yoruba cosmology are not however utterly distinct or mutually exclusive as Morton-Williams suggests.[7] There are rituals and occasions when the physical earth, *ayé*, taken to embrace the abode of the living and the earth of the earth goddess, feature together in contradistinction to the spiritual realm. At other times, the distinction between the spiritual world *ọ̀run*, and the earth, *ilẹ*, disappears as both merge into one realm, as it were, from which spirits of the dead are summoned. As a case in point the Egun which celebrates the visit of the ancestors from the spirit world to their progeny, are summoned from the earth. *Ọ̀run* the spiritual world then includes the sky, but also beyond the sky and below the earth (Olajubu and Ojo 1977:253-5). The Yoruba idea of reincarnation provides the ideological base for the dynamic interdependence of the three realms.

The Bini world-view has two divisions; the spirit world (*erinmwin*) and the abode of the living (*agbọn*). The former is the invisible, non-physical world of the Supreme Being, the divinities and ancestors. Also in the *erinmwin* are other mystical powers like hero-deities associated with natural phenomena and spiritual elements who have never been incarnated. In this realm *Osanobua* is the supreme authority and the creator of the tangible visible world of the *agbọn*. Rivers serve as the passage linking these two worlds and the Bini mortuary rites specifically enshrine this in practice by positioning the corpse in the grave in such a way that the feet point toward Ughoton, the old port of Benin, where the dead are said to embark on their journey to the celestial realm in canoes.[8] The significance of the river as a demarcating factor in cosmology is enhanced and transformed into geographical categories by the fact that the major boundaries are set with rivers (Bradbury 1957:18).

The visible world, *agbon*, is subdivided into the land and the waters (embracing the rivers which flow into the sea). *Olókun*, the first son of the Creator, *Osanobua*, is the supreme authority over the waters. The *Ọba* is effectively the divinity of the land as the abode of the living. *Ogiuwu* is worshipped as the king of the earth. By earth is meant the place of burial for the deceased ancestors. His messenger is *Ofoe*, death.

The Bini explain their idea of the creation of their world in a story whose variants agree at least in their major outline.[9] It was *Osanobua*, the Supreme Being's initiative to create the earth. He assembled his children, three sons in all, and commanded them to take only one item for the journey to the watery abode. The Ọba of Benin was the youngest of these three sons. The other two were Olókun, his first son, and the king of the Europeans.[10] The elder brothers chose wealth and craft implements respectively. While pondering on what of value was left for him, the youngest son was advised to his consternation by a primordial bird, *Owonwon*, the toucan, to take a snail shell with sand in it. Doubtful of the competitive value of sand among such an array of impressively valuable gifts taken by his siblings, he allowed himself to be persuaded and took the shell of a snail. They all set sail in the primordial canoe and were amazed to find that down below was covered in water. After travelling on what seemed an endless expanse of water the toucan whispered to the Ọba of Bini that he should turn the shell upside-down. When he carried out this instruction he found to his surprise and joy that the sand spread itself to become solid and from it emerged houses, trees and all the things that give the earth such variation. His siblings were afraid to get out of the canoe and on account of his careful movement, *uwenrhoten* (the chameleon) was sent to find how solid the earth was. With his approval, all came down at the Ọba of Bini's instruction and bartered their gifts with him for a portion of the earth. Osanobua descended on the spot where the earth started to form from the sand in the shell; that spot became known as *agbon*. Osanobua demarcated the land from the spirit world there and made the Ọba of Bini the owner of the world. He exerts his supremacy over the land in the annual ritual of Igue (the feast dedicated to the strengthening of the mystical power of the king) when he ritually kills a leopard, the king of the forest (*ugbo*). (Photo page 22a.)

A comparative look at the main outlines of the Bini and Yoruba world-view shows an interesting range of similarities and dissimilarities. They both agree that the creation of the world was of divine origin and at divine initiative. They equally confirm that this creative work was accomplished by the son of the Supreme Being who subsequently became the ruler. Those who accomplished these creative tasks were not the eldest of the children of the Supreme Being. They achieved their creator role due to the display of some virtuous character; in the one, obedience, in the other, ingenuity. The Ọba of Bini was obedient to the advice of *owonwon*, the toucan, and eventually owned the earth. Oduduwa, the culture-hero of the Yoruba, was full of ingenuity. Having been sent by the Supreme Being to find out what was delaying his brother in this task of creating the world, he went down, saw his brother drunk, and the task not yet accomplished; he then proceeded to usurp his brother's role as creator by accomplishing the task himself.

An element of opposition appears to characterize relations between certain siblings in each case of creation. In the Yoruba account, the opposition was between Oduduwa the creator of the earth, the first king of Ilẹ̀-Ife, and his brother Obatala, the arch-divinity and sculptor of the physique of man.[11] In the Bini story, the opposition is between the Ọba of Benin, the fulcrum of social and political organization of the Bini, and Olókun, the Bini arch-divinity and the first son of Osaobua. In the latter case, the opposition has become institutionalized in the dichotomous division of the universe into *erinmwin* and *agbọn*, the spirit world and the abode of the living, with Olókun identified more with the heavenward dimension and the Ọba with the earthward dimension. On a second plane of dichotomy, the opposition occurs with the physical earth partitioned into the land under the Ọba and the waters under Olókun, whose domain is the link between both the spirit-world and the abode of the living.

The basic dissimilarity between both world-views, concerns the division of the universe. The Yoruba have a tripartite scheme of cosmology as opposed to the essentially dualistic structure of Benin cosmology. This singular fact introduces a wide range of differences between each group's conception of ideas that appear similar to both. Each sociolinguistic group's structure of the universe serves as a conceptual model by which its own members understand and at times define their social circumstances, belief pattern and political relationships. Thus, in relation to reincarnation, the tripartite scheme manifests itself in the three modes of existence, the participation in each of which constitutes the Yoruba idea of salvation, itself the reward of a successful life. In Benin society, the group to which the individual belongs in the larger society exists to support the political control exerted at the palace, the hub of political organization, the lineages not being corporate[12] as are those of the Yoruba. The divergence between the understanding of an idea common to the two people may now be illustrated with regard to reincarnation.

Reincarnation in the Bini and Yoruba World-views

Yoruba metaphysics is devoted above all to account for death and deal with man's natural fear of it. If the Yoruba partially succeeds in using art to neutralize that fear (Lawal 1977:50), he finds a better solution in a metaphysical world-view. Central to this metaphysical world-view, cyclical in nature, is reincarnation, the basic dogma of Yoruba traditional religion (Finnegan 1977:15; Ferguson 1980:29; Cordwell 1952:30). In Bini traditional religion, reincarnation (*ariavbehe*) is so basic that the certainty of the individual elder who has lived what the Bini regard as a successful life being reincarnated is taken for granted. Thus, such Bini proverbs as "the aged lady is about to die, so she sells her mortar; she forgets her life in her next generation" (*Omaen ra wu omaen mu odo khien; umaen ma ghi ye agbon no gha re ariavbehe*) or more to the point the adage "to die for a worthy person is not painful; but to die for a worthless person pains one till one's next reincarnation" (*A gha ra wu ne omwan esi e ida egbe, sokpan a gha wu ne omwan oya ta vie egbe se ariavbehe*) manifests this certainty.

For the Yoruba, the three salient points of this world-view correspond to the three phases of the Yoruba conception of existence and bring back to mind the tripartite scheme of conceptualization discussed earlier. These three phases are; the hereafter (*ọrun*), the here-and-now (*ilé-aiyé*) and the yet-to-come or the world of the unborn,[13] easily assimilated to the earth (*ilẹ́* as the transitional abode of the deceased who wish to be reincarnated and the unborn whose potentiality is to be actualized by proceeding to the abode of the living). The here-and-now world of the living is sandwiched between the hereafter and the yet-to-come. These modes of being correspond to the main outline of those described in Morton-Williams' work on Yoruba cosmology (1960:224-7).

The aspect of this tripartite division is that the boundaries are not rigid but that there is frequent intermixing between the beings of the *ile* (earth) and the abode of the Supreme Being, divinities and ancestors. Thus, although the ancestors are in the spirit world, they are said to pay visits to their progeny in the Egúngún masquerade dance. In this form, they emerge from the earth and go back to their spirit world at the completion of their visit by disappearing into the bowels of the earth. Cordwell's observation on this orientation of the Yoruba is worth noting here. She stated that it is "...based upon the knowledge that life and death are but aspects or a continuum extending from before birth, through life, and into the realm of death in the ancestral world (1952:30)."

The boundaries between the levels of existence are not rigid as they lead into one another. Wole Soyinka observes in relation to the dynamic cycle of the Yoruba world-view:

> ...the traditional thought operates, not a linear conception of time but a cyclical reality. One does not suggest for a moment that this is peculiar to the Yoruba or the African world-view...But the degree of the integrated acceptance of this temporal sense in the life rhythm, mores and social organization of Yoruba society is certainly worth emphasizing, being a reflection of that same reality which denies periodicity to the existencies of the dead, the living and the unborn. The expression the child is father of the man becomes within the context of this time structure, not merely metaphor of development, one that is rooted in a system of representative individuation, but a proverb of human continuity which is not unidirectional. Neither child nor father is a closed or chronological concept. The world of the unborn, in the Yoruba world-view, is evidently older than the world of the living as the world of the living is older than the ancestor-world. And of course, the other way round. We cannot insist that the world of the living is older than the world of the ancestors in the same breath as we declare that the deities preceded humanity into the universe (1976:10).

This rather compressed account of the cyclical world-view is understandable in terms of Yoruba soteriology. Contrary to the view that

Yoruba religious thought is not moralistic in the sense that good and evil done on earth would be rewarded by peace or punishment hereafter (Bascom 1953), Yoruba religious notions are moralistic if seen in terms of its own conception of salvation. It is not surprising that a culture whose essential metaphysical thought is cyclically dynamic could conceive of salvation in terms of the underpinning principle of this thought pattern.

Although Yoruba believe that certain divinities punish certain crimes immediately, there is no doubt that the ultimate and most telling reward or punishment awaits the individual after death. The rewards of a good life in Yoruba society, a life characterized by respect for elders (*ìtẹriba fágbà*), cautious behaviour (*ìwà pẹ̀lẹ́*), truthfulness (*òtító ṣíṣe*) and dedicated devotion to duty (*akíkanjú*) are devoted children, the force of whose combined funerary ritual and ceremonial feasting propels the dead onto the next phase of being.

The admission into the ancestral world is neither the end of all rewards nor the termination of active participation in being. It is the most important reward since it qualifies one to reincarnate oneself through one's progeny. One acquires the power to attach oneself to the being of a yet-to-be-born and to return to the abode of living human beings (*ilé-ayé*). Asked why people who have died and who enjoy the status of the ancestor do not remain in the coveted mode of existence, one informant said:

> The heavenly abode is good, but for one to be stable immobile is not good; to be in the midst of one's own people is comforting. That is why the Supreme Being decreed that that part of the person that can go to the heaven and return may go. Is that not the reason why you are called Babatunde (father comes back)?[14]

It has been suggested in the literature on ancestor veneration that since, at death, the departed soul is deprived of the body and its natural means of knowledge, it is no longer possible for him to remain in a habitual relationship with the living (Laroche 1968:299). More relevant to the Yoruba, Awolalu has suggested that the Yoruba idea of ancestor veneration and the idea of reincarnation are basically contradictory and paradoxical (1979:60). While these points are indisputable when one employs the conceptual categories of traditional Western metaphysical thought to the Yoruba, it should be pointed out that the categories of Yoruba philosophy of the person excludes this contradiction. This outlook stipulates the facets of the personality and identifies the specific one that undergoes change at death into the ancestral spirit and the ancestral guardian soul which is reborn (Bascom 1960a:404-5; Eades 1980:122). The ancestral spirit which occupies its distinguished place in the spiritual realm is taken by the Yoruba to participate at a higher mode of being. They mean that he becomes more capable of doing all that he did on earth, since his human attributes have become heightened rather than destroyed at death.

Among the Bini, the idea of reincarnation is tied to the two-tier conception of the world, the spiritual ancestral world of *erinmwin* and the physical world of *agbọn*. The link between Bini concept of reincarnation and world-view lies in the belief that each individual has fourteen lives and alternates the process of coming into being with his spirit double *Ehi*. As one informant stated:

> There is a lot of activity after death. For us the Bini death at old age is not the end. It opens the way to a new beginning. To be able to come back and live on earth fresh and strong, we have to die. Each individual has fourteen lives. He shares these fourteen lives with his *ehi*. *Ehi* is his other self who stays with Osanobua. Between them they have seven lives each to lead. An individual Bini who has completed his cycle melts into an ancestral being.[15]

Each individual and his spirit double passes from *erinmwin* to *agbon* seven times in a process made automatic by the individual living up to the Bini standard of a successful life. This life is characterized in its quality by the manifestation, in behaviour in the society, of such virtues as truthfulness (*emwanta*), kindness (*itohan*) and at time of war, bravery (*udinmwen*). The successful life is placed at the service of the king because not to be the king's enemy is equivalent to wealth (*A ire oghian oba se vbe efe*). A manifestation of this wealth is in the number of children begotten. Not to have children at all is to remain junior perpetually because the barren wife is always regarded as a junior (*Ne oma bie o re ovbokhan*). The Bini word for the impotent, *awuekia*, literally means tabooed man.

A successful life enables the individual's *ehi*, spirit double, to take its own turn while the individual becomes transformed to the *ehi*. The *ehi* attaches itself to a new child to be born within the circle of his related kingroup. If either party, through living a life unbefitting an individual forfeits his right to readmission into the spirit-world, he destroys the chances of both himself and his partner to ancestorhood. Ancestorhood is conferred on the pair which succeeds in completing its apportioned times of reincarnation.

Although both the Bini and the Yoruba are agreed upon the fact that human fertility is the essential insurance premium for reincarnation (hence, the living and the dead have a contractual obligation and interest in its continuity), essential details surrounding reincarnation differ somewhat considerably. Among the Yoruba, it is conceived in the dynamic term of eternal return in which the successful individual goes through the three phases of being. Among the Bini it is conditioned by the number of times the individual alternates with his *ehi*. Among the Bini, it is virtually a right due to the individual which he throws away by his own choice, while among the Yoruba it is earned, not taken for granted.

The most basic difference perhaps, concerns orientation of this expectation in both societies. Among the Bini it is oriented to the individual, but it is oriented to the group among the Yoruba. In the Bini understanding, the focus is the individual concerned with the attempt to enjoy the projected number of existences that are due to him as he alternates with his spirit double. A forfeiture of that right will ultimately affect the individual's *ehi*. The great exception to this individualist orientation is the royal ancestral spirits of Bini (*erinmwin idu*), the veneration of which, in the light of the Bini Ọba's central focus in society, has a group dimension to it. The forfeiture of the right to reincarnation would involve, for the Yoruba, three persons; the culprit, the ancestor determined to come back among his progeny, and the unborn child through whom the process of reincarnation is kept alive.

It may be that differences in the concepts of reincarnation are related to differences in the nature and content of the domestic group. It would be easy to point to the fact that the Yoruba lineage is corporate and membership in it is important for success in society, while the Bini corporate group is the village and not the immediate kinship group. It would follow that in the former group, interpretations of concepts important to the society would take the line of group involvement while those belonging to the latter would stress the point of individual achievement in a wider competitive group composed of non-kinsmen. Perhaps further research would confirm the correlation.

The Ancestors: Edion Ebho, Ará-Ọ̀run

A basic generalization in recent scholarship on ancestorhood is that there is a noticeable broad uniformity in African patterns of ancestor veneration in consequence of their basis in the family, kinship and descent structure (Fortes and Dieterlen 1965:11-13; Bradbury 1965; 1973:213; Fortes 1959: 28-30; 1976:4-6; 1974:82-103; 1976:7). This appears to be confirmed by my research among the Bini and the Yoruba. Prior to the establishment of this generalization, Talbot had emphasized the importance of ancestors to the people of Southern Nigeria, when he stated that:

> No one can hope to appreciate the thought and feelings of the black man who does not realize that to him the dead are not dead but living (1926:298).

The Bini and the Yoruba believe that the deceased elders are present to them and that they can punish or reward their descendants for ritual neglect and moral transgressions. They share with other ancestor-venerating societies such as the Tallensi (Fortes 1959), the Chinese (Ahern 1973) three crucial basic points about ancestorhood. The first is that death, though necessary to the transition, does not put an end to the deceased. It merely releases him to participate in a more unique mode of being which enables him to influence mystically and powerfully the life of his descendants. At the moment of death, the soul is freed from the body and transformed to participate in a spiritual existence (Lawal 1977:50). Secondly, the manner of death must be one that is in accordance with what a people's collective representations accept as normal. The normality of death is judged in terms of whether the deceased has fulfilled certain expectations in society. Thirdly, the deceased achieved the status of ancestorhood more proximately through the provision of accepted funerary rites by the right group of descendants.

Both the Bini and Yoruba provide ideological and structural grounds for the veneration of their ancestors. The ideological ground is manifest in a world view that teaches as a dogma of belief, that death is not the end but only a release from one limited mode of existence to a more mystically fulfilling mode made possible by the imperishable nature of the human soul. Through the canons of the undying quality of the soul and life-after-death, an ideological basis has been created for the acceptance of a mode of existence which serves as a solution to the fearful possibility that death means oblivion to the deceased.

The structural ground for ancestor veneration, relevant to kinship and descent, is the final condition that the deceased must have begotten descendants whose feasts and ritual celebrations alone can guarantee his admission to the circle of ancestors. This demand has a double effect on the individual in society. The individual whose society has assigned procreation as the basic condition for ancestorhood puts a high premium on human fertility and the procreation of children in an attempt to realize his desired status. The energy and strains expended and incurred in ensuring this realization is repaid by the belief that his relations with his descendants will not cease at death. More important to the society, however, is the fact that in ensuring that the deceased has children, he has made his greatest contribution to it, for they will, in obedience to the same demand ensure that the society survives.

The apparent contradiction inherent in a culture's stress on ancestorhood and reincarnation is resolved, among the Bini, by their concept of reincarnation which is an extension of the full space of an individual's existence and which he enjoys in a process of alternation with his *ehi*. After the completion, the individual melts into ancestorhood. For the Bini, therefore, one phase is a step to the next, hence there is no contradiction.

The Yoruba, too, do not experience any element of contradiction in their conception of both phases. The Yoruba idea of the components of human personality (to be explored in depth later) resolves any contradiction that would have arisen. The Yoruba notions of the personality are not unlike those of the Dogon. The Dogon conceive of the person as made up of eight souls, four attached to the body and its senses and four linked with the individual's sexual and reproductive capacities. It is two of the sex-related souls that get enshrined in the ancestral spirit (Dieterlen 1966). The Yoruba[16] divide the person into the body (*ara*) and soul (*ẹ̀mí*) (Idowu 1962:70). There are distinct types that make up the soul. *Orí-inú* is the essence of the individual as an extension of the Supreme Being because it is that part of him which participates in the divine essence. There is *Alájọbi* or *Ẹlẹ́da* that re- enters the reincarnation cycle while the *orí-inó*, though part of the divine, has its own unique individuality which is not compromised by nearness to the numinousity of the Supreme Being.

The attitude to death and subsequent funerary rites of the Bini and the Yoruba will serve to illuminate both groups' responses to death. The statements of Bradbury, the authoritative Edo scholar were confirmed in detail by my fieldwork research, and what he says in relation to death is applicable not only to the Bini but also to the Yoruba:

> The older a man is, the more descendants he has, the higher his rank and prestige, the more acceptable does his death become. The peaceful demise of an old chief with numerous progeny is as much an occasion for rejoicing in his life; achievement as for sorrow. To die childless and sonless, is the most dreaded fate, and when one asks: Why do you want many children? the reply is often: So that they may bury me well. The Edo believe that one who is not properly buried cannot enter the society of his dead kin and associates, for his survival as a social being is dependent on the performance of the mortuary ritual by his children (1965:98).

Death of the young is abhorrent to the people of both societies. The word young is the significant operative word as it is relative and meant to be applied as such by both the Bini and the Yoruba. It is an age continuum from a teenager to an adult of fifty years whose parents are still living. The impression gathered from informants of both groups is that any member of the localized kinship group who is not in the category of living elders is said to be young. Both groups believe in the importance of seniority as an ordering principle, both in life and at death. This implies that, according to the law of proportionality, seniors ought to die before their juniors. It is, therefore, the customary expectation that juniors should bury (*re*), (*sin*), the Bini and Yoruba elders respectively.

<u>Bini Responses to the Fear of Death</u>

The death of the young disrupts these accepted expectations. It brings about the reversed spectacle of one burying those who would have buried and venerated one. Besides, if the deceased youth has many children, who can adequately perform his funerary rites which would qualify him for admission into the company of ancestors; this introduces another complication. It has reversed seniority in the spiritual ancestral world thereby giving way to confusion. Although the living elders in his own kinship unit do not have to venerate him at his shrine since the rule of primogeniture establishes a lineal ritual connection, they are, however, in an inferior state to him as he has been admitted to a state they have not reached.

The death of a minor is even more abhorrent. Not only has he not lived up to any of the expectations of the society, his right to reincarnation is jeopardized. Unlike certain Japanese societies where the elevation to ancestorhood is not limited to the reproductive members of the lineage (*ie*) but embraces deceased collaterals and children (Takeda 1976:119-21; Fortes 1976:8-9), among the Bini and the Yoruba minors are not commemorated. Of the three divisions of Bini polities, the Elders (*edionwere*), the warriors (*ighele*) and the little ones (*iroghae*) who sweep the villages and provided related services, the Bini expect death to take people from the Elders category. As the Bini say, the sun should shrine on those standing before it touches those stooping and kneeling.

The Bini funerary rites display the classical attributes of the *rites de passage* discussed by Arnold van Genep (1909). They also confirm in their attitudes certain of Hertz's claims in his study of death representations (1910). Death itself is seen as the commencement of the transition for the elder who is separated from his kin group in the world of the living. He is not immediately integrated into the company of the ancestors at death. He becomes totally dependent upon his descendants from the moment of the cessation of life to the time when he acquires the status of an ancestor. Until this is ensured through the performance of the funerary rites, he is in the liminal, unclassified, restless state in which he becomes dangerous to his children. It is, therefore, in the interests of both his children and himself that the integration be made as quickly as possible.

The two most important groups at the funeral of a Bini elder are the children of the deceased (*Ovbi orinmwin*), and the senior men of the bereaved kinship group (*egbee*). Among the children of the deceased, the most important for the funeral rites is the first son (*omodion*). He was described by an informant, Chief Ebohon, as the one who was the reward for the pains of the waist (*ekun*). The most important duty of the omodion is to plant (*ko*) (or bury) his father. When he is properly planted, he becomes the living dead (*kebh'erinbhin*) and he has the opportunity to germinate by completing his reincarnation cycles. Perhaps it is to ensure that a child (*omomo*) plants his father properly that good planting is made the condition for the *omodion* to inherit the status and largest share of his deceased father's property. It is implied that the father (*erha*) properly planted (*re*) would enjoy all the rights and privileges that belonged to him as a member of his group in the ancestral world. The thorough extent and rapid pace to which the *omodion* initiates and executes the integration of his father into the ancestral status is correlated to the rapidity with which he is recognized by the group of living elders as the heir to the status, property and privileges of the deceased. Much stress is laid on the importance of the performance of these rites to the extent that a senior son who finds himself unable to do this will have his rights and prerogatives usurped by any son who decides to perform the rites according to expectation. When this occurs, the celebrant automatically replaces the senior son in seniority and has all rights to inheritance and succession accruing to his achieved kinship position.

In preparation for interment, the *Egbee* demand (and are given by the *omodion*) a new white cloth, a mat (*ewa*) and a sponge. The *omodion* and some of his father's children (preferably the first sons of other wives of the deceased) sprinkle water on the dead person after *omodion* has first done this. Then, members of the group of elders who are junior to the dead person *orinbhin*, then proceed to wash the corpse. They shave his hair, cut his nails and stick these into white chalk. This is kept as it signifies the deceased. It is called *akpa*. The incorruptible nature of these clippings and their capacity for growth singles them out for their ritual significance.

When the washing is concluded, a goat (*ewe*) provided by the *omodion* is killed and its blood sprinkled over the bowl and sponge that were used to do the washing. My informants told me that the goat is killed for two purposes; in honour of the waist (*ekun*) of the deceased, since it is the waist that bears the brunt of the suffering that goes with sexual activity and reproduction. The blood of the slaughtered goat, it is alleged, has a cooling effect on the spirit of the deceased. It circumscribes the movement of the dead person thus preventing him from aimless wandering, a state in which it becomes dangerous to its descendants. My informants were unanimous in stating that the goat meat is then cooked and eaten in a ritual meal[17] exclusive to the elders. Subsequently, an elder of the lineage then goes to mark out the position of the grave with chalk. The *omodion* strikes along the marked lines seven times, after which the sons-in-law of the deceased dig the grave. The corpse is laid with its feet pointing to Ughoton, the old Bini river port from where the deceased are said to depart for the spirit world. The rivers are of great ritual significance in Bini because they are said to be the link between the world of the living and the dead.

The funeral rites last for seven days and are in seven stages. The main actor and the centre of ritual and festive attraction is the first born, *omodion*, the senior son. The interment takes place before him and the elders of the bereaved lineage in the ritual of *Iwaorinbhin* or the spreading out of the corpse. On the third afternoon, the ritual of taking out bath (*Izaluve*) is performed. A goat is killed and the traditional portions of the head, the right foreleg and the left hindleg which normally belong to the deceased as the head of the family, go to the first son. Two days after the performance of the living out ritual, the Isoton dance is performed. This is a big procession around the town at the expense of the first son. Again he kills a goat and sends the left hindleg and right foreleg to the *Egbee* (elders). Along with this he gives them a mat, a white piece of cloth, yam tubers, a container of kola-nuts, sticks of chalk and a container of palm-oil. On the eve of the seventh day, the *arha* rite and *Isuerhanta* (wake-keeping ceremony) are held. One of the younger brothers of the *omodion* is dressed up like the deceased and treated as if he were the dead person. After some initial gifts of money, cloth, and a live goat, there is a confrontation which ends by the *omodion* seizing the bigger outer garment of the deceased from the ritual representative. This is concluded with the rite of *nkonben*, when the juniors of the lineage greet *omodion* as our father (*erha ven*). The number of times goats are killed in the Bini funerary ceremony clarifies the point of the Bini proverb: It is unnecessary to ask a Bini if he knows how to eat the flesh of a goat; with what does he venerate his departed fathers yearly? (*A ino ovbi Edo he o guara ri ewe, ubo ghi ya ru erhae ukpakpo?*)

Scholars have drawn attention to the fact that a kind of ambivalent and ambiguous tendency manifests itself in the rituals of this sort. They stressed that there is a feeling of guilt in knowing that one will replace those from whom one inherits (Fortes 1959; 1966; 1976). Goody characterized this mixed guilt feeling as holder-heir relationship (1965:435). He asserted that the tension created by this ambivalent relationship is transformed on the ideological plane to the harsh treatment which a deceased parent may mete out to his progeny because of ritual neglect. It would appear from the data on Bini funerary rites that what is at stake and central to the rites themselves is not the resolution at death of a supposed tension arising from a father and his son who would eventually replace him. The consuming desire of the Bini is to beget children who will inherit from them. The central purpose is to be found in the society's readiness to fill the vacancy and transfer the status and authority associated with it in the group smoothly by crediting it with ancestral sanction. It is not surprising that the degree to which the first-born performs the funerary rites is the degree to which he establishes his authority as heir. Thus, although it would appear that ancestor veneration is a consecration of the past, seen in the light of redistribution of status in society, ancestor-making and ancestor beliefs are much more concerned with the present concerns, the synchronic event in the society. The good Bini man, the proper self in society, therefore, in making sure that his father is admitted into the ancestral world, ensures in the same process and by virtue of the discharge of his duties to the deceased, the discharge of the duty to the living by having his new status confirmed and supported with metaphysical sanctions.

Yoruba Response to the Fear of Death

The Yoruba fears the idea of being taken away by death. He expresses this fear in proverbs and in attempts to conquer death, either through the use of magic alleged to keep death at bay, or in systems of belief which appear to remove the sting of death by dramatizing that death at an old age is a most welcome transition to the more powerful mode of existence of the ancestor in the spiritual realm, *orun* (Morton-Williams 1960:34; Lawal 1977:50-1). The Yoruba minimizes the stark reality of his eventual extinction by death in the belief that:

> ...death is not the end of life. It is merely an dematerialization of the vital breath or soul, and hence a transformation from earthly to spiritual existence (a land of Afterlife), where the dematerialized soul may choose to stay forever although it can make periodic returns to earth through reincarnation (*atunwa*) (Lawal 1977:51).

This belief notwithstanding, the Yoruba still express fear about death. They say in one of their proverbs, "the elderly man is sick unto death, the young ones around him ask him to greet all relatives in the spirit world. Do they think that he is in such a hurry to see the ancestors?" (*Àgbàlagbà nlọ sòrun, ẹniki okile ki oki ọ̀nà. Oju lasan lo fi nlọ sòrun bi?*) Therefore, the Yoruba actively engage in preserving life. A verse of *Ejiogbe*, one of the sixteen principal verses (*odù*) of the corpus of Ifá divination notes the primordial attempt of the Yoruba to overcome death:

Oyinikange
Ifá divination was made on Òrúnmìlà's behalf
On the day that Òrúnmìlà was going to partake of the seed of long life
On the day that Òrúnmìlà was going to sign an agreement with death.
That death may not take him (kill him) in his youth
He consulted Oyinikange about what to do.
A very old *orose*, shea butter, black soap
He should take the sand at the bottom of a gourd,
He should also have a very heavy straight iron-road
He should use this in the sacrifice against death.
He heard the instructions and followed them to the letter adding a pebble from the river.
Òrúnmìlà then said,
I have become like the old orose
I will not die
I have become like the protected sand under the growing gourd
I have become stout and solid (I am too strong)
I will know everything.
I will know everything in the heavens and on earth
I will keep my mouth shut,
I wandered far and near without getting lost.
They said they would bring evil (misfortune).
But my eyes do not see misfortune.
Òrúnmìlà is walking along the road
The breeze unwraps clothes from the body,
The breeze is removing clothes.[18]

The Yoruba identify longevity and perfection that comes with ritual purity with the elements of the sacrifice, like *orose*, shea butter, black soap. Thus, in this verse of Ifá, the operative concept which lends efficacy to Òrúnmìlà's hard-won immunity from death at a young age is that the ritual elements are thought to shed their qualities of undyingness and longevity on the maker of sacrifice. Thus they are expected to affect, homeopathically, the life of the donor by conferring long life on him. The essence of this sacrifice is not as a remedy for death, which the Yoruba accept as inevitable, but in the conferment of old age - an essential condition for ancestorhood.

Seen in the context of transition to the ancestral status, the Yoruba accept the inevitability of death at old age when a person's achievements have become established, as a new beginning. These achievements which manifest the blessings of God on the individual include, besides long life, increasing prosperity and many children (Morton-Williams 1960:55; Awolalu, 1979:54). These blessings aid in the integration of the individual into the ancestral world when he becomes an ancestor himself. Awolabi noted about the Yoruba that when they speak of ancestors:

> ...they think of the departed spirit of their forebears with whom the living maintain a filial and affectionate relationship. It is not every dead person that comes in for consideration. To qualify, such men and women must have lived well, attained an enviable old age before dying, must have left behind good children and good memory. Children and youths who die a premature death, barren women, and all who die a bad death, e.g. killed by Ayelala or Sango or Sopanno are excluded from this respectable group (1979:54).

The Yoruba announce the death of an elderly person with the booming of the gun. The immediate response of the people, particularly women, is to weep.[19] Informants of the Egba Yoruba maintained that the tears shed are tears of joy that the bereaved lineage will soon acquire an additional mediator in the spirit world. The corpse is washed and its head is shaven if a man. If a woman, her hair is plaited. The corpse (*ara*) is laid on a mat (*eni*) having been wrapped in a white garment (*aso funfun*). A container holding some traditional medicinal concoctions thought to prevent the immediate decay of the corpse is placed on its chest.[20] The corpse itself, or more frequently, its effigy, is taken around the town on its last tour on the second day. If all the children cannot be assembled in the space of a day, the interment is done on the third day when it is buried in the house at a depth of about seven feet and in such a way that its head is located in the centre of the room. The location of its burial practically acts out the symbolic beliefs of the Yoruba that the living are not free from the dead and that the deceased have more power and sanctions on the living. It is interred amidst the wailing admonition of the descendants:

Má mà jẹ òkùn
Má mà jẹ ekòló
Ohun tiwon ba njẹ la jule Ọrun
Niki obawọn jẹ

Do not eat millipedes
Do not eat worms
Eat only what is eaten in the heavens
That you should eat

Relatives pray that the deceased may come back in his children - *Ya omo wa.*

The ceremony of burial continues on the seventh day with the second burial ceremony. This is called in certain parts of Yorubaland, *Gbeye*, Carry the honour of the deceased. This often takes one of two forms. The first is that the effigy of the deceased taken around for his last tour of the village is dressed and taken now through all the major quarters of the village. It is then returned and buried accordingly (Willet 1966:34-45; Abiodun 1976; Lawal 1977:52). The second form is to dress up a descendant of the deceased in the finest clothes of the dead person. This ritual representative is led through the town and receives the obeisance and respect due to the deceased. Neither he nor the garments used are buried.

Among the Ọ̀họ̀ri Yoruba[21] astride the Nigeria-Republic of Benin (Dahomey) boundary, who live in the swampy area of Ipobe, there still exists an ancient Yoruba ritual which ends the funerary rites. This is called *Mawe*, taking away the fasting that comes with bereavement It takes place about three months after the interment. My informants, Chief Edun, *Chef de Canton* of the central Ọ̀họ̀ri village of Issaba and Ọ̀dọ̀fin Adenle of Oke-Ola Quarters, Ipobe, asserted independently of each other that this custom was brought back from Ife and Ọ̀yọ̀ respectively.

Ifá oracle, the Yoruba divination process is consulted as to which of the maidens in the kinship group the deceased would like to use as his medium when he is called from the dead to the ceremony. Once chosen, the family of the deceased provide a container in which are kept household utensils. This container is carried by the virgin. Also, the hair and nails of the deceased are added to the contents of the container. In the afternoon, the girl leads the crowd of performers and spectators with the medicinal container balanced on her head. The onlookers sing ritual songs that are said to have the power of calling the spirit of the dead to take possession of the girl. Three types of these possession songs, collected at Issaba, are as follows:

1. Ọmọ nsọkun nile ọlọjọ Ifẹ ko wa gbe
Ọ̀mọ̀ nsọ̀kun nile Ẹ̀rọ̀ Ifẹ kowa gbe
Ọ̀mọ̀ nsọ̀kun nile Ero Aiba kowa gbe

The child is crying, the deceased come and take her
The child is crying, one from the past come and take her
The child is crying, one from Aiba come and take her

2. Ko ya ṣasà, ẹ̀gà ki i kọle imọ tikodọla
ko ya ṣaṣa

Be quick, the weaverbird does not postpone its weaving till tomorrow
Be quick

3. Olúbòdé ṣẹkù o
Olúbòdé ṣẹku ona
Olele o oriṣa ṣa ṣa olele
Kaya ko ya
Oriṣa ṣa ṣa olele

Olúbòdé open
Olúbòdé open the door
Quickly, divinity, quickly
Let it be quick
Divinity open the day

These songs continue for a long time in slow and gloomy monotonous rhythm, meant to hypnotise the virgin medium. After protracted repetition of these rhythms, the girl is alleged to become spasmic, indicating that she has been possessed by the dead person. She is alleged to remain in this state for about one day. The deceased gives the instructions through the girl. These include the location of some buried wealth, exhortation to all lineage members to respect and reverence the eldest surviving member of the lineage. In cases of sickness in the family, the deceased gives prescriptions of medicinal herbs to be used in the medicine that will cure the sick. The ceremony end with the sacrifice of a goat, the blood of which is poured on the position of the head of the deceased in the grave at the centre of the house. In most parts of Yorubaland the annual performance and ritual outing of the Egúngún masquerade, representative of the deceased, constantly keep alive the memory of the deceased in the family. Theses masquerades emerge from the deep recesses of the earth in order to pay a visit to their descendants (Olajubu and Ojo 1977:253-5; Morton-Williams 1960:36-8).

The foregoing data on the Bini and Yoruba responses to death and obsequies make interesting comparison. They confirm that for both groups ancestorhood is conferred not just on any deceased, but on those who have performed their duties to the society and are considered to have lived successful lives. The social indices of a successful life include the bearing of children, the most fundamental duty to the survival of the group. Thus, conferment of ancestorhood is limited to the productive members of the group. To the extent to which it focuses attention on the transfer of status and the filling of the vacancy created by death, the evidence shows that ancestor veneration has more immediate sociological values for the living, as statuses are reallocated and group mores are reinforced by mystical sanctions of the ancestors. The participation of all members in these obsequies provides the occasion and the solemn atmosphere for the internalization of social values and expectations about the self in society.

There is, however, a basic difference as to the main actors in the obsequies. This divergence derives from the basic difference between the rules for inheritance of property and those of succession to status. Among the Bini, *omodion* is the main actor and the funerary rites are more a demonstration of his acquired status of leadership as they are of an admission of the deceased into the ancestral world. The rule of primogeniture makes the first son in Bini the central focus. Among the Yoruba succession to office is not by the rule of primogeniture. The next eligible elder becomes the main focus.

Yoruba rules of inheritance recognize two types of wealth classified according to their source of accumulation. Wealth acquired by membership of the kinship group reverts back to the group at death, the next surviving elder becoming the leader and dispenser of the wealth in this category. Wealth accumulated by an individual due to his own efforts is passed over to his children (Lloyd 1955, 1962; Schwab 1955; Bascom 1969; Peel 1968). Privately acquired clothes and status symbols that go with old age and its

Yoruba correlation with authority do not pass to the children of the owner. They are passed to junior siblings of the deceased whose life mirrors the value of the symbols.

There is an everwidening circle of group inclusiveness among the Bini and the Yoruba, from the compound family of a man and his wives and children to the families of collateral kinsmen and wider kinship groups, until the whole lineage is embraced. This is duplicated in the metaphysical plane with an hierarchy of ancestors. Among the Bini in particular, jural and ritual authority resides in all men who are fathers. Each head of a family will have his admission to the status of an ancestor guaranteed by the obsequies made by his *omodion* and other children. Yet, until the father dies, the *omodion* and his other children, *de jure* and *de facto*, do not have either jural or ritual independence. They are extensions of their father. They achieve independence only when they have performed what Fortes described as the supreme act of filial piety, the performance of mortuary and funerary ceremonies for the parents (1959:29).

The situation where the child becomes free and important only after his father's death, it has been suggested, gives rise to generational hostility (Fortes 1959:29). As an analytical category it has been conceptualized as the holder-heir relationship - the variable of the anticipated, and achieved, inheritance (Goody 1965:438). It is said to be characterized by a feeling of guilt in those who realize that their ambition for the status of their father can only be achieved by willing his death. In the ancestor ideology, therefore, the ancestor who must be inherited from is consoled with the idea that death does not terminate the parent-child relationship, but enhances it - crediting him with greater mystical powers to control the behaviour of his inheritors. Thus, the traditional world view makes a symbolic restitution to counteract the dilemma in human experience. It is suggested that the ritualization of filial piety continued through death is insitutionalized in the harsh reality of ancestral punishment (Goody 1965:399-400). Ancestor veneration in these societies is practical in form as it is intended to keep the ancestors happy so that they do not punish their descendants.

Although Bradbury (1965:14) stresses the ritualization of generational conflict in the mortuary rites of the Edo, I was told that it would be unwise for the would-be ancestor who is still adrift prior to his acquisition of the status to punish his descendants. The deceased needs their filial piety to integrate him into the ancestral world just as they need his ancestral blessings.

This generational conflict is a feature decidedly absent from Yoruba funerary rites. The Yoruba data with reference to the transfer of status and rank contradict Goody's general thesis that sacrifices are made to those from whom we inherit. The children of the deceased are only entitled to those parts of the deceased's wealth acquired by his own efforts, excluding big clothes (*agbádá*), which go with old age and authority. In terms of the Yoruba world-view, the cyclical nature of life and the constant possibility of reincarnation (a thing not conceived by the Yoruba as paradoxical to ancestorhood) intensifies the desire to have many children and thereby gain pleasure by transferring one's rights to them at death.

A common Yoruba prayer is:

The children of the hand (fingers) do not die before the hand
The children of the leg (toes) do not die before the leg
When the embers are put out, they are covered by ashes.
If the banana tree dies (is cut down) its shoots come forth
When the maker of native pomade is away, her daughter replaces her
May children inherit all that is beautiful about us.[22]

Yoruba ideas of the greatest good of all good things - the begetting of children, who will inherit one removes the harshness of the generational hostility which conflicts with the idea that one be inherited from by one's children. The Yoruba goes to great length to ensure that his children replace him. A verse of the sixteen corpus of Ifá divination called *Iyeku Meji* enshrines this attitude in the most authoritative corpus of divination for the Yoruba:

1. When a tethered horse escapes it goes to the house of the noble.
2. When the instrument of divination is lost, it finds its way to Ijero (place of divination).
3. Cultic secret ought to be kept in the forest or in the grassland.
4. Ifá was consulted on behalf of Alapa of Rawe.

5. Who was going to the house of Rawe.
6. They were advised to make a sacrifice for good replacement.
7. Because if the tethered horse escapes,
8. It leaves its beautiful tail behind (as a replacement).
9. Our children, they are our inheritors (our good replacement).
10. The medicine is that of the one leaving a good replacement behind.
11. Our children are our replacement.
12. Because if the tethered horse escapes, it runs to the house of the noble.
13. When the divination instrument gets lost, it finds its way to Ijero.
14. The cultic secret ought to be kept both in the forest and grassland.
15. Ifá oracle was consulted for Enilojo (owner of the day) of Apa.
16. Who was on his way to Alapa's house at Rawe.
17. They were advised to make a sacrifice of,
18. Seven hundred and eighty cowries
19. A horse tail
20. The leaf called "a replacement is good", sixteen pigeons and one medicine pot.
21. So that they may have very many children to replace them.
22. They heard and made the sacrifice.
23. They gave birth to many children.
24. The children grew up to be important.
25. One of them was Ògún (divinity of iron, patron of first son).
26. Then they began to say.
27. So it is when horses escape,
28. They leave their tails behind them.
29. It is our children that we leave behind as our tails.[23]

In this chapter, Bini and Yoruba metaphysical beliefs in relation to the different modes of being have been discussed. The response of the two peoples to the fear of death and the manner in which after-life is conceived have been explored. The importance of reincarnation itself lies in keeping open the frontiers between the earthly and the heavenly abodes.

Death itself ceases to be an end but a new beginning of participating in an essential spiritual mode of existence. The Bini and the Yoruba are able to transcend their finiteness by acquiring power to participate at their level of being. The importance of the spiritual world to the understanding of the human personality will be discussed in the following chapter on Yoruba and Bini divinities as epitomies of the human.

CHAPTER TWO

PART 2

BINI AND YORUBA DIVINITIES AS EPITOMES OF HUMAN CHARACTERISTICS

The Bini spiritual universe, in common with that of the Yoruba, has, in addition to the ancestors (the representatives of the kinship groups) more important spiritual beings. The supreme deity, Osanubowa, rules the spiritual and earthly domains, *erinmwin* and *agbon*, which he created. He delegated the day-to-day running of human affairs to his representatives. The Bini regard seven of these representatives as his most important children. The first child of Osanubowa and Anume his wife is Obienmwen, the female divinity of safe delivery. Olókun, the first son of Osanubowa, is the divinity of wealth and fertility. Although he is the second child, being the first son of the supreme deity of the Bini society whose principal rule of succession to office is primogeniture, he is taken as the arch-divinity. His area of dominance is the waters.[24] The third divinity, Ogiuwu, has ownership of the earth as the burial ground or graveyard of the dead. His messenger is Ofoe - death. Ògún, the fourth divinity in the Bini spiritual universe is the mediating spiritual factor that combines in his essence the qualities of the good and the bad, the auspicious and the inauspicious, two dichotomous categories into which the Bini metaphysical realm is divided. These categories are the lifegiving, life-sustaining and rank-ascribing positive world of Osanobuwa, Olókun and Obiemwen on the one hand, while we have the life-taking, life-diminishing negative world of Ogiuwu, and Ofoe on the other.

If Ògún is the mediating spiritual force in the Bini spiritual universe between the positive life-giving and the negative life-taking elements of that realm, the Bini king (Oba) the last son of the supreme being, Osanubowa, is the mediating link between the two separate realms of *agbon*, the earth, and *erinmwin*, the heavens. In the king, who as a divinity belongs to heaven (though of the earth), the polar concepts of the spiritual and material fuse together and remain for ever. This undying essence of the king, not only as the son of the Supreme Being, but as divinity himself is symbolized in the annual worship of the royal ancestors, the veneration of whom is common to all Bini people. The other two Bini divinities of the seven most-important divinities are Osun, the divinity of medicine and Ovia, the divinity of fertility. Bini medicine experts and devotees of Osun, Osain, tap the forces inherent in natural phenomena like certain leaves and trees in making medicines that are said to bring health to the king and, by extension, to his people. In connection with the many divinities of the Bini spiritual universe, Chief J. Egharevba, the Bini historian noted:

> The almighty God, Osanubowa, created this earth, (otagbonhia fefe osayi) and the unknown spiritual world (kevbe erinmwin). Obiemwen muheniro was his first child but she was female. Olókun, Osanobuwa's first son was his second child, but having the right sex, he superseded his sister in importance. He is the highest of our divinities. Then there is Ogiuwu whose fearful messenger is Ofoe - death. Ògún, that you will always see represented in the dangerous colour of red comes next and there is Osun and Ovia. Of course, the Oba belongs to this category because he is not an ordinary person but the son of Osanobuwa, whose wisdom created the earth and made him superior to every other being on earth. These are not all the divinities because we have very many divinities (1980). (Recorded interview).

The Yoruba earthly and heavenly domains, *aiye* and *Òrun* belong to the Supreme Being Olódùmaré. He is the great god who, having created the realms, as befits his royal protocol, delegated the control of sections of the universe to his different divinities, who are very many (Crowther 1847; Ojo

1966:184).[25] The most important Yoruba divinity, Òrìshà-nlá, is the moulder of human physique. He is, on that account, held responsible for all malformations in children who then become his priests and devotees. Òrúnmìlà, the omniscience of the supreme being provides, through his divination process, *Ifá*, the knowledge of future events and the diagnosis of a present illness or predicament. Ògún is the Yoruba divinity of war, the owner of iron,[26] and the protector of all first sons. Èsù is the chief implementor of the will of the divinities and the censor of all sacrifices. Sango, the deified fourth king of Ọ̀yọ̀ is taken as the fiery divinity of thunder and the symbol of the wrath of Olódùmaré. In addition to these divinities and many others, the Yoruba recognize a peculiar group of forces to which they attribute independent existence in *Òrun*. These include; death - *iku*, sickness - *àrùn*, loss - *òfò*, paralysis - *ẹ̀gbà*, trouble - *ọ̀ràn*, curse - *èpè*, and afflictions - *èṣe*.[27] These forces are collectively referred to as *ajogún*.

The striking aspect of traditional religion as far as the aforementioned spiritual forces are concerned is that the very good or the very bad aspects of human experience are developed into archetypal symbols of belief which are accorded independent existence in their own right. It appears as if, in building up these symbols, the societies use their images of these experiences to attract their occurrence if good and positive or to prevent it if bad and dangerous. It is the experiences that people fear or desire most that they transform into symbolic forces. This tendency has, among the Yoruba, been given a scholarly confirmation in the work of S.A. Babalola. In his study of Yoruba hunters' songs, *Ijálá*, he showed - among other things - that animals like elephant, duiker, baboon, buffalo and colobus monkey (highly prized as quarry by the Yoruba) became the object of poetic songs (Babalola 1976:87-116). The Yoruba hunters' salute to the baboon (*akiti*) will serve as an illustration:

> Possessor of eyes like a bride's, seeing the farmer's wives on their husband's farms.
> Bulky fellow on the *igba* tree, uncle to the red patas monkey.
> Gentleman on the tree-top, whose fine figure intoxicates him.

Ladoogi whose mouth is protuburent and long
like a ginning rod
Whose jaws are like wooden spoons and whose
chest looks as if it has a wooden bar in it.
Four hundred while going through the farm.
Twelve hundred while returning to the bush.
He said it was a pity
It was the farm of his relatives-in-law
Otherwise he would have eaten two hundred
more.
He whom his mother gazed and gazed upon and
burst out weeping
Saying her child's handsomeness would be his
ruin.
Possessor of a hair-denuded posterior.
He whose claws are mischievously sharp.
Whose female's udders are never left in peace,
Nursing mother who continually clings to the
branches of trees.

Song:

Stout and noisy,
A baboon I saw on my forest farm,
As it was munching away.

Chorus:

Stout it was, munching away

(Babalola, 1976:96-7).

In this song, the hunter treats the baboon as a person, although a mean and marginal one, since its manners seem to contradict those associated with the person in the society. It lacks the sense to know that it may fall victim to dangerous tricks that it teaches others. Its voracious appetite is a curse to the labours of the farmer. Its ugliness is satirized as the cause of anxiety to its mother, who feels that the baboon may die due to its extreme handsomeness (a euphemism). It commits the offence against Yoruba etiquette when, instead of protecting the property and farms of its affinal relatives it proceeds to destroy them, boasting that the destruction is limited in scope because of the special affinal links between it and its in-laws. Thus, in the light of all these reasons as well as the more proximate reason of need for its juicy meat, it is temporarily raised to the level of a human being as if to enable it to apprehend the reasons that justify its death in hunting. This tendency to personalize aspects of natural phenomena also extends to and influences the Bini and Yoruba ideas about the spiritual world and the beings associated with it.

The Bini and the Yoruba world-views conceive the spiritual universe as if functioning on the same pattern as the natural world of human beings. The divinities associated with this realm are conceived in terms that present them as supermen and symbolic markers of the qualities approved and desired in men in the society. While the Bini divinities are either wholly good like Olókun and Obiemwen or wholly bad like Ogiuwu, except Ògún who, as a mediator between the good and bad has some aspects of both the Yoruba divinities on the other hand, are never wholly good or bad. They are not perfect beings. Like the hero in Shakespearean tragedy, their near-perfection is always compromised by an intractable flaw. Òrìshà-nlá, the moulder of human physique is a drunkard whose weakness for palm wine results in malformations in human beings. Ògún, the protector of first sons and the symbol of creative initiative is also a figure of cruelty whose thirst is only satisfied with blood-letting. Òrunmila, the refraction of divine omniscience lacks the ability to take care of his precious wife Iwa (good character). Shango's magnificence is compromised by his short temper and Èsù, the divinity of order in ritual sacrifices, undermines the solemnity of ritual occasions because of his tireless desire to play tricks on worshippers. Thus, the Yoruba is able to identify with the divinities of his spiritual universe since these are, in the way they are presented, models in which adhere the qualities envied or disapproved of in society.

In Bini and Yoruba cultural systems certain divinities are presented as polar concepts to each other. The Òrìshà-nlá and Ògún polarity symbolize the life-giving and the life-taking principles. The two divinities constitute symbolic epitomes of the Yoruba people's experiences about the beauty and wealth inherent in the act of creating a new being as well as the pathos and ugliness attendant upon death and bereavement. To a large extent, therefore, G. A. Ojo's observation about Yoruba gods being a reflection of the harsh realities of Yoruba environment is equally applicable to the Bini: In them (Yoruba gods) they (The Yoruba) use the environment to counter its own problems all the time (1966:184). On account of this, therefore, the manner of behaviour and the nature of the functions attributed to the divinities provide cultural reference points for determining the qualities, good or bad, to be found in persons in the societies.

The Òrìshà-nlá/Ògún Polarity in Yoruba Belief System

The Yoruba arch-divinity, Òrìshà-nlá (Obatala) is the moulder of human physique. His duty is to form children and once his work of formation is concluded, he leaves the animation of the forms to Olódùmaré, who imparts the breath of life, a share in his own divine essence in the forms (Talbot 1927:31, 33; Peel 1968:30; Beier 1958; Ijimere 1966:10). He is also taken by the Yoruba to be the divinity of morality and purity. His praise-song is indicative of his functions:

> Òrìshà-nlá is the one who moulds the nose and the eyes,
> He is the one who moulds the eyes of the father and the mouth of his child.
> He moulded the child and moulded the mother,
> He who changes suddenly his manner of behavior
> He is the one who moulds the world like a hoe is easily moulded.
> You are the king, you are the divinity.[28]

His greatest asset in the discharge of his duty is patience. Through the exercise of patience (*sùuru*) he is able to accomplish his tasks excellently. If he were completely pure, all of creation - and human beings in particular - would be well-formed and radiant. His greatest weakness is for palm wine, the potent beverage tapped from the palm or raffia tree.[29] Since all human beings are not well-formed, although their creator is a purist and a perfectionist the Yoruba resolve the contradiction by attributing malformation to the weakness of an otherwise excellent creator. The badly-moulded human beings resulted from a hang-over Òrìshà-nlá had when, one day, he drank vast quantities of palm wine. Two consequences follow from the disharmony caused by his drunkenness. Firstly, he admits his fault and offers restitution by making all the malformed people his special devotees and priests. This removes the malformed from the precarious and marginal life of the unwanted to a central position in traditional religious worship.[30] Secondly, to atone for his offence, he must make an appointment with the divinity of fate, Ẹ̀ṣù, and by a cleansing rite of passage in suffering and degradation, seek a restoration to his prior, near-perfect state, even though the consequences of his act are irreversible. The case against Òrìshà-nlá (Obatala) is well stated in the drama of the imprisonment of Obatala when the diviner whom he consulted on his fate and due atonement, retorted to him:

Obatala,
Who turns blood into children!
Obatala who can turn a single man into two hundred!
Divine craftsman, second only to the owner of heaven
You have an account to settle with the God of fate
Olódùmaré, the immovable rock, who never dies,
Olódùmaré, the eye of heaven that does not grow any grass
Olódùmaré the owner of the sun, the sky and the earth
Appointed you his craftsman,
To mould the features of man.
Obatala who turns blood into children,
You make nose and eyes,
You make penis and vagina,
You betrayed the trust of Olódùmaré.
You drank the milky wine of the palm
Cool and sizzling it was in the morning,
Fermenting in the calabash.
Its sweet form overflowed
Like the eyes of a woman in love.
You refreshed yourself in the morning.
But by evening time your hands were unsteady,
Your senses were dull, your fingertips numbed,
And then,
You made the blind man who cannot see
The whiteness of the cattle egret,
Nor the blackness of the hornbill,
Nor the redness of the cuckal.
You made a red-eyed albino
Who is frightened of the sun,
Whose skin is sore like the leper's.
You made the hunchback,
Laughing-stock of children,

Shunned by women,
A living calabash of medicine
You must pay for your sins.
As soon as you leave this sacred city

Eshu will be waiting for you behind the iroko tree,
He will be hidden in ant-hills,
You will meet him on the road and in the bush,
In the savanna and in the farm. (Ijimere 1966:10).

The Yoruba idea of the purist and perfectionist divinity, Òrìshà-nlá, is cast in terms of this human weakness. The irony of the situation is that the arch-divinity whose symbolic colour is white, a manifestation of his purity and power, is brought down by the potent power of the foaming white palm wine. The only way in which he could regain the essence of his being, his creatorship, was to undergo suffering. Since he was so important in the spiritual universe, if he undertook his particular rite of passage through suffering, he would easily be recognized and those who were to perform the duties of his expiation would either shirk their duties in fear, or make light the burden of suffering that he had to bear. So he had to prevent these situations which would nullify his piacular rite by disguising himself as an ordinary man and, for the duration of the rite, leave aside his duties to the universe. He abandoned himself in the hand of the trickster divinity Eshu whose machinations he had to endure in an extreme display of patience.

Eshu, the chief guardian of the Yoruba spiritual universe and the one who ensures that rituals are carried out to the standard demanded if they are to be efficacious, led Obatala through the most difficult aspects of the piacular exercise. He led him to a farmer and confused both Obatala and the farmer through his won trick of appearing with each half of his body painted in red and black colours. The confusion caused between Obatala and the farmer is graphically recorded in Ulli Beier's English rendering of Ijimere's play on Obatala:

Farmer: Who was that cheeky fellow dressed in red?
His presence made me feel cold in the heart:
He portends evil.

Obatala: Cheeky he was indeed
And I agree with you
That his uncanny presence
May likely mean disaster.
But was he dressed in red?
Surely his dress was black!

Farmer: Are you trying to provoke me?
Have I not eyes in my head?
My eyes like birds
Are wont to fly over two hundred trees.
I see the weaver bird hiding
In the silk cotton tree.
The antelope stiffening in the grass
Cannot elude me.
My gun has hit the hawk
When it stands in the centre of the sky
Quivering
Ready to pounce on my chicken
That man - stranger - wore red!

Obatala: I am a man of peace.
Far be it from me to quarrel with a stranger
Yet I could swear by the iron that digs the bleeding soil
That this man's dress was black (Ijimere 1966:16)

This altercation which began on the note of the awareness that Eshu was going to cause confusion actually led to the confusion that was feared. The confusion was compounded when the trickster divinity, Eshu, appeared to the disputants from another direction. Each disputant, on seeing what he had not seen at the first passing of Eshu, thought he was wrong and the other was right in the first place. The end result of this quarrel was that Obatala, the great and patient creator-divinity was knocked down by the farmer who considered him a liar. Obatala then proceeded on his piacular journey to his friend Shango's house, only to be accused on reaching there, that he was a thief. He was subsequently thrown into prison by his friend's servants.

The paradox in this ritual of restitution was that the condition for Obatala's atonement which forced him to abandon temporarily his official duties caused an imbalance in the ordering of the universe. The temporary neutralization of Obatala's creative and life-sustaining duties which counter-balanced the blood-letting and life-taking tendencies of Ògún, the divinity of war created an imbalance in favor of the life-taking services of Ògún. The main outline of this story of Obatala's imprisonment collected from an informant, Babaláwo Osanyinyeju Ojubona, receives yet another confirmation in Ulli Beier's rendering of Ijimere's play on the consequences of Obatala's imprisonment. This is made clear by Ọ̀yá, the wife of Shango, who stated:

My Lord,
Even now the imprisonment of Obatala spells disaster
The bringer of peace, the father of laughter in gaol,
You have unleashed Ògún, who bathes in blood.
Even now his reign begins:
He kills suddenly in the house and suddenly in the field.
He kills the child with the iron with which it plays.
Ògún kills the owner of the slaves and the slaves as well.
He kills the owner of the house, and paints the hearth with his blood (Ijimere 1966:27).

The consequences are not only on such general terms. The basic fabric of the social and biological life of the Yoruba had been touched because, in Obatala's imprisonment:

...a curse had fallen on the city:
Some women die in childbirth; they bled
Until their body is drained and dry.
Or else the fruit rots in their womb
Before sometime now, the swelling belly
And the pendulous heavy breasts, a woman's pride,
Seem like a death sentence.
The women fear the king, when he returns
For a brief spell from the war
His ankles crusted with blood
His body sweaty and caked with red earth,
The women tremble when he calls them to his mat
And he must force their thighs asunder
And the heat of lust in their bodies
Mingles with the cold sweat of fear.
A curse has fallen on Ọ̀yọ̀.
The corn on its stalk is worm-eaten
And hollow like an old honeycomb.
The yam in the earth is dry and stringy like palm wood
I fear that we are paying now
For the king's injustice.
No one can maltreat the father of laughter
With impunity. Creation comes to a standstill
When he who turns blood into children
Is lingering in gaol (Ijimere 1966:30-31).

In the act of expiation itself, Obatala's imprisonment introduced an element of imbalance in favour of Ògún, the divinity of war, whose favourite colour is red. When his reign is not counter-balanced by that of his opposite number, the creator-divinity, destruction is unleashed on the earth, a destruction which affects all different living things. The fertility of the soil is killed and it yields no harvest. The plants die from lack of nutrition and the prized tuber vegetable - yam - shrivels and - more importantly - the foetus dies in pregnant women while others die at childbirth. Ògún's reign is one in which blood flows freely instead of life-giving water. In the flow of blood, life ebbs away. It is the concatenation of all the fearful things about Ògún's reign that the Yoruba encapsulate in the proverb "Whoever says Ògún is of no consequence, will eat his hot yams with his hands" (*Enití ó wípe t'Ogun ko tonkan, Olúwarẹ̀ a fọwọ lasan jẹsụ gbígboná*). Seen against the backdrop of Ògún's involvement in an individual's life, it becomes clear why the Yoruba emphatically declare for Òrìshà-nlá:

Ẹniti sọjú sẹmú	He who makes the eyes and the nose
Orịsa ni maasin	I will always serve the Orịsa
A-dá-ni bóti rí	He who created us as he is
Orịsa ni maasin	I will always serve the Orịsa
Eni ran mi wa	He who sends one to come here
Orịsa ni maasin	I will always serve Orịsa.[31]

Thus, the expiatory rite of passage of Òrìshà-nlá proved dangerous to the well-being of the human society, for the society realized only in the temporary absence of the protective and creative power of the creator-divinity how valuable was his contribution to the survival of man. Òrìshà-nlá's patient endurance of such suffering was rewarded, not only by the consolation of purification for the purist divinity, but also by his importance, which rose with the people's realisation of the value of his presence and the danger inherent in his absence. Even Ògún acknowledges the reign of peace ushered in by the timely restoration of Òrìshà-nlá to his position in the ordering of the universe, for he was alleged to have said:

Father of laughter
Your reign has begun.
Once more you have come to us
To turn blood into children.

I bow to the master craftsman
Who moulds the red clay
Who makes eyes and makes nose.
The child in the womb will live again:
Your shielding hand once more
Blesses our women.
I shall retire from your dazzling presence,
Your immaculate whiteness
Drives me back into the darkness of my forest.
Now the blood will dry on swords and the arrows.
The elders forging weapons in the smithy
Will grow fat.
The river of blood that fed me has dried up.
I will have to be satisfied with a trickle.
That flows from circumcisions and tribal markings
...I will return to the silent darkness of my forest
Death and creation cannot live close together
Yet remember: They cannot live too far apart either.
(Ijimere 1966:37-38)

The basic idea of Yoruba beliefs about Òrìshà-nlá and Ògún reiterates that the presence of good does not exclude the existence of evil. Good manifested in life-giving is counterbalanced by evil in life-taking. Both remain ideal aspects of the human condition. The ever present reality of the evil in human experience is lessened by the consolation of the blessings of life. The important thing is that Òrìshà-nlá who symbolizes the permanence of that balance remains unmolested in the order of things. When his position is weakened, then:

Ògún will burst out of his forest
To cool his parched throat with blood.
Then the father of laughter will be driven from the city
And the rule of iron returns.
For if Obatala is the right arm of the owner of heaven
Ògún is his left arm.
If Obatala's love is the right eye of the owner of the sun
Ògún's iron is his left eye.
For the owner of the world has interlocked
Creation and death
Inseparably, like mating dogs (Ijimere 1966:44).

Thus, the presence of one principle does not exclude the other, for human experience which is transformed into spiritual categories remain aware of the presence of the good and the evil.

The Yoruba people's conception of the functions and activities of the divinities, Ò̀rìshà-nlá and Ògún, in terms of polarity reaches a high point in the ideas about the human weaknesses that keep both from being wholly pure and perfect spiritual beings. Reactions of both to palm wine manifested the contradictory attitudes of the divinities to similar events. Òrìshà-nlá the creator divinity whose hands slipped in his creative duty after he had become drunk on palm wine and in consequence caused malformations in creation proscribed the drinking of palm wine to his priests and priestesses. Ògún who, under the influence of palm wine, committed the mass murder of his kin and followers who had made him king, on the contrary, approved the drinking of palm wine and vast quantities of it are ceremonially consumed at the concluding rites of Ògún's annual festival as an obligatory liturgical act (Soyinka 1976:15-16). It has been pointed out that this differing attitude to both divinities manifests an important cultural trait, the compensating principle of the Yoruba world-view, for:

> ...the Yoruba can be reassuringly pragmatic, Unless one is in the unfortunate position of being actually marked for priesthood in the worship of Obatala, it is possible still to be a sincere follower of that deity, stay ecstatically sober at his outing, then wind up the festival of the gods by getting beatifically drunk on Ògún's day (Soyinka 1976:16).

Ògún was said, by a second tradition, to have been a human being, not a primordial divinity. He was the powerful warrior-son of Oduduwa, the culture-hero of the Yoruba. In one of his campaigns, he was alleged to have called on the Ire people among the Ekiti Yoruba. Dazzled by his reputation and magical power, they made a move to make him a king. He rejected their offers until, as if to give himself some respite, he accepted. As king of Ire he led campaigns against the enemies of his people as well as defending them. However, during one such campaign, having taken vast quantities of the potent palm wine, he routed the enemy with ease, and, in a state of stupor, turned on his followers and massacred a considerable number of them. When he had recovered from his hang-over, he realized the destruction he had caused, and rather than prohibit the cause of the carnage, he made it obligatory. Thus, at the end of each annual Ògún festival, there is a commemoration of the carnage, when the followers of Ògún sit in a strangely violent way singing songs that would have been taken to be in bad taste at normal periods.[32] The auspicious aspects of Ògún notwithstanding, in the mind of the Yoruba, he is immediately associated with blood and death. On this account, most ritual attempts to Ògún are aimed at placating him and inducing him to keep his distance. The intention is not to form a friendship or enter into his patronage (except for the hunters). A hunter's salute to their patron, Ògún, provides a clear commentary on the relationship of Ògún and his devotees:

> Now I will chant a salute to my Ògún
> O belligerent One, you are cruel.
> The Ejemu, foremost chief of Iworan Town,
> He who smartly accountres himself and goes to the fight.
> A butterfly chances upon a civet-cat's faeces
> and flies high up into the air.
> Ògún, don't fight against me.
> Don't play with me.
> Just be to me a giver of good luck.
> You said you were playing with a child.
> I saw much blood flowing from the girl's private parts
> Ògún don't fight against me.
> You said you were playing with a boy.
> I saw much blood flowing from the boy's private parts.
> Ògún don't fight against me.
> Don't play with me.
> You were playing with a pigeon.
> The pigeon's head was torn from his neck.
> Ògún, don't fight against me.
> Don't play with me.
> You were playing with a sheep.
> the sheep was slaughtered with a knife.
> Ògún, don't fight with me.
> Don't play with me.
> You were playing with a male dog.
> The male dog was beheaded.
> Ògún don't fight with me.
> Don't play with me.[33]

Compared with the desire to get under the protection of Òrìshà-nlá, the message of the salute to Ògún confirms the fact that in certain ritual aspects, the Yoruba see Ògún as the opposite of Òrìshà-nlá.

The Òrúnmìlà/Èṣù Partnership in Yoruba Belief System

Òrúnmìlà is the Yoruba refraction of the omniscience of Olódùmaré, the supreme being. Since he participates in the all-knowing quality of Olódùmaré, he is the divinity that foretells the future through the divination processes Ifá. On account of his knowledge, Òrúnmìlà has been taken by some as the most important divinity under the over-all power of Olódùmaré (Farrow 1926; Abimbola 1976). The Yoruba refer to him as:

Akéré finú sọgbọ́n,
Akọni lọrọ bì iyekan eni
Gbàyẹ-gbọ̀rin, Ibikeji Edumare
Ẹlẹri ipín.

Small, but the essence of wisdom
The one who advises another like his kinsman
One who lives both on the earth and in the heavens
Next in rank with Olódùmaré
The one who witnesses to the choice of destiny.

He symbolizes, therefore, the permanence of the supreme being and the fact that he (the supreme being) lives outside of time. For him, the past, the present and the future are an eternal now. Òrúnmìlà, who represents the essence of his all-knowing power lives, as it were, outside of time and is therefore able to reveal to man in the present what his fate will be in the future. The Yoruba, who like to know ahead of time the projected consequence of an action to be taken in the present, find meaning, a sense of direction and purpose in consulting Òrúnmìlà through the Ifá divination processes. They express the timelessness of Òrúnmìlà, the owner of Ifá when they constantly report, as an act of faith, before consultation that:

Ifá owns today (master of today)
Ifá owns yesterday
Ifá owns the day after tomorrow
To Ifá belongs all the four days established
by Ooṣa on earth.

Ifá lo lòni
Ifá lo ni àná
Ifá lo lòtúnla pẹlu e
Ọrun mila loni ọjọ mérèrin Oosa daiye.

Since the Yoruba believe that the world has been divided into department under the auspices of the different divinities, whose will can be ascertained during any period only through Ifá divination process, the position of Òrúnmìlà becomes unique as the mouthpiece of the divinities. When Òrúnmìlà makes known the mind of his fellow divinities, he always recommends sacrifices to be made, either to improve the good chances that have been divined or to overcome or neutralize evil, for:

> ...it is the belief of the Yoruba that if the prediction of Ifá is good, a sacrifice will help further to make it come to pass and if the prediction is evil, a sacrifice will help the client to dispel the evil (Abimbola 1976:35).

It is in connection with the enforcement of the obligations of clients to make sacrifices prescribed that the Èṣù trickster, order-maintaining, law-enforcement divinity of the Yoruba co-operates with Òrúnmìlà. Before the terms of partnership existing between them are explored, more ought to be said about Òrúnmìlà and his divination processes.

The priests of Òrúnmìlà and the manipulators of Ifá divination process are called the father of secrets (Babaláwo). There are five classes of Babaláwo: the first category is that of Babaláwo Olódù, diviners of Odù, Odu is alleged in myths to be the wife of Ifá. These fathers of secrets are the most qualified because they combine the work of healing with that of divining. The second category is made up of equally qualified diviners who are restricted in the practice of healing and divining to their household. The third group have the instruments of divination but have not been fully initiated. The fourth group consists of those who divine solely for healing. The last group of Babaláwo are Ifá priests who neither divine nor heal but are recognized as priests. Each of the priests in this category is fully employed in occupations of his own, but attend Ifá divining sessions.[34]

The Babaláwo divines in one of four ways. He may decide to use Ikin, the sixteen sacred palm-nuts (Abimbola, 1976:11; Bascom 1980). He employs the simple method of casting these sacred cowries, all at once, into a shallow reed tray. The number that land mouth up is observed and seen against those that land with mouth down; the configuration that they represent has certain prophetic verses attached to it. The diviner interprets the configuration in the light of the sixteen verses attached to it for the benefit of the client and mentions the sacrifice that the configuration carries. The most frequently used method of divination is *ọ̀pẹ̀lẹ̀*, the sacred chain of Ifá divination shaped like a fork with eight half-nuts of *ọ̀pẹ̀lẹ̀* tree (*Schrebera golungensis*) tied to its two sides. Each nut has a concave and four convex sides give a definite Odù.[35]

The complex literary corpus of Ifá has two main divisions; the *Odù* and the *esè*. *Odù* is a collection or volume of verses of Ifá. There are 256 Odu volumes in all. Each Odu is broken down into many chapters called *esè*. The first sixteen volumes (Odù) in the corpus of Ifá are the most important and are called *Ojú Odù* - the central or core Odù:[36] the remaining 240 Odù are called *Omo Odù*, little Odù. The sixteen core or principal Odù contain the most important chapters of Ifá. It is obligatory on all Ifá priests to know these sixteen Odù and their various *ẹsẹ̀*.[37]

The partnership between Ọ̀rúnmìlà and Ẹ̀ṣù, the mouthpiece and the public relations officer of all the other Yoruba gods (Abimbola 1965:4) began very early in the life of the Yoruba group when, on account of the limited population, the divinities were stinted of sacrifices. They were said to have gone so hungry since there were not many people to offer sacrifices to them that some of them took to foraging for survival. Even Ọ̀rúnmìlà was so hungry that he took to fishing. When he met with little success, he became so desperate that he consulted Ẹ̀ṣù on what to do next. Ẹ̀ṣù, it was alleged:

> ... told him that if he could obtain sixteen palm-nuts from the two palm trees of Ọrungan, the chief man, he would show Ifá how to forecast the future. Ifá could then use his knowledge to forecast the future to benefit mankind and so receive abundance of offerings in return; these offerings should be his. Ifá agreed... (Farrow 1926:37).

Èsù subsequently taught Òrúnmìlà the divination and Òrúnmìlà taught the first man, *Òrungan*, who became the first Babaláwo. The terms of agreement have always been carried out by each Babaláwo, and each client who wants successful divination, by setting apart a good portion of the sacrifice recommended to any divinity for the use of Èṣù.

The more auspicious qualities associated with Òrúnmìlà pertain to his ability to cause wealth, and pregnancy, and to combat the machinations of evil forces. As the possessor of these abilities, and the provider of these blessings, the Yoruba who count success in terms of the number of wives and children they possess, seek the protection of Òrúnmìlà against the witches who may destroy their chances of benefiting from such blessings. A typical Yoruba incantation which manifests these powers in Òrúnmìlà is:

> Abisere
> Assanmenmen
> He-that-used-sixteen-buildings for his divinitory activities.
> They made a strong incantation for Òrúnmìlà.
> On the day the Sire was coming from heaven to earth.
> When Òrúnmìlà arrived, he settled on the ground belonging to the witches.
> The witches complained he was on their ground.
> They asked him what he wanted to do.
> Òrúnmìlà replied he wanted to have money,
> Òrúnmìlà replied he wanted to have wives.
> Òrúnmìlà replied he wanted to have children.
> The witches retorted he would have none of them
> Òrúnmìlà said he would have everything before their very eyes.
> He said it is before the landlord's very eyes that the spider makes it web in his building.
> It is before the very eyes of the Lord of the forest that the spider makes its web in the forest.
> No one knows with what the bees build their own comb.
> No one knows with what the porcupine makes its quills.
> When the sun shines forth, everyone is enveloped by its light.
> Ogunda commands that you surround me with the good things of life (Olabintan 1979:9).[38]

In this extract from the Ifá volume of Ogunda, Òrúnmìlà identifies with all adults who wish to be successful in life. He narrates his desire to have the three Yoruba indices of a successful life; wives, children and money. To achieve his desire, he had to overcome powers inimical to his success in a way reminiscent of the Bini proverb whoever must succeed in life, must not heed the bird of prophecy (*No gha yin agbon e idanmweho ahianwen nukioya*) Òrúnmìlà drew attention to the achievement of animals in the face of inimical opposition as assurance of the fact that he would succeed. The spider who succeeds in building a home for itself against the odds created by the determination of the householder to keep his house clean of webs, was a case in point. The operative principle in drawing on the success cases is that they, in turn, will guarantee homeopathically the success of Òrúnmìlà. Through such experience as this, the Yoruba who identifies with Òrúnmìlà's success, forefigures success in his own undertaken.

The legend of the origin of the relationship between Òrúnmìlà and Èsù, collected from Babaláwo Ifatogun will serve as a conclusion to the consideration of the Èṣù and Òrúnmìlà partnership. The story is contained in the Oṣalogbe volume or Odù of the Ifá literary corpus. It states that:

> ...at the early stage of human existence, Èṣù led an army of divinities to wage war against Ogbomekun segi (primordial enemy). It was very important that all the divinities take part in the primordial battle - the 301 divinities of the right of Olódùmaré and the 300 divinities of the left. The battle also held great promise of gathering booty. In anticipation of the battle, divinities like Ogún and Shango took no time to get ready and hastened to the battle field. Òrunmila on his part took the natural step of consulting Ifá to find the auspiciousness of his intended journey to the battlefront. Ifá told him to make a sacrifice and to behave patiently because, on his intended journey, patience would have its reward. On the completion of his sacrifice, he started on his journey to the front. About the same time, Imi, the mother of Èṣù, the warrior-leader of the divinities, was seized by an incurable disease and when she realized that her end was near, she struggled on to the road that led to the battlefront in the hope that she would see some kind person to send to her son Èsù, to inform him about the imminence of her death. (It was part of a child's duty to her parents, that she attend to them on their deathbed). On reaching a crossroad, she saw Òrúnmìlà going to the battlefront. She told him to wait and bury her first, then burn a stick of firewood on her grave for seven days before proceeding to the battlefront. Òrúnmìlà was at first reluctant as he wanted to press forward to take part in the battle so that some portion of the booty would be his. However, he remembered the terms of divination and decided to exercise patience. He carried out the wishes of Imi and on the last day of burning firewood, word having reached Èṣù, he met Òrúnmìlà and asked what he was doing. Òrúnmìlà told him

> that it was Imi, a woman, who had delayed him, but that now the obsequies were completed, he would hurry up and join forces with other divinities. On hearing that Òrúnmìlà had attended his mother at her dying moments, Èṣù thanked him and told him not to go the battlefield. In appreciation for the sacred duty Òrúnmìlà had performed for his mother, Èṣù gave him one hundred and twenty slaves, one hundred and twenty horses and considerable number of clothes. Èṣù then instructed Òrúnmìlà that if anyone should ask him how he came to have all that property since he did not go to war, he should tell them I have buried Imi, the mother of Èṣù, I will not work again (Babaláwo Ifatogun - translation mine).

The partnership between Òrúnmìlà and Èṣù is rooted, therefore, in the fact that like great friends, one stood for the other to perform an important filial duty. The story also reveals the reason why professional friends of Òrúnmìlà who are custodians of his divination process do not engage in manual labour. They perform vital sacred duties to the people who like Èṣù, bring means of sustenance in appreciation of the services of the friends. It communicates the exclusion of priests from manual labour through the subtle play on words; *sin mi* means "take a rest." Hence in the act of burying the mother of Èṣù called Imi, the Yoruba say *sin'mi*, "bury Imi." Through the different meanings generated by the deep structures of *sin mi* the Yoruba give an explanation for the reason why traditional priests do not engage in manual labour. Furthermore, the Èṣù/Òrúnmìlà partnership expresses a basic axiom of Yoruba philosophy that wisdom, without the some physical strength to back it up, is prone to failure as a life that is controlled by brute force without some element of wisdom to regulate its excesses will end in destruction.

Shango is another of the Yoruba divinities whose nature has some relevance to a consideration of the qualities expected in men in society. As a deified hero, he participates more in the human condition and symbolizes two tendencies in man - the one envied, the other despised. Although there are many legends linked with him (Idowu, 1962; Awolalu 1979), the most widespread depict him as the fourth Alaafin, King of Ọ̀yọ́. His three wives were said to be Ọ́yà (the Yoruba word for the River Niger), Ọ̀ṣun and Ọba (two other rivers in Yorubaland). It was claimed that he was a powerful medicine man who belched smoke and fire when he spoke to his subjects. He was short-tempered and vengeful. At one period, he had two powerful warlords under him, Tìmì Àgbàlé and Gbọnka Ebiri, who became, on account of success in battle, difficult to control. In an attempt to rid himself of both of them, he engineered the important chiefs of the town to instigate both men to fight each other. Gbọnka was victorious in the test of nerves that ensued. Since the menance they constituted was unresolved, a second combat was proposed. Timi was killed by Gbọnka who, realising the meaning of the conspiracy implied in the fight between Timi and himself, decided to depose Shango the King. He challenged Shango to a display of magical prowess boasting that should he be thrown into a furnace, he would come out unscathed. Shango ordered that Gbọnka should be cast into the fire, and when Gbọnka emerged unscathed as he promised, he was alleged to have asked Shango to abdicate and go back to his mother's place of Tapaland. Deserted by friends and wives, Shango is a burst of anger, hung himself. Since it was taboo that the king should hang, Ọ̀yọ́ people were forbidden to say so. The elders stated that *Ọba Koso*, the king did not hang but that he disappeared into the heavens. Subsequently, the qualities of the primordial representatives of the wrath of Olódùmaré were assimilated to those of Shango, thus finalising his apotheosis. These qualities of Jakuta (one who fights with stones) as the guardian of morality in society, included a penchant for fair play and justice, an aversion to stealing, lying and witchcraft, and a readiness to administer immediate punishment to the offender. A praise-song of Shango describes him as the one:

> ... who rides fire like a horse,
> Draped in the cloth of death.
> Shango who kills money with a big stick,
> Shango strikes the one who is striped,
> Shango who wrinkles his nose and the liar runs.
> (Ijimere, 1966:21)

Shango as a deified human being with all the qualities the Yoruba desire in their men, is relevant to a study of the qualities of man in society. He also fits perfectly into the model of the Yoruba divinities, who like heroes in Shakespearean tragedy, have their good qualities compromised by some flaw. In the case of Shango, the big fall was caused by short-temper and high-handedness when angry. These weaknesses do not lead to the rejection of the divinity since a major belief in the Yoruba is that no one is perfect (*kòsí eniti kò ni àbùkù lara*). The rules regulating social morality naturally draw attention to the ideal manifested in acts aimed at reducing the weaknesses and strengthening the positive aspects. The flaw notwithstanding, Shango is apotheosized and becomes the object of veneration. In Shango and other divinities, therefore, the Yoruba conceive of various qualities which they can identify in their own moral constitution. They present these qualities as having an independent existence, in which however, they in some sense partake. W. Soyinka's observation on Ògún as the fusion of the will's tendencies to create and destroy is, therefore, applicable to other divinities that each

> ... one who has himself undergone the experience of disintegration, whose spirit has been tested and whose psychic resources laid under stress by the forces most inimical to individual assertion, only he can understand and be the force of fusion between the two contradictions (1976:150).

Such divinities are not just the passive recipients of the veneration of followers, but beings in whom those followers can relate to in the confidence that comes with the knowledge that the objects of worship have gone through the experience that impel the worshipper to take recourse to the divinities.

Olókun, Ògún, Ogiuwu in Bini Belief System

The second child but the first son of Osanubowa is Olókun, the foremost divinity of the Bini. Like Osanobuwa, his father, Olókun enjoys all the positive qualities and stands for all the positive social expectations in the successful Bini first son. As the sovereign over the waters, his abode is said to be a lavishly furnished palace under the sea and it serves as the source of peace, wealth and beauty, all of which bring some considerable amount of joy to the successful Bini man. As the power that controls movement in and over the waters, his position is unique to the Bini in two ways. The Bini regard the waters (rivers) as the passageway to the heavens, *erinmwin*, the abode of the spirits, of the ancestors, of the double of the individual, *ehi*, with whom the individual alternates seven times before being assumed to the position of an elder. Thus, Olókun commands respect as the one who allows the transition of the deceased to the ancestral world. He is also the divinity who controls the blessings of fertility in people. He controls the passage of the unborn children through the waters to the earth, *agbọn*. It is in this sense that he is venerated as the divinity of fertility.

The role of Olókun in terms of these two functions of promoting the transition of the deceased to the *erinmwin*, and consequently to the envied status of an ancestor, as well as affording the unborn children the opportunity of coming down to earth among the living, provides a paradigm for the roles and obligations of the first son. The Bini inheritance principle of primogeniture (as shown in the section on ancestorhood) obliges the first son to effect the transition of his deceased father into the abode of the dead and to the status of ancestor. It is the extent to which he has satisfactorily discharged this sacred filial duty that will improve his chance of admission to the group of elders of the lineage. The first son ensures that he is capable of discharging his sacred duty by receiving from Olókun, through the petitions of his wives, many children - the *summum bonum* of Bini value system. Olókun gives wealth too, and the first son, who must live up to his responsibilities will seek the blessings of Olókun. All who wish to be successful, therefore, must constantly seek the blessings of Olókun. The Bini say this graphically in their proverb, "all rivers that do not flow to the sea (Olókun's palace) eventually become nothing but lakes" (*Eze in ma le gie okun odighi etua ren*). The importance the Bini attach to Olókun as the source of wealth and the fullness of being finds expression in the fact that although Olókun is the first son of Osanobuwa, the supreme deity, he is taken to have superseded his father. Perhaps to justify this contradiction on the metaphysical plane, a Bini proverb asserts that, "one's child is greater than one is not a curse" (*Ovbi omwan se omwan i ru omwan ihen*). An informant mentioned, while talking about Bini divinities that:

> Olókun and Obiemwen are the only spiritual beings who do not kill. Olókun gives wealth, makes the farms fertile, and the yams big, and gives children. Obiemwen ensures the safe delivery of the children. Ogiuwu takes the living away by sending his messenger Ofoe to kill. Ògún is very fearful as the divinity of iron and accidents that make human blood to flow, hence red is his colour. The best divinities are Olókun and his sister, Obiemwen (Ebohon, a translation).

The Bini, therefore, have a symbolic triad. Olókun and Obiemwen as divinities, positive attributes, are balanced by Ogiuwu and Ofoe, with their negative life-taking capacity. The middle ground is maintained by Ògún, who as a fearful divinity of iron and as the enforcer of sacred obligations in a manner reminiscent of Èṣù in Yoruba belief system, is a fearful but necessary symbolic force. As the patron of farmers, hunters, craftsmen and warriors, all of whom use iron tools in the discharge of their duties, Ògún is positive and important to the social needs of the people. Information gathered in the field confirms the observation of Ben-Amos who stated that:

> In Benin thought, Ògún is conceived in both abstract and anthropomorphic forms. As an abstract concept, Ògún represents the force inherent in metal, a mystical power with the potential to create or destroy....Yet Ògún also appears in the oral literature as a junior son of Osanobuwa sent out into the world with two cutlasses to make farms and to make war (1980:51).

It is the context that determines the auspiciousness or inauspiciousness of Ògún's qualities as a Bini divinity. In the context of war, the fierce fighter is described in reference to the blood- spilling tendencies of Ògún as having red eyes. He is hailed and his victories bring prestige and wealth to the king and to himself. He is regarded as a good powerful man. Most men in the *Ighele* (adult) group of warriors in the tripartite social grouping of the Edo would aspire to emulate the conquering will and warlike qualities of Ògún. In the context of the patron of farmers and the controller of the tools of craftsmen, Ògún is a positive creative force and people venerate him so that he can keep accidents away from the farmer and the craftsmen. In both contexts he is auspicious. In the context of childbirth when, against the desires of Obiemwen, the divinity of safe-delivery, blood flows more than is desirable causing the death of the would- be mother, Ògún as the one who lets blood flow freely is inauspicious. He is also dreaded as an abstract power inherent in metals which drives them to cause grievous bodily harm to those who employ such tools in the discharge of their duties. It is on account of his alleged pervading presence in all metal tools that the Bini teach their young ones to treat metal tools with caution. Any misuse of a tool would bring instant retribution on the offending person, and it is alleged that to entice people to misuse metal tools so as to punish them, Ògún allows for iron tools to be in large supply. As a Bini proverb states, "If Ògún were something to be beaten, would iron have been so common on the ground?" (*Evabaghe Ògún Khin ona vb oto?*)

The final aspect of both Bini and Yoruba belief systems is the place of the Supreme Being and his relevance to the qualities of man in society. The divinities are seen as children of the Supreme Deity, to whom has been delegated the power of ruling over different departments of social life. To the extent to which they are seen in this light, they reveal opinions or ideas of the Bini and Yoruba about what the deity expects from man in society and what he disapproves of in human behaviour. In eliciting the rank of the divinities and their relationship to the supreme being, there is a propensity for a divinity's priests, priestesses and devotees to think and speak in ways that suggest that their divinity is the greatest. Consequent upon this propensity is a tendency to ascribe to their divinity an independent existence. This resùlts in a situation where the supreme being whom these divinities represent is pushed further off from the lives of the people and becomes a remote god or *Deus otiosus et absconditus*. Abimbola's observation about the Yoruba worshipper's tendency to exaggerate the importance of his god is applicable to a large extent to most worshippers in both cultures:

> If one asks worshippers of each of the other Yoruba major deities one finds that each group claims that its own god is the most important one (1976:8).

The divinities who are supposed to reveal certain attributes and aspects of the supreme deity, become at the hands of their zealous devotees, symbolic forces that obscure the facts that they ought to reveal. The Bini accept that Olókun, the first son of the supreme deity Osanobuwa became so important that he eclipsed his father. They express this fact in art by representing the supreme deity as a kingly figure smaller than and sitting at the right hand of the much bigger sculpture of Olókun. Perhaps such deliberate increase in Olókun's importance as the king of the waters and the sea is in accord with an axiom of Bini political and religious regulation stated in the proverb, "A king does not live with another king as a servant; each has his own court" (*Ọba igue Ọba dia, domwande ugha o mwen*).[39]

The Yoruba Olódùmarè is not represented in art. It has not been claimed that he has a wife. Neither Òrìshà-nlá or Ifá (Òrúnmìlà) is treated as being great enough to have superseded Olódùmarè, although each is treated by his devotees as being a divinity of unequalled importance under the over all authority of the supreme deity.

Conclusion

The divinities in the spiritual universes of the Bini and the Yoruba reveal in the nature attributed to them, certain virtues and vices which the societies associate with the properly human in the society. In accordance with the experience of the societies which gave rise, in their collective representations, to the spiritual forces, the divinities are not presented as wholly good. Some have much-feared characteristics and are detested in the society and represent, on the account, symbols of what is morally detestable in society. Veneration of such spiritual forces is aimed at keeping them at bay and at drawing the attention of members in the society to characteristics that are disapproved of, and in so doing, serve to reinforce social disapproval of them.

But for the Bini Obienwen and Olókun who are regarded as being wholly good, other divinities in both Bini and Yoruba spiritual universes have good and inauspicious aspects to them. Thus, Ogiuwu, the divinity of the earth as the graveyard of the deceased, has *Ofoe*, death, as its messenger. To the extent to which he takes the living non-elders of the society in premature death, he is regarded as evil. When he takes the elderly who have fulfilled their obligations to society and have been judged by society to have led successful lives, he performs the unique duty of effecting the process of transfer of the deceased to the ancestral abode of *erinmwin*.

The major Yoruba divinities mentioned have signficance for most of the Yoruba people. These divinities are not wholly good as their near-perfect nature is compromised by a flaw.[40] This flaw brings him down to experience the human condition in the process of seeking reparation through a structure of rite of passage. Like Òrìshà-nlá (Obatala) he is separated from his unique position in the social universe; for the transitional period of reparation, a halt is put to his duties. He experiences suffering and pain, after which he is reinstated in his new position which is not wholly pure. He comes to terms with his flaw; thus, unlike the Shakespearean hero, the flaw does not lead to his total rejection. In terms of the experience of Yoruba religious symbolism, it would appear that the flaw itself was desirable so as to enable the spiritual to experience the human condition fully. Precisely through that experience, the Yoruba are able to identify with the divinity and to nurse the hope that since the divinity has met with and overcome his problem, they too will overcome the crisis that impels them to identify with the divinity. The divinities are, thus, symbolic markers to the societies of the qualities desirable in man as ell as those which he must try to overcome. In their spiritual forces, both societies develop symbols from their experiences about life. They employ these symbols to fight and counteract the experiences they are frightened of, as well as to express their satisfaction with those experiences that account for success in life.

CHAPTER TWO NOTES

REFERENCES

1. At the beginning of what turned out to be a long and fruitful series of interviews, an informant, Prince Edun Akenzua, was asked the question What are the essential elements of Bini religion? After a brief silence, he answered with the Bini proverb, The closer one gets to Benin, the farther away Benin is (*A gha se Edo, Edo rre*). This was taken to mean that the exercise of studying Bini religion was as difficult as trying to know the dynamic features of Bini culture. On a note of desperation, he was pressed to explain the puzzle. He responded with yet another proverb, Whoever wishes to succeed in life, must not heed the bird of prophecy (*No gha yin agbon e idanmweho ahianwen nukioya*). He then explained that although learning the essence of Bini religion was very difficult, I should not think that it was impossible and give up on that account. It was important to know from the beginning that it was difficult. It was equally important that the fact of it being difficult should not discourage research into it. To give up in the face of difficulty was not manly. Hence, although he had warned of the difficulty, anyone who wishes to succeed must not listen to predictions. He must apply his efforts to his work. Prince Edun Akenzua is the brother of the reigning Oba of Benin, Uku Akpolokpolo Omo n'Ọba n"Edo, Ọba Erediauwa. He is one of the leading authorities on Bini culture and acts as a liaison between the palace and researchers.

2. Interview with Baale Tewure, 35 miles north-west of Ogbomosho on 24 November 1980.

3. The Egba Ogbóni institution was derived from Ile-Ife (Biobaku 1957:5).

4. Professor Asiwaju, a Ketu-man, who has done scholarly work on the Ketu has pointed out to me in a personal communication that the occurrence of Ogbóni in Imeko is a unique occurrence of cultural borrowing. Although Imèko is a Ketu town (Parinder 1956; Folayan 1974), the Ogbóni cult is not present in Ketu. Imeko not only has the Ogbóni cult but also a vigorous Ẹ́ẹ̀lẹ̀dẹ̀ cult.

5. Ulli Beier (1958), Harper (1970a, 1970b), Drewal (1973; 1974a; 1974b; 1974c; Drewal and Drewal 1975) have drawn attention to the role of this cultic ritual in connection with procurement of fertility. More will be written about this cult in the chapter on female rituals and female status.

6. This verse collected at Abeokuta during an interview with Babaláwo Osayinpeju Ojubona, Ba Onifa, Ijemo, Abeokuta (17.10.80). *See* appendix for vernacular text 1.

7. Dr. Morton-Williams gave a perceptive exposition of the different institutions of the Ọba, Ọ̀yọ̀-Mesi and Ogbóni acting as checks on one another. While the Ọ̀yọ̀-Mesi acts as a check on the Ọba, the Ogbóni acts as

a check on the Ọ̀yọ̀-Mesi in return. Each institution represents a cosmological realm, such that there is a perceived logical connection between the different realms. It would be wrong, as was suggested by Babaloa, that Morton- Williams treated the domains as if mutually exclusive (Abimbola 1977:74-5).

8. Personal communication Prince Edun, 6 Plymouth Road, Benin City and Chief Edomoyin of Mission Street, Benin City.

9. Two variants of this story are recorded in Bradbury (1957:19) and Ben-Amos (1980:45).

10. Contrary to the view held by such scholars as Cordwell who hold that unlike the Yoruba, the Benin people are not receptive to change, and since this includes both basic and surface patterns, one finds no mechanisms for great deviation or radical innovations and the society appears to have a greater homogeneity than can be claimed by the confines of Yoruba ethnic groups (1952:56), the Bini are actually open to change. The inclusion of the King of Europeans in their story of creation is an attempt to integrate a people of foreign provenance into their world-view. This becomes particularly important as the traditional Bini attitude to white skin pigmentation is one of avoidance, especially in ritual matters. (Personal communication by Chief Priest Ebohon, 21 Igbinadolo Street, Benin City.) This was corrobated by Chief Edomoyin, Mission St., Benin City, Prince Edun, Plymouth Road, Benin City and Sir Augustine Emumwen, 22 Agbado St., Benin City. In a later interview, Chief Ebohon stated that *Osanobua*, had along with those children some other purely spiritual one who preceded these; the first was Obiemwen, female goddess of safe delivery; the second *Olókun*, a male divinity of wealth and the controller of the waters; the third was *Ugiuwu*, the owner of the earth as a burial place of the ancestors, and his messenger Ofoe, death. Each of these came down with the tools suited to their function.

11. The opposition in the Yoruba case has often been overplayed and used as a key to decipher early Yoruba history. For instance, Dr. Benjamin C. Ray in *African Religions* has, in an attempt to maintain a set of binary oppositions useful in the trend of his analysis, confused myth and history. He created two bounded categories of obatala the arch-divinity and autochtones and a second category of the Oduduwa and the migrants. Obatala was alleged by him to have returned to Ile-Ife and subsequently become the fourth king of Ile-Ife (1976:43). While recent research support the idea of a foreign group mixing with autochtone at Ife to inaugurate a centralized political system (Obayemi 1976:211), there is no confusion in Yoruba oral literature about the figure of Obatala as a celestial being. Yoruba folklore and divination processes tend to create human circumstances around the divinities.

12. Corporate is employed here to connote land-owning interest groups as used by Jack Goody (1961:7-10).

13. Interview with Chief E. Sanni Ojedeji Baale Tewure, 32 miles northwest of Ogbomosho, 24.11.80.

14. Interview with Asipa Oguntegbe, of Apogere Compound, Imeko, 9 December 1980. *See* appendix for vernacular text 2.

15. Chief Priest Ebohon, 21 Igbinadolo Street, Benin City.

16. Recent scholarship on Yoruba ideas of the soul, taking after Bascom (1960a) have given the impression that it is only Ketu Yoruba that thinks along the lines of the multiple soul which resolves the contradiction between ancestorhood and reincarnation. My fieldwork data which were gathered from interviews as far afield as the Ogbomosho area, Ado Ekiti confirm the explanation given. Special mention is to be made of the interview held at Tewure, near Ogbomosho, with the Elders of the town.

17. Bradbury asserted that the intestines and the head of the goat killed are cooked with yam and used to propitiate the deceased so that it may not bother his progeny (1965:112-14). My fieldwork findings on this showed that the blood of the goat was to achieve the end of restricting the corpse. Chief Edomonyin stated that a dead person who troubles his progeny unduly at this time will jeopardize the chances of his own entry into the ancestral world.

18. For the vernacular, *see* Appendix V Text 3.

19. Reverend Monsignor Oguntuyi stated that among the Ekiti Yoruba, Tears were believed to be provisions for the journey of the deceased to the other world (Oguntuyi 1979:34).

20. Its contents include Asparagus of the sea, Spondiers Anacarcliacees, the cut nails and hair from the deceased, all wrapped in a piece of white linen (personal communication, Chief Odofin Adenle, Oke-Ola Quarters, Pobe, 19.11.80).

21. The Ohori (Hollije) are a unique subgroup of the Yoruba. Although they are located primarily in the Republic of Benin they resisted all attempts by the French to subjugate them. Parrinder described their location as follows. "It is a wild place, inaccessible to outsiders for six months of the year. The people are barbaric, but appear to be akin to the Egbado branch of the Yoruba" (1956:19). Professor A.I. Asiwaju, whose specialist interest covers the Ohori and other sub-groups of Yoruba of Western Yorubaland, described them as belonging to a well organized conglomerate of eighteen separate quarters (1976:16). The series of interviews I conducted at Issaba which is claimed to be their central quarter or village, gave me an insight into their impressive social organization, the traits of which resemble those of the Ọ̀yọ̀ centre from which they claimed to have migrated. Chief Edun, *Chef de Canton*, Issaba, 16.11.80.

22. *See* Appendix for vernacular. Text 4.

23. *See* Appendix for vernacular Text 5.

24. In the Bini system of thought and belief, the waters, constitute the gateway to the spiritual world as well as the source of material wealth from trading with people from across the seas. Thus Olókun's position as owner of the waters is of particular significance to the Bini. By passing through his domain, the deceased whose cycle of lives is completed, becomes an ancestor. The unborn children pass through Olókun's domain in order to actuate their potency to be born. He also dispenses wealth to the people.

25. Crowther, S.A., Bishop. Letter to G.C. Greenway, 15 September 1847. *See*, *Letters and Journals*, C.M.S. Archives, London CA 2/031(a).

26. With the introduction of motor vehicles and heavy industrial machines that could inflict great injuries or cause death, the patronage of Ògún has been extended to cover them.

27. Abimbola (1971:73-4) includes imprisonment - *ewon* (introduced with the establishment of European law) into this category.

28. Collected from Babaláwo Ifatogun. *See* appendix for vernacular Text 6.

29. M. D. W. Jeffreys who gave a hamitic explanation for the presence of palm wine in southern Nigeria as having come from the Nile valley, gave a description of...it as follows "I have found it a drink that grows on one. Consumed in quantities, it lulls away the cares of the world and gives one a bland contented outlook on the troubles of life" (1957:45).

30. Ulli Beier (1958) draws attention to the fact that such religious provisions, which made the malformed priests and priestesses of Obatala, manifest a deep-seated humane tendency in Yoruba culture.

31. Collected from Babaláwo Ifatoye, Igbehin Quarters, Abeokuta. A close version of this was quoted by Awolalu (1979:27).

32. Ògún, as a primordial divinity, was alleged to have led the divinities of the Yoruba down to the earth and cleared the way for their passage. In this sense he is associated with creative progress and adventure and he is taken as the explorer-divinity. This auspicious aspect of Ògún was stressed in interviews with Babaláwo, Ifatogun, and Babaláwo Osanifinpeju of Abeokuta, Babaláwo Oguntegbe of Imeko. It has also been given attention by Parrinder 1949:33-35, 65 & 71; 1952:25-27; Idowu 1962:85-89; Lucas 1948:106-109; Soyinka 1976:140-60; Babalola 1976:168-73; 1979:23-26.

33. Part of a longer Ijala hunter's salute to Ògún collected from Ashipa Oguntegbe of Imeko, rendered in Ketu dialect. It is remarkable that the same was recorded by Babalola and the Ketu dialect of Yoruba seems to have been preserved in writing rather than the *Kione* Yoruba. *See* appendix for vernacular.

34. These five categories were furnished by Babaláwo Oguntegbe of Apogere Compound Meko and Babaláwo Ifatoye of Isale-Ake, Abeokuta,

independently of each other and correspond accurately to those sketched out by Babalola (1976:13).

35. The two other ways of divining are *ibo*, the sacred cowry and sacred bone used from casting lots, and *iroke*. *Iroke* consist of carved club-like objects used to invoke the spirit of Ifá during the divination process.

36. Abimbola translates *Ojú Odù* as the principal Odu(1976:26).

37. References in this work to the authoritative voice of Odu, Ifá have been quoted in various chapters to illuminate points made.

38. *See* appendix for vernacular Text 8.

39. Although most Bini agree that Olókun is the greatest Bini divinity, there is no such agreement among the Yoruba because the point of seniority is not as precise nor as significant as in a society with primogeniture as the principle of inheritance to office. Although Idowu claimed that Òrìshà-nlá (Obatala) is senior and most important (1962:71), Ifá priests interviewed stress the line of thought put forward by Farrow that Ifá is the most important orisa (1926:3). Abimbola feels it is difficult to establish seniority (1976:8).

40. The flaw of Òrúnmìlà has not been dealt with here because it concerns the sum total of the Yoruba idea of good character (*iwa rere*); it will be discussed later.

This Bini art form represents the arms of the Oba being supported on the right by the Ezomo and on the left by the Edaiken, two of the seven members of the Uzama, the highest ranking Bini chiefly group. The Ezomo was one of the two commanders of the Bini forces. He was a constant source of wealth to the king as he disbursed the booty. Edaiken was, and still is, the heir to the throne. Thus, the picture represents the wealth and continuity of kingship.

CHAPTER THREE

THE QUALITIES OF THE GOOD PERSON AMONG THE BINI AND THE YORUBA

Preamble

In literature, a discussion of the qualities of man among the Bini and the Yoruba has been characterized by an overtly negative or positive tendency. Following the British punitive military conquest of the Bini in 1987, the literature that subsequently emerged presented, but for fascination with Bini art, an image of Benin, called "the city of blood" and the Bini in a somewhat negative posture (Bacon 1895). These views seemed to have endured, as the otherwise brilliant comparative study of the Bini and Yoruba art forms by Cordwell (1952) revealed. They began to clear up with the brief but consistently scholarly contributions of Bradbury.

The contributions of certain Yoruba scholars on the Yoruba have been too positive to be properly representative of the Yoruba (Abimbola 1975; Olaniyan 1975; Awoniyi 1975; Awolabi 1974; Fajana 1966). The Yoruba, like other human beings, recognize their limitations, make a clear distinction between the extremes of human behaviour, none of which they approve of, and have a preference for moderation. In terms of this preference, there is an agreement between both the Bini and the Yoruba. The discussion of these qualities will employ, in order to stay closely to the Yoruba and Bini expectations, the more representative paradigm of

Aristotelian Nicomachean ethics. This paradigm presents each quality in a tripartite form - the positive and negative extremes or polar-ends with a mediating tendency to moderation (Artistotle, *Nich, Ethics Book IV*).

A didactic feature noticeable in Yoruba and Bini explanations is the tendency to personify the qualities. This tendency is noticeable also in ideas about the divinities. This way of looking at non-physical attributes has, perhaps, the advantage of making their inculcation in the individual easier than if they were presented in an abstract way. A second feature in the explanations of the attributes is that members of both groups, when interviewed, showed more willingness to illustrate the meaning of such attributes practically by calling on personal experiences than to talk about the ideas that make up each quality.

A final observation of particular relevance to this discussion of attributes is that the demands or expectations connected with each are unique to it. There appears not to be a logical connection between the demands of one and another. Thus, the demands of truthfulness, *emwanta*, may at times offend against kindness, *itohan*, in the Bini understanding of both attributes just as *otito siso*, "speaking the truth", may offend against *inu rere*, "kindness", in the Yoruba understandings of both. Thus, while the Bini or Yoruba may be perfectly aware of the demands of such attributes, if a strict adherence to them would lead to a greater evil in the community (i.e. friction or fission), he is expected - according to the demands of yet another attribute - *ìṣóra sọ̀rọ̀, Ọ̀yọ́* "cautious or diplomatic language", to exercise "mental reservation" by not speaking the truth. Since among the Yoruba, as among the Tallensi (Fortes 1945), the fundamental duty of the corporate lineage is to ensure its survival as a united whole, offenses against truthfulness have a less damaging effect than those against lineage unity. In not speaking the truth, he has chosen, the lesser of two evils. This important attitude to the attributes of man in society will be given a fuller treatment when the process of "dissembling" is discussed.

Kindness: Itohan, Inúrere

Unlike the Yoruba Ọba who is not an absolute ruler and forms a centripetal, over-arching authority over the competing, quasi-autonomous town lineages, the Bini Oba was more of an absolute ruler like the King of Bunyoro (Beattie 1974). Thus, while most Yoruba will baulk at the idea of being called "the slaves of Ọba" (*erú oba*) or even his subjects, the Bini willingly accept the appellation *Ovb*i *Ọba*, "Ọba's subjects or slaves", as depicting correctly their pattern of relationship to the King. The King, as the ruler of the land, is the immediate manifestation of the kindness of *Osanobuwa* and an embodiment of *itohan*, kindness. Since he has power of life and death, one who is alive must recognize that he is alive through the kindness of the king. More specifically, kindness has a hierarchical perspective to it. In Benin society, where rights and obligations consequent upon membership in the larger group, the town - or the smaller group - the family - are seen in terms of a master-servant relationship (Bradbury 1957:19), the extraobligatory duties of the subject to the authority, or the son to the father are not seen as kindness. Conversely, however, the same pattern of relationship does not permit the subject or son to take the services of the father or king for granted. He ought to see them as acts of kindness because he cannot command their performance.

Acts which bring relief to the stranger in need are seen as acts of kindness if they do not bring gains to the one who performs them, and if they are not performed out of obligation. As an illustration, an informant recalled this event in his family:

> *Itohan* is exemplified in this event. During the 1918 influenza epidemic, my father Emumwen was on his farm Urora about ten kilometers from Benin City, on the Ekpoma-Ubiaja Road. My mother, Iyoha, was stricken with the influenza and since there was no one to treat her at the farm, my father decided to take her back to Benin City. One of the symptoms of that dreadful disease was that it induces thirst in its victim so that one stricken tends to drink vast amount of water. The supply of water we took on our journey was depleted as we went along and when it was finished, we had reached Ikpoba, about four kilometers from Benin. Since my mother was asking for more water, my father decided to ask for water when we reached the Bini Ward called, *Eyanugie.* This ward belongs to the blacksmiths guild. In those days, Benin was associated with one craft or another (or one service or another that it performs for the Ọba and the people). By the time we came to the Eyanugiẹ ward, night had fallen. My father tried the first door we came to, tapped it lightly and explained our needs to the

> people inside, since we had heard voices from within the house. They refused to open to give us water. The second group of people in the second house, opened their door, heard my father's explanation and immediately slammed the door shut. We tried about four more doors without success. My father decided to make a last attempt and when he tapped on the door, a fairly young man opened it and to our consternation, gave my mother water, not only to drink then but also for the remaining journey to Benin City. This gesture saved my mother.
>
> Years later, after our mother had recovered, my father sent a messenger to *Eyanugie* Ward to find out and bring back our helper - Iyamu - to our ward *Iwevernwen* - the ward of arrow-shooters. When Iyamu came, my father told him that he was going to honour Iyamu for his *itohan*. My father took his daughter, Iyabo, and handed her over to Iyamu as his wife. This was to thank him for saving the life of our mother. (Papa Emumwen, recorded interview).

Crucial to the consideration of what is involved in Iyamu's act of kindness, *itohan*, is the spontaneous nature of the act; the element of sacrifice and danger and the fact that in performing the act Iyamu did not seek any reward. Since the parties involved were complete strangers, the element of rank and its obligation was not relevant to the act. The influenza epidemic referred to prevailed all over southern Nigeria and was at its peak in October of 1918 when the Superior of the Catholic Mission, Lagos, noted in his log book:

> The most terrible month in the history of Lagos. The influenza raged furiously - death toll very high - hundreds died. One day one hundred and forty-nine cases of death were registered - decrease of the sickness towards the end of the month. No regular services at the Holy Cross Cathedral - all the Schools were closed - no ringing of bells.[1]

Iyamu gave relief to the sick at some danger to himself by giving up some quantity of water that was regarded as a palliative. Thus, the element of danger and deprivation involved heightened the impact of kindness in the act. Since the Bini in particular, and the Edo in general, believe that "the man who has done good does not need to solicit for prayers" (*Onon elu non sen iwa ohi na len*) since goodness will repay itself, the act won him, eventually, a bride. The summary way in which the daughter was given to Iyamu confirms the pattern of father/child relationship.

Although the Bini put emphasis on the need to be kind, they frown at the excess of kindness. A common Bini proverb stated that "too much kindness is foolishness". Iyamu would have been guilty of "over-kindness" according to the Bini if he had not only given water to the sick, but knowing the infectious nature of the influenza, he had harboured the sick in his house. He would not only jeopardize his own well-being, but also that of his household. Had he gone to that extent, he would not have been called "a kind man" but a "foolish man". A measure of consideration for the individual's interest is crucial to what the Bini see as distinguishing "kindness" from foolhardiness. The extreme consideration for one's own interest to the total exclusion of those of other people is taken as cruelty. The lack of thought for one's interest, the other extreme, is foolhardiness. In line with the provisions of Nichomachean ethics, the mean between these two constitutes the right attribute for the "proper" man in Bini society.

Cruelty isolates the individual from his group members who single him out for corrective attacks. In the traditional Bini society, with its division of the male ppopulation of society into the three groups of *Edion* (elders), *Ighele* (adults) and *Iroghae* (the young), group-belonging is very vital to success. Since the Bini lineages are traditionally non-corporate, land for farming and support for occupational and social progress come to one not from his lineage but as a member of his group in society. Isolation from one's peers has lasting punitive effects. It would be in one's own interest, therefore, to cultivate - among other qualities - kindness, because it has the tendency of integrating one firmly in one's group as a focus of attention.

The hierarchical touch to kindness, *itohan*, and the lack of kindness, *emhin-dan*, surfaces in the story of the influenza epidemic. It was considered perfectly normal for the husband of the victim to give his daughter in marriage in appreciation for the act of kindness received. The father was the owner of his child and in the pattern of relationship that informs dealings between parent and child, the daughter, as expected, took this without protest and adjusted to a change in life occasioned by her father's act of appreciation. It would have been seen as a great act of unkindness on the part of the daughter if she had refused to co-operate with her father in the matter of becoming Iyamu's wife. When asked what would have been the consequences of such a rebellious act, the elderly informants who confirmed the veracity of the story stated that, at that time, there was no precedent and it would have been difficult to deal with it. They insisted that the child would have become a symbol of *emhin-dan* (lack of kindness) for the village. It would have been viewed by the village as "over-kindness" for the father of such a daughter to have anything to do with her or even allow her to live in the village. The *Edion* (elder) who told the story, as if to conclude the discussion, reminded the group of the Bini proverb "when kindness is too much, it becomes the act of a fool" (*Ese gha bungbe O khien oghe ozuo*).

The Yoruba word for kindness and its extreme manifestations are connected with the stomach, *inú, ikùn*. The same word also embraces all that is within man. It could refer to the stomach and the heart or to non-physical inner essence. Kindness, *inú-rere*, literally means either "a good stomach and heart" - what constitutes for the Yoruba the totality of the physical things within man - or "a good inside (stomach)". Cruelty, or lack of kindness, is referred to as *sónú*. One who is cruel is referred to a *ọ́sónú*; that is, he has bitter inner-self or within (or a warped stomach). Anyone who is "over-kind", that is, so kind as not to have some thoughts for himself and the interests of his own Kinsmen is called *Òpònú* - one with a distorted stomach or inner-self.

The stomach, *inú*, is an important repository for the Yoruba. Although they clearly distinguish between the chest, *àyà*, and the stomach, *inú* is used in a context that ignores this distinction and embraces not only the stomach and the chest (the cage of the heart) but also the reproductive organs. The Yoruba stress in their proverbs that "we do not keep what is black in our stomach and spit out what is purely white" (*A ki i fi dúdú sínú ki a tu funfun jade*). White is auspicious colour in most rituals and it symbolizes purity. Black, in most contexts, stands for ritual impurity. Colour symbolism is transformed into categories of evaluation and the Yoruba personality. One who has an evil and dangerous inner-self cannot be expected to perform good acts that bring peace. The inner-self which, for the Yoruba, includes the physical parts of man such as the heart and the stomach (excluding the head) is the seat and source of important human acts. For the Yoruba female it is even more important. The womb is located in the area referred to as *inú*. *Inú*, the stomach, is also the repository for witchcraft paraphernalia. A woman with a "bad stomach" and a distorted inner-self is a woman with black stomach and she could not be expected to bring out good things. She could not speak words of peace (*ọ̀rọ̀ àlàáfíà*) and reconciliation (*ìlàjà*). She would not bring forth good or peaceful children either. Conversely, a woman with a white inner-self or stomach is thought to be incapable of bringing out evil works which threaten family group unity or bad children who disrupt soceity. Thus, when people in the village have, through their actions and words as well as through the behaviour of their children, acquired the reputation for being *oninu rere* ("good people" - people with good inner-self", or "good stomach", more literally), this image stays in people's estimation. If for some unknown reason unfavorable acts are attributed to kind people and positive and favorable acts are linked with unkind people, these are taken as a typical and temporary. It is assumed that the individual will keep to type in acts and behaviour that reflects his or her inner stomach. Temperamental people, *onínú fùfù* (literally, people with erupting stomachs[2]) fluctuate between the two rigid sets of classifications. What the Yoruba regard as the period of their normal behaviour is when they are not agitated or upset. In this state they are prone to be kind and are, therefore, *onínú rere*. When they experience temperamental fits during which they are prone to do or say things that are unwholesome, on account of the nature of their *in*ú they are unkind people. The Latin principle of *nemo dat quod non habit* (no one gives what he does not possess) which underlies this approach to kindness, *inu rere*, supports the idea that kindness is physically conditioned in adulthood. The implication is that since the child is still to be formed, all attempts ought to be made to socialize him to develop into a kind person.

Kindness *inú rere* should be commensurate with position in life. In particular, a position achieved through the dint of hard work and the exploitation of human resources is highly regarded. It bestows achieved status and is a condition of the worth of the individual as an illustrous worker. However, achieved status, of its nature, places an obligation on the achiever to be kind, that is to spread the fruit of his success around his relations and followers. The wealthy achiever in Yoruba society is privileged. He attracts friendly gestures of gifts of wives by fathers who, in order to establish contact with him, give him their daughters. He can exploit these connections for political reasons and he is likely to have good following. As Simpson noted:

> The Yoruba is fond of community life and forms societies for all sorts of purposes. This gregarious characteristics is reflected politically in the crowds of followers who attach themselves to a chief whose importance is measured in the terms of the numbers of his attendants and in his propensity for outward display (1937:6).

These attractive appendages to wealth are balanced by the demands on the Yoruba wealthy achiever. Just as the successful man can and often does command not only respect and admiration as well as services which help to maximize his profits and increase the gap between himself and his dependents, he is under a moral imperative to be kind. He ought constantly to give out to his dependents. He is expected to take care, not only his own children, but also the children of relatives. Included in the category of relatives, along with his siblings and their children, are cousins, and in fact, those who can convincingly trace their connections with him particularly through father and less frequently through the mother.

A successful man would be regarded as being unkind and indeed cruel if he failed to try to be benevolent. This moral imperative performs the duty of ensuring that he does not become so wealthy as to be too conspicuous in the community. His kindly gestures ensure the redistribution of wealth in his immediate group and in his village, and prevent him from becoming atypical by being over-wealthy. This outstanding position offends against the traditional Yoruba caution against dictatorship which easily comes about through one individual out-distancing others and through the concentration of power in the hands of this outstanding man. He is thus having to be reduced to manageable size through the extended obligations that are associated with his position. If he fails to do this, he is branded *ènìa burúkú*, and people wonder whether he has achieved his position by evil means, suspecting him of witchcraft and eventually feeling that their suspicions are justified. He is accused of witchcraft, which creates ill-will for him in the society, with the consequence that his following is considerably reduced. If he remains adamant and refuses to fulfill his traditional role of making "kindly" gestures that enhance his popularity and reduce his substance, public furore is increased until lack of popularity forces a reduction in his property.

The Yoruba disapprove of what they call *àpọ̀jù inúrere*, "too much kindness". When one neglects his duties to himself and performs those same duties for others, the people ridicule him. They would remind him of his duties to himself with the proverb "if embers fall on you and your child simultaneously, you should first remove the one on your body" (*tí 'ná bá jóni jó ọmọ ẹni ti ara ẹni laa kókó yan*). They insist that one ought to begin these acts of kindness at home by making the advantages or benefits of one's position to members of one's extended family before one distributes largesse to the society because "it is from the home that we take treasures to the larger society" (*Ile lati nkó ẹ̀ṣọ̀ ròde*). Anyone who prefers to show his generosity to outsiders without a thought for his own people is reminded that "one does not, in the attempt to protect others from harm, lose his own head" (*Akii du orí olóri kí àgbìgbò gbé tẹni lọ*).

Àpọ̀jù inú rere, "over-kindness", it is not disapproved of because it involves no apparent interest for the one who performs it. The Yoruba encourage people to reach out of themselves and help others in need. This lack of selfishness implied in such acts is one of the criteria for determining the good person *ọmọlúwàbí*. The inherent fallacy of *àpòjù inú rere* is that it involves in its performance, a simultaneous unkindness to the self and those connected with the performer. Thus, a man who spends much of his time doing good to the village community and has little time to look after his own affairs or bring up his children properly is committing an act of unkindness to his children. Yoruba parents are severe in the way they correct their children. They are meticulous in their insistence that their children grow up to be well-behaved adults. They make sure that children respect (*bọ̀wọ̀*) their elders and carry out their domestic responsibilities. When children fail, they are often severely flogged. The flogging is seen as an act of kindness aimed at preventing the child from becoming a difficult person. These apparently harsh corrective measures are justified in the proverb "the child behaves foolishly and instead of correcting him sternly, one prays that he may not die; what kills more quickly than foolishness?" (*Ọmọ kògbọ́n, aní ki omaku, kíní onpa ọmọ bi àìgbọ́n?*). It is essential, therefore, that if an act is to be regarded as kind, it ought not to prove inimical or dangerous to one's own interests and, particularly, to the interests of one's kinsmen. Thus, the duties of the father to his children are more important to the society at large and most severe acts are aimed at turning them into responsible members of that society. The Yoruba insist that if these steps are not taken, the children will become more stepped in their wrongdoing and would be atypical, marginal and dangerous people to the society. The Yoruba art form *Ìjálá*, the hunter's songs, graphically records the consequences of uncorrected demeanor:

> ...when a she-goat hardens and hardens in behaviour, She ultimately turns into a tough he-goat. When an ewe becomes confirmed in wild behavior, she in due course becomes a ram. A newly-wed wife plays the bully resolutely and usurps the title of "Iyaale" (senior wife).

The father must prevent his children from becoming such problems to the society by performing his parental duties towards of close supervision of his children.

Truthfulness: Enwata/Ìsòtító

It has been observed earlier that both the Bini and the Yoruba have a tendency to attribute human traits to non-physical objects of discussion. This tendency is shown in both people's tendency to discuss truthfulness in terms of one of the five senses - taste. The Bini and the Yoruba maintain, in their proverbs, that truth is bitter. Although appeal is made to the sense of taste in this description, it is not the felt, distasteful quality of a thing that is important but the effect of repulsion and consequent isolation that it brings about that forms the common ground of comparison between the sense of taste and the quality of truthfulness. Truthfulness is an admirable quality in the Bini or Yoruba person and children are, among other things, socialized to be truthful in a way acceptable to the community. Thus it is not just sufficient to be a truthful person. The context of truthfulness and the good or evil it can do to the community are essential criteria that go into the idea of *emwata or òtítọ́ síṣọ*. The auspiciousness or inauspiciousness of speaking the truth are part of the criteria that determine the maturity of an individual in the community

The Bini attach great importance to the inculcation of *emwata* in their young ones. Children are taught to speak the truth and are beaten when they are discovered to have behaved untruthfully. Papa Augustine Emumwen, an elderly informant, made a distinction between a fearless speaker of the truth and one who speaks the truth only when matters under discussion do not concern him. He alleged that the Bini admire and respect the person who speaks the truth fearlessly. All attempts were made to get at the truth in the olden days. Ordeals were used and such ordeals included one that was thought very effective. A fortune-teller, *Obọ*, used the ordeal of the feather. In this ordeal, the suspects were brought to the *Obọ* who proceeded to pierce their tongue with the pointed end of the feather on which some native medicine had been rubbed. If, after an interval, he found it difficult to remove the feather, this pointed out the untruthful person, who was then severely punished. Honesty in marital dealings or fidelity to the obligations of marriage also shows concern for *enwata*. The poison ordeal was used to find out the truth in allegations of adultery. If the accused to whom the poison was administered died, he was taken as guilty and had, by his death, paid for it. In cases where adultery was proved, the punishment was very severe before the coming of the *pax Britannica* in 1897. The punishment varied according to the status of the woman. If she was the wife of the Ọba the act was sacrilege and the accused paid with his life. This penalty also extended to the wives of the very important Bini chiefs, the Uzama. Banishment was considered a less severe punishment for adultery (Igbafe 1973:77). Adultery with wives of common men was punished by a fine.

The Bini have a more practical approach to truth, *emwata*, in dealings which concern business or political matters. Truthfulness for its own sake is less important than the desire to keep society united and peaceful. If truthfulness would bring a crisis, attempts are made to preserve peaceful relations in society. The Bini support this attitude with the proverb "When people deceive each other there will be no quarrel" (*A gha rere eghe a i gui*). Again, in a situation where a Bini is faced with choosing between speaking the truth and surviving, traditional wisdom advises that he should opt for survival because "one cannot speak the truth with hunger" (*A iy ohanmwem ta emwata*). When truth will hurt a close relative, it is advisable to tell a lie in order to avoid doing a greater harm. The Bini show how they rate compassion over the desire to stick to principle in their proverb "it is in order that a mother may not cry herself to death that one says that her child's eye is only deformed" (*Ne iye omo ghe vie wu ore a na we ovbi ere reghe aro*).

The Bini, who admire eloquence - especially in their leaders and in those who deal in state matters - warn against the tendency to take every word or action that surround any event related to one as true. Allowance ought to be made for exaggeration in recapitulating events because "without exaggerating facts they are not interesting" (*Ama fian ye ots e irhienrhien*). Thus, although the Bini insist that it is desirable to be truthful and admire truthfulness in people, they expect people who are confronted with the choice of maintaining the principle or allowing peace to prevail to put the interest of the community above the maintenance of any principle.

The Yoruba say *òtítọ́ korò*, "the truth is bitter". They recognize and teach their children to speak the truth (*sọ òtótó*). Yet they disapprove of speaking the truth in certain contexts. Truth is not just the conformity of the mind to reality as Immanuel Kant asserted. To the Yoruba, truth is the faithful and factual recollection of a past event that can illuminate problems of the present and contribute to their solution. Truthfulness embraces reliability as it does among the Hausa of Northern Nigeria (Kirk-Greene 1974:4). Reliability itself presupposes "trust", *ìgbọ́kànlé*, which introduces a judicious use of prudence which works in two ways to affect the tendency to be truthful. While a truthful person would be relied upon to speak the truth when occasion demands, if he is reliable he would not speak the "truth" if it were harmful to the one who has confided in him. Should he fail to make this subtle distinction, he would not be considered reliable, and therefore be seen as untrustworthy. Thus the frame of reference for truthfulness is the social context. Yet the Yoruba teach their children such songs as:

Òtító korò, jòwó ọrẹ́ mi,
Ẹjẹ k'a sotítọ́,
ìwà rere Ló'n maíye yẹ ni
Ọtító nínú ilé, lónmu tọkọ taiya gbáiyé rere
Òtító nile aiye ló nmu gbogbo wa gbáiyé rere
Ẹjẹ k'asotito,
ìwà rere Ló'n maiye yeni

The truth is bitter, please my friend,
Let us be truthful,
good character makes us live happily
Truthfulness in the house, makes the husband and wife to live in peace.
Truthfulness in the house makes all of us to be happy on earth.
Let us be truthful,
good character is what makes life happy.

Although the Yoruba admire the truthful person, they disapprove of one who provides truthful information that implicates others and causes conflict within the society. In ridiculing such an act, they say "telling the truth on others does not win much money, it only guarantees worthless praise" (*Aṣòfófó kò gbẹgbaa, kòjú kó mu omi toro ọbẹ̀ lọ̀*). However, the attitude of the Yoruba shifts from disapproval to approval when someone takes it upon himself to inform the king or the elders about the plan of others to cause civil disobedience in the community or to undermine constituted authority. In another proverb they maintain that "the king hears all that is said in farmlands and in the towns; it is people who make this feat possible" (*etí Ọba wa nílé, etí Ọba wa lóko ènìà ló njẹ bẹ*). Implicit in the shifts is the fact that the consequence or goal of truthfulness constitutes its context of rationality.

The Yoruba traditional manner of child-rearing requires, all the same, that a child be taught the benefits of being truthful in his relations with others. He ought to inform his parents about the kind gestures of others to him. He ought to show gifts that he has received. He ought to avoid the habit of telling lies (*puró*) and he is taught to desist from informing on his mates. It is believed that as he matures he will gradually learn the art of subtle discrimination between what he ought to say about what he had seen and what he ought not to say, because "it is not all that the eye sees that the mouth speaks" (*Kìn-nse gbogbo nkan t'oju bárí ni ẹnu nso*). Yet he ought to be honest in his dealings with himself and his kinsmen. They offer him protection, provide for his needs and support him in his ventures. Dishonesty to the close group of relatives is dishonesty to oneself and it implies self-deceit (*itanra ẹnijẹ*). In clear disapproval of self-deceit (*itanra ẹnijẹ*) the Yoruba provide the proverb "he who plants a hundred seedlings of yam and calls it two hundred in order to impress others, when he has finished eating one hundred true yams, he would eat one hundred false yams" (*Enití ógbin ọgọ́run isu tí ope ní igba, tí óbá jẹ ọgọ́run òtítọ́, yio je ogórun irọ́tán*).

To counteract this relative application of truthfulness, the Yoruba widen the scope of trust and reliability beyond the immediate kinship circle through the appeal to Ogun, the divinity of iron and the patron of all firstborn sons. His worship is prevalent all over Yorubaland. One of its taboos is lying. He is alleged to abhor lies and any kind of devious behaviour between friends. Informants in different areas of Yorubaland agree that "Ogun hates lies" (*Ogún kò féke*). Ogun's sanctions against dishonesty are very strong. He is the fearful divinity of hunters who, in their praise-song Ìjálá, refer to him as:

Ogun is god	*Òrìṣa l'Ògun*
Ogun is god	*Òrìṣa l'Ògun*
Anyone who knows Ogun	*Ẹní bá m'Ògun*
Must not jest with Ogun	*K'ómá f'Ògun ṣiré*
Ogun is a god	*Orìṣa l'Ògun*

All sorts of dishonest acts are affronts directed at Ogun, the lover of all that is reliable in man. He is alleged to punish unreliable people (*awon alágàbàgebè*) with sudden injuries from iron implements. He causes the death of those who do not stand by their word of honour.

To appreciate the force of Ogun's sanctions against dishonesty and injustice, the roles of Ogun in the life of the Yoruba should be discussed. Ogun is the patron of all first sons. To the patrilineal Yoruba whose *summum bonum* is procreation of children, especially male children, the favors of Ogun - who protects their sons from dying in a society with a high infant mortality rate, is most eagerly sought. Ogun is the bloodthirsty divinity and the owner of all implements made of iron. He is alleged to cause grievous bodily harm, and even death, to all who use these implements after engaging in acts of dishonesty and fraud. The capacity of the Yoruba to absorb new things and re-arrange them according to their cultural categories is reflected in the phenomenon of the absorption of all vehicles especially motor-vehicles under the tutelage of Ogun. Deaths and grievous injuries from motor accidents which are very frequent in the country are alleged to be consequent on offenses of dishonesty, breach of contract, or fraudulence caused by Ogun in punishment for undisclosed unethical ways of acquiring money. Passenger lorries in areas of Yorubaland often carry two sets of prayerful names, one with Christian orientation such as "Save me O God" or "Jesus is my protector" boldly imprinted on the front of the lorry and a second wish like "May we not experience the wrath of Ogun" equally boldly written at the rear. Ogun is also associated with causing the excessive flow of blood through prolonged labor in childbirth. An instance of prolonged birth throe brings accusations of infidelity against the woman who may then be expected to make confessions of her alleged wrongdoing as a condition for recovering from the pangs. Thus, Ogun's sanctions give rise to a set of strongly held beliefs which strengthen the contracts between people of different lineages.

The Yoruba, who teach and expect that people be truthful in dealings with one another, put the importance of truthfulness for its own sake in second place to the judicious use of truthfulness to maintain smooth human relations. Aware of the dangers of this subjective and selective approach to truthfulness, an approach that is of immense practical use in society, they make up for this shortcoming at a symbolic level. At the level of religious beliefs, the consequences of breaking Ogun's sanctions against lying and fraudulent practices constitute a binding principle regulating activities. The strength of the belief that Ogun will punish such offenses severelly becomes, as it were, the basis of a contract ensuring that words are judiciously kept and promises are fulfilled. Thus, shortcomings which arise at the level of existential relations in the society are remedied at the level of symbolism through the force of deeply held internalized beliefs. As a corollary to the entranched force of this belief in the exacting nature of Ogun on all who cheat or perpetrate fraudulent practices, Yoruba, whether they are adherents of Traditional Religion, Christians or Muslims, who are brought before Courts or Communities when they have erred prefer, not on account of faith but of fear of Ogun, to take Oath on the Bible and the Koran rather than the symbol of Ogun.

Diplomacy as a Pre-requisite Human Characteristic in the Yoruba and Bini

The possession of a diplomatic acumen is crucial to the complete image of the leader as a good person among the Bini and the Yoruba. The analysis of traditional Bini and Yoruba diplomacy has two aspects; activities which concerns the relationship of the autonomous Bini and Yoruba kingdoms and their neighbours and activities which regulate the relationship between the quasi-autonomous wards within the Yoruba towns. Among the Bini, the tripartite division of the society into the elders (*edion*), the adults (*ighele*) and the young (*iroghae*) coupled with the non-corporate nature of the lineages, has the unique effect of not allowing the lineages to operate as interest groups. Since an individual Bini (In the village) makes progress as a member of his division of the village society and not as a member of his lineage or family group, the basis of competition between lineages, ownership of a common property (Goody 1966:63) is removed. The rule of primogeniture also weakens the family as an interest group because it invests rights of inheritance, succession to office and property-ownership in the first son (Bradbury 1956; Ighafe 1973;90). This often leads to conflict within the family between groups of "mother's childrens" at father's death. In this way, the family and the lineage among the Bini traditionally, do not constitute interest groups and cannot, therefore, compete with one another. Besides, since the only true rank among the Bini, with the exception of the Uzama hereditary chiefs is that granted by the oba, there is a tendency for all activities to rotate around the king (Cordwell 1952; Ben-Amos 1980; Igbafe 1973). In this respect, therefore, the second aspect of diplomacy is not of such moment to the Bini as it is to the Yoruba. The Bini kingdom has engaged in diplomatic relations with European countries since the fifteenth century, beginning with the Portuguese, the Spanish, the Dutch and the British (Ryder 1969; 24-194). The terms of this relationship do not come into the discussion of "traditional diplomacy" since they were not dictated by and operated on the terms of Bini customary ways of dealing with its indigenous neighbouring kingdoms and communities.

The duties in the palace were divided between the three palace associations of *Iwebo*, caretakers of the royal wardrobe, *Iweguae*, the providers of domestic service and *Ibiwe*, those who look after the harem of the king.[3] These formed the palace chiefly ranks of *Eghaevbo n"ogbe*. Counterpoised, as it were, against them as a check were the chiefly rank of the town, *Eghaevbo n"Ore*.[4] In addition to those two opposing groups, there was the Uzama, originally made up of the five important chiefs who represented the autochthonous elements in the Bini kingdom. He (the Oba) was able to stave off problems through the way he expertly manipulated the groups (Photo page 86a).

The situation of the Bini king was quite different from that of the Yoruba. Unlike those of the latter, the Bini lineages were not corporate and did not form interest-groups with the exception of the Uzama chiefly families. The Bini do not have a set of equally important and generally accepted alternative means of acquiring status besides that provided by the king (except the Uzama). Thus, the king remained the only source of effecting a rise in rank and status. All who aspired to positions would, therefore, fit themselves into associations set up by the king and accept their positions in the power structure, a position which could be altered for better or worse by the king alone. In this way the king enjoyed:

> ...control of a delicate mechanism through which he could reward services, satisfy ambitions, stimulate loyalty, neutralize conflict and counter hostility. Indeed, much of the political history of Benin turns upon the strivings of important men and families to win place or advancement in the hierarchies of town and palace (Ryder 1969:9).

When the situation was normal and things took their traditional, customary expectation, the power of the king was greatly enhanced.[5] It was the recognition of this power that the Bini express symbolically in their story of creation and their ideas of Bini theocracy when they insist, as informants do even now, that the king was the god of the earth. An able king reduced instances of conflict by judiciously dispensing his gifts of rank and duty. Again, tradition supports the manner in which he chooses to dispense them as they originate from him and can only be rescinded by him. An informant stated that the king was free to act as he pleased. The giving of dispensations or gifts by the king are not obligatory.[6] In support of this claim, he quoted the Bini proverb: "If one salutes the king and he answers, it is reckoned as one of the kind acts he has done for one" (*A gha tue Ọba igbe okhuemnien omwan a ghi kae ba ese no ru re*).

The impact of this image of the powerful kingship of the Bini and the fear it generated amongst the neighbouring communities with which Benin maintained political and economic relationships was great. Benin traded with its hinterland and Yoruba neighbour. This trading enterprise was organized into different branches controlled by special trading associations called *Ekhen*. Each *Ekhen* or trade mission to a specific area had the Ọba himself as the patron and a delegated leader in the person of one of the palace chiefs, most often from the *Iwebo* palace association. The three most important of such missions were: Ekhen-Iruhuen, traders to Ivbiosakon and Etsako area (in the modern day Bendel State); Ekhen-Oria "traders to the Esan or the Ishan" (of the modern-day Bendel State) and Ekhen-Egbo, "traders to the bush areas" salt, coral beads, brass utensils and iron implements for home-made cloth, leather goods, some ivory, palm oil and kernels, and delicacies like locust beans (Akintoye 1969:545) were some of the items of trade.[7]

The relevant point is that these Bini traders were seen as ambassadors of the Ọba of Benin and treated as such. An injury suffered by any of these was often sufficient to bring a punitive army from Benin and through military conquests the north-eastern districts of Yorubaland became part of the Bini kingdom (Akintoye 1969:550). Hunters in these areas of Ọwọ, Ekiti and Akoko who killed leopards were under the obligation to take the animals to the Ọba of Bini Kingdom.[8] Fear was an important determinant in the factors that regulated the response of the Bini neighbours to Bini traders and Bini Kingdom. A clear expression of this all pervading fear was alleged to have been given in a Bini proverb by the king of the north-eastern Yoruba town of Akure:

> The Bini (King) of Akure says: what must befall one cannot be avoided. Without carrying load I become bald, without going to Benin I become the King's enemy (Aigbe 1960:15).

It is the ability to carry on a silent communication between the hidden private selves or to engage in the "inner activity of getting the unspoken message from an adult about an imminent action to be taken on a sensitive issue that singles out the well brought-up, young man. The Yoruba say, in reference to that ability, that the "grunt of the pig remains within him" (*hùnhùn elédè inú rí nó gbé*). The Yoruba town, made up of autonomous competing corporate patrilineages (Frobenius 1913; Lloyd 1955; Schwab 1955, 1962), recognizes, besides the rank bestowed by the king, also the rank achieved by individuals as members of the lineage. The segments of the lineage, *idile* are politically articulate as action of members, good or bad are often predicated of their segment, the residential corporate compound (Agbo-ile). Thus, among the Yoruba the king has to delicately balance the weight of demands between the competing lineages.

The diplomatic activities of the Yoruba kingdom are best exemplified by the Ọ̀yọ́-Yoruba sub-group. The Ọ̀yọ́ (Yoruba) kingdom serves as apt illustration because through its military power from the seventeenth to the nineteenth century, it held sway over much of Yorubaland and on that account it had to deal with other hitherto-autonomous Yoruba kingdoms which it had to administer. R. Smith, who undertook the first study of Yoruba diplomacy, remarked that, to the Yoruba

> ...diplomacy was a fine and familiar art. Their numerous kingdoms negotiated both among themselves and with their neighbours, and this international intercourse was conducted along recognized lines and according to a strict and practical protocol (1969:40).

R. Olaniyan subsequently built on Smith's contribution by providing a scholarly work on Ọ̀yọ́-Yoruba nineteenth-century diplomacy. His restriction of this study to the activities of the Ọ̀yọ́ kingdom with other Yoruba kingdoms did not allow him to appreciate the level to which diplomacy pervaded the dealings of the Yoruba among themselves.

In seeking the approximate Yoruba word for "diplomacy", informants from different parts of Yorubaland surprisingly gave, along with other words, *Ọ̀yọ́*. Ọ̀yọ́ is the name of the Yoruba kingdom whose military power spanned four centuries until it was reduced in the nineteenth century through the combined efforts of the Fulani Jihadists from the North and the Dahomey from the West as well as intrigue from within. What is surprising about the consensus on "Ọ̀yọ́" as translating diplomacy, is that it is made synonymous with other words like "cunning" (*Ọgbọ́n ẹ̀wẹ́*) or *àrékéreké* "wise in a devious way". Although the Reverend S. Johnson, an Ọ̀yọ́ man, described the Ọ̀yọ́ as "very diplomatic, cautious almost to timidity, provokingly conservative, and withal very masterful" (1921), most informants are in agreement with the view of the informant who said that:

> We use "*Ọ̀yọ́*" for a man or a group of people who shy away from committing themselves to any stated view or principle, who manipulate others to achieve their interest and whose language though apparently conciliatory contains innuendoes.

There is an agreement, therefore, that the connotation of diplomacy in Yoruba is not completely positive.

The Alafin, King of Ọ̀yọ́, the head of Ọ̀yọ́ kingdom's traditional government, was the final source of authority. He was not absolute as his power was checked by the Ọ̀yọ́ Mesi, the seven most senior chiefs. The authority of the Ọ̀yọ́ Mesi was equally checked by Ògbóni (Morton-Williams 1960). The Ọba and the Ọ̀yọ́ Mesi, as the body with the executive, judicial and legislative powers (Olaniyan 1975:302-303) were responsible for formulating the policy of relations between the kingdom and its neighbours, whether this was expressed in gestures of peace or acts of war. It is as characteristic of Yoruba traditional government, that although the Alafin, the symbol of Ọ̀yọ́ collective power and unity, was to all intents and purposes the ruler of the empire, in his kingdom as well as in other Yoruba kingdoms like Ẹ̀gbá (Biobaku 1957), the real rulers were his chiefs, heads of wards and lineages in the capital. Each important chief acted as a patron to a vassal

Yoruba town in the periphery of the kingdom. In this role, he protected their interests and brought their grievances to the palace of the Alafin.

The king maintained a direct presence in the vassal towns in two ways. The first was through the liaison of a special group of his representatives called *Ajẹ́lẹ̀*; these were hand-picked slaves of the palace whose loyalty was beyond any question. The patron chiefs of vassal towns pass on messages to the Ọba through the offices of the Ajẹ́lẹ̀. The second group of palace representatives were the *ìlàrí*. Again, they were a corps of well-trusted slaves or distinguished warriors (Johnson 1921: 171-72). These stayed in the towns and kept the king well-informed about events of any relevance to the palace. Including the warriors in this category had the added advantage of keeping such powerful people at some distance and in reserve from the capital. Having been chosen and specially prepared for their duties by rituals which bind them in loyalty to the king, they were given important names, which served as a statement of policies of the king (Johnson 1921:60-63; Ellis 1893:168).

The Ìlarí names were clearly diplomatic in nature as they tended to be general and avoided further clarification.[9] Thus when the Alafin sends an Ilari with the name "do not challenge him" (*Madarikan*) to a troublesome vassal town, warning is provided. No further clarification is made until the ruler of the vassal town unleashes a series of diplomatic moves through the town's patron with the help of the Ajẹlẹ. to avoid the full impact of Ọ̀yọ́'s wrath, amends are then made. If the king (Alafin) is satisfied by the amends, he may recall the first Ilari and send a second named "there is no more fight" (*kòsíjà mó*). A vassal town of Ọ̀yọ́ which having remained loyal suddenly changed its attitude to Ọ̀yọ́ was sent an Ilari named "do not make the Ọba uncomfortable" (*máni Ọba lára*). If it refused to heed the warning, a new Ilari named "let us have it strong" (*káfilegbon*) was sent. This policy would subsequently be translated into action by the organization of a punitive force to bring the erring town into line. A vassal town that went to this extreme would have to pay the price and seek a gradual restoration to the good graces of the Ọba Alaafin of Ọ̀yọ́. Attempts at reconciliation may meet with the rebuff of receiving an Ilari from the Ọba with the name "the king is not ready", (*Ọba- kò-se-tán*). Through this Ilari, the king states that it is himself who will decide when sufficient punishment has been given to the erring town.

An example of the poor diplomacy along this line was recorded by the Reverend Johnson (1921:407) when the Alafin of Ọ̀yọ́ sought the help of the British colonial officers in Lagos to bring an end to internecine warfare that ravaged much of Yorubaland. Unable to control the carnage that resulted from the demise of its empire (Smith and Ajayi 1964) Alafin Adeyemi appealed, in 1881, to Governor W. B. Griffiths and Reverend J. B. Wood, Secretary of the Church Missionary Society, to put pressure on the British government to stop the fighting. In contravention of the rules that regulate the sending of an Ilari whose name unequivocally states the commitment of the king to a move he started, the king sent an Ilari with the name "the king is not ready" (*Ọba-kò-setán*). The observers of Ọ̀yọ́ diplomacy advised the British officials not to take any positive action since the terms of the message contained a contradiction between the intention and policy statement of the king. When a similar demand was made in 1893 through the same Ilari, Governor Carter took advice and refused to have anything to do with the king until he sent an Ilari with a name that marked the desire of the king (Johnson 1921:627; Olaniyan 1975:310). The king complied by sending an Ilari with the name "the king is the Chief" (*Ọbalolú*).[10] Thus the delicate business of diplomacy was carried on in symbolic messages which more often left unclear or deliberately confusing the intention of the king on any given sensitive subject.

The kings and elders of Yorubaland also maintained communication through the use of symbols. These means of communication took two forms - the use of *owo eyo* (cowries) which were then used as the medium of exchange and the employment of items whose Yoruba names form the meaning or content of the message intended to be conveyed by the prestation. In apparent confirmation of views of certain Yoruba writers (Johnson 1921:486; Akinyele 1952:114-8; Lucas 1948: Appendix 11) but unaware of it, an informant in Ọ̀yọ́ Palace said:

> In the olden days, our fathers sent messages in very many interesting ways. These messages were meant to be understood only by the wise. They used different items like

> cowries, feathers and special leaves. When they send the hyacinth plant to a person, it is meant to warn him that his affairs are in the open and he should make some attempt to conceal them because when you touch hyacinth, the leaves close up immediately. When two cowries facing each other are tied together with a red cord, it symbolizes that the two people are so agreed on a policy or are so much united in friendship that only death can separate them. In this way, our elders send secret messages to themselves. That is why the elders say that it is with proverbs that we beat the drum of *agidigbo* (traditional violin) only the wise dance to it, and only those with incisive minds decipher its message (Kudefu 1980) (Translation).[11]

An instance of this communication through the use of symbols was recorded by Johnson (1921:486) when the leader of the Yoruba town of Ibadan, originally a war camp (Awe 1967), sought to improve relations between his town and the king of the Ijebu Yoruba. He sent a parcel containing a fan (*abèbè*) a feather of the water-bird *osìn*, and a white sash. *Abèbè*, the Yoruba for fan, derives from the root *bè*, which means "to beg". *Osìn* derives from *sin* which means "to serve" and white, acknowledged internationally as the colour of peace, conveyed the plea for peace. The message conveyed by those items was, "we beg you, we will serve you, let there be peace between us" (Johnson 1921:486; Olaniya 1975:320). This, then, was the way sophisticated messages were sent in symbolic codes.

The second context of the employment of diplomacy and tact in regulating affairs in the society was noticeable in the king's subtle way of balancing the power of the competing lineages. As has been noted:

> The Yoruba traditional political system...consists of a number of separate lineages. The lineages are independent of one another, each endeavouring to maintain its identity and autonomy...(Lloyd 1955:21).

As corporate bodies, the lineages compete to maintain their interests as well as to be superior to others. Their leaders, often the eldest surviving male, represent the interests of the group in the government of the town. Frobenius provides an insight into the intense competition between the lineages, a competition which the king has to endure and palliate when he observed, in reference to the elders of Ifè town that:

> ...each one watches his neighbour and his fellows with the utmost sharpness, and is patently concerned that none should get a greater pull on the ruler than himself. It is an uncommonly petty sort, a disgusting matching of the smallest of the importance of one's own personality and family against that of others (1913:280)

The peculiar situation imposed the obligation of caution on the king in relation to the members of the lineages that formed his town. The members of the lineages themselves reciprocate with caution in dealing with the king and members of other lineages. The members of the lineages are socialized in the art of tactful relationships with non-lineage members so as to maintain the family interest. Thus, the king finds it perhaps, less demanding to maintain inter-city diplomatic relations than to keep the balance between the competing lineages. In the former diplomatic context, all the lineages fuse together to give support to the king in dealing with another town. However, within the town, the king is by himself as the lineages form exclusive groups which fight among themselves to maintain or improve their rank in the town. A Yoruba folk-tale quoted by R. G. Lienhardt provides an apt commentary on the king's tactful response to the competition of the lineages:

> The king invited the animals to a great feast, and offered a prize to the best dancer. The animals danced energetically before him, each showing off its own most striking qualities - the elephant its grave dignity, the leopard it beautiful coat and sinuous agility, the gazelle its spectacular leaps and so forth. When, at the end of the dance, they gathered around the king to hear his judgement, to their surprise and displeasure he awarded the prize to the tortoise. Answering their complaints, the king asked them who had provided the feast, and who was giving the prize, to which they could only reply "it is you O king". "And so it is that I award the prize to the tortoise" said the king, "for it is only I who can see the dance of the tortoise: his dance is entirely inside him" (1980:71).

In choosing the winner, the king, characteristic of Yoruba royal balance-maintaining caution, has avoided the rancour and ill-feeling that a more popular choice would have engendered. He has picked on the least likely figure and his choice neither enhances nor reduces the rank of such powerful and difficult competitors as the elephant, the leopard and the python. Yet the choice itself is not lacking in wisdom for:

> the success of the slow, ungainly tortoise is an extreme example of the deceptiveness of outward appearance, though the moral is not that hidden intellectual agility is preferred, as such, to physical display: both are parts of the dance. The tortoise too, now public and exposed, now withdrawn and hidden, is a fitting and subtle image for the self (Lienhardt 1980:71).

Even within the lineage segment, the compound family, the elder must behave constantly in a way that shows that there are no favorites but that all are important to the family and its interests. In allocating family property, he would very often serve his own children last. When he gives what he has refused his own child to the child of his sibling, his own child will gradually learn that the act of his father was not an instance of discrimination but of caution. Through the gradual introduction to the art of tactful relationships with others in the community and through the frequent use of folktales and other didactic methods, it becomes clear that:

> ...from childhood the Yoruba are not only supposed to have an idea of a hidden, private self-here an inner *activity*...but to understand that it may ultimately be more important than the outer activity, the *persona*, or mask, in Mauss's terms, presented to others (*Ibid*).

Bravery: Udinwin/Agbára

Among the Bini and the Yoruba, the conception of bravery embraces ideas about power and wisdom. Power itself is of three types; physical power, metaphysical or medicinal power and moral power. Each of these types of power submits to the tripartite division Characteristic of the Aristotelian approach to the analysis of the qualities of the person.

The Bini admire bravery in the individual but insist that *enwan* "wisdom" is superior to physical strength and forms the distinguishing criterion between what is permissible and what is *ozuo* (foolhardiness). Bravery, *udinmwen*, is admired, particularly in the *Ighele* division of male society. The Ighele society forms the military section of the community and members are expected to display bravery and tenacity during the military campaigns. Members of the Ighele organization, like all other subjects of the Ọba, are expected to give service to the community to the best of their ability. To refuse to serve as best one can is to invite trouble. Young men who acquit themselves well at war are compensated in many ways by the king or by their own community. A young distinguished warrior could be rewarded by being named an elder and incorporated into the association of elders where he enjoys all the rights and privileges of his hard-won status. The Ọba could reward the services of a warrior with the gift of his daughter as wife to the warrior because he has demonstrated by his performance at war that he was a friendly and loyal subject of the king and "not to be the king's enemy is equivalent to wealth" (*A ire oghian oba se vbe efe*).

Members of the community who show themselves to be unaccountably weak and engage in acts that border on disloyalty, automatically make themselves the enemies of the Ọba and the community. They face the consequences which the enemies of the Ọba bring upon themselves. Wherever in the kingdom they might be, they would be brought to justice because "no forest can accommodate the enemy of the king" (*Oha igua oghian ọba*).[12] Members of the community may refuse to allow their daughters to marry such people. If they have received titles, they could be stripped of them.

While the Bini admire bravery in their young men and socialize them through rewards and punishments to live up to their calling, the Bini are quick to disapprove of any act that borders on being brave in an unwise way. They caution their young ones to use their sense in discriminating between situations that call for a display of bravery and another that encourages the attitude of a weakling. As a Benin informant said, "it is nice and admirable to be brave, but on occasions it is nicer to be a weakling for we often stand in the compound of the weak to point to the ruins where the strong man used to live". It is to inculcate this discriminatory attitude in the young that the Bini say "If a person stronger than one snatches a sword from one's hand, one would say, "I am on the way to your farm sir" (*Ase emwan gha mien omwan ikhu, a we, "odugbo rue i te rie"*). Thus, while it is essentially admirable to be brave, an unwise display of bravery would be rejected just as the Bini rejected weakness in their young. Weakness and the unwise show of bravery amounts to foolishness and the Bini are uncomfortable with both.

The Yoruba regard bravery as an essential attribute in the person whether male or female. The brave person is called *akínkanjú*. A courageous wrestler (*akínkanjú elemu*) is one who does not give up easily and puts all his best to turn moments of apparent defeat into victory. A Yoruba woman at child-birth is called *akínkanjú obínrín* if she bears the pangs of birth without giving much trouble. However, when an extreme situation shows that any act of courage or bravery would be most harmful to the individual, the Yoruba ridicule anyone who musters courage in such a situation. Such an individual may be referred to as "one of brutal physical energy but no sense" (*alágbára má mèrò baba òle*). He would be reminded that "wisdom is superior to brutal force". The Yoruba regard an uncalled-for show of strength as provoking harmful retaliation. They call the act itself foolhardiness (*àìlọ́gbọ́nlóri*). A Yoruba who shows lack of courage (or weakness) when some courage and a moderate show of strength is called for is ridiculed as a weakling - *ọ̀lẹ́*. He is reminded that if he does not improve by showing some courage, the strong and the courageous will appropriate what belongs to him because "it is the wealthy (courageous worker) who often marries the spouse of the lazy man" (*Olówó, ló má a gbàyàwó ọ̀lẹ́*).

The brave man who possesses metaphysical or medicinal power is also highly regarded. He is a sort of medical doctor in the community. His power is in demand at times of crisis or sudden illness. He is credited with knowing the medicinal power of different leaves in the forest and that he is able to tap the force (*agbába*) inherent in them because of his knowledge of the secret names of the leaves which when pronounced activate their medicinal potential. *Babaláwo*, "father of secrets", is one who is credited with such power. He is consulted at such times and having diagnosed the sickness prescribes the medicinal concoction that will treat the ailment.[13] As a case in point, a Babaláwo, medicine man, may be called in to assist in effecting an easy delivery particularly when a woman is undergoing prolonged labour. An informant claimed that in most areas of Yorubaland the items that made up the ingredients of the medicine which the medicine man uses to effect easy delivery include the breast of a goat *oyàn ewúré*, the reproductive organs of a sheep, the horn of a he-goat, a little piece of human skull (*agbárí*), alligator pepper (*ata rere*), and a red sash (aṣọ pupa). The medicinal items are, with the exception of the horn, ground and put into the horn. Holes are made in the red sash which is subsequently used to cover the open end of the horn. The medicine man then goes into the house and stays beside the woman in labour. He holds the horn with the left hand pointing towards the woman and chants the following incantation:

> The goats do not have midwives
> The sheep do not have midwives
> When the goat is pregnant, she is safely delivered
> When the sheep is pregnant, she is safely delivered
> The alligator pepper reawakens the body
> Anywhere death takes becomes the path
> You, woman, bring forth what is inside you quickly.

The underlying principle on which the medicine is alleged to operate is the homoeopathic principle of like causing similar reactions. My informant insisted that this medicinal assistance was always effective.

The possession of moral power (*inú rere*) is vital to the criteria which distinguish a brave person from a fool (*òpònu*) and a weakling (*ọ̀lẹ*). It also differentiates the good medicine man from the bad medicine man. Moral power is the courage to refuse to use one's knowledge about the magical use of medicine to hurt or harm others. One who is reputed to lack this moral power because he hurts others by his masterly control of bad medicine is called *oninu burúkú*. Anyone with such a stigma in Yoruba society may find it difficult to find a wife as the people like to keep him at a distance. At times of crisis such as periods of war, however, the man who is feared for his ability to use bad medicine (*ogun burúkú*) to hurt others becomes very important to the community. He is expected to employ all the reserves of his ability to hurt the enemy. If he succeeds he is admired and praised and his rank increases in the society as his esteem rises among the people. Thus, the context in which any given ability or power is used is vital to determining its auspiciousness to the community.

Another quality in the person associated with the idea of bravery by the Yoruba is the ability to endure. Endurance is taken by the Yoruba as a prerequisite for success. They say that "consistent perservance is the medicine of success and wealth" (*Adó-isí-loogun ọrọ̀*). The Yoruba teach their children that they must persist in facing a difficult problem. Not until one has tried at any worthwhile venture and failed three times is he exonerated from the accusation of lack of endurance. The number three stands for finality. Thus, any hardship that does not resolve itself after three conscious efforts at seeking a solution may be abandoned without loss of face. To persist when all indications show that no solution is forthcoming after the third attempt is regarded by the Yoruba as foolhardiness.

One way of teaching Yoruba children the virtue of endurance is folklore. Yoruba folklore teaches the merit of endurance by showing the loss that lack of it entails. Such folklore was given by an informant about the fate of the tortoise who wanted to marry the daughter of the king. As has been noted "the tortoise represents intelligence, resourcefulness, trickery and luck" (Lienhardt 1980:71). He is also employed to portray, through his response to situations, the consequences of failing to persevere. The folktale is summarized thus:

> The King invited all eligible bachelors to make a bid for the hand of his elegant daughter. He promised that anyone who succeeded in winning the hand of his daughter would have, in addition to his wife, half of all he owned and would be installed as the ruler over half his kingdom. The only condition for qualification was a test of endurance. Any bachelor who could endure staying in a filthy toilet for seven days would win the hand of the princess. Powerful animals came and tried. The elephant could not last the first day. The leopard was carried out in a coma on the evening of the second day. The hedgehog thought that its very narrow nose would reduce the volume of the odour to be endured, but it lasted only four days. The king got desperate as he was afraid that none would qualify. However, he felt the trial was worth the effort since it was an indication of the quality of character of his would- be son-in-law and a sign that the marriage would endure. Other animals

> came forward and tried. The hyena made a desperate attempt and lost its howl after the fourth day. Finally, the tortoise came along and started. No-one expected it to last two days but it endured one day after another. After the fifth day, the king and his chiefs shifted from cynicism to hope that the tortoise would endure the test. On the sixth day, the king commanded his movable property to be divided in two in readiness to give half to the tortoise. On the eve of the sixth day he commanded the town to begin the festivity of thanksgiving that at last his beautiful daughter would be happily married. The dances continued until about four hours to the end of the endurance test when the tortoise insisted, to the consternation of everybody, that it could no longer complete the test. All begged him to no avail. When he was released two hours later, he saw the valuable property and the beautiful gowns and heard about the great towns over which he would have ruled had he completed. In a final desperate attempt, he pleaded to go back. Since he had failed, he was refused another try and so lost the hand of the princess. He remained a wretched, lonely figure thereafter.

Endurance was, therefore, shown as vital to success in any venture in life. The tortoise (*ìjàpá*) was not strong enough and lost the contest.

Respect for Seniority: Ekpen/Ìteriba

The Bini and the Yoruba teach their children to show respect for elders. Seniority is a means of maintaining order as anyone who is senior in age in any group is automatically regarded as the leader (except if he is senile).

The Bini division of the male population into three groups of the young, the adult and the elders, clearly demonstrates the factor of seniority as a determinant of political organization. Normally, the *iroghae* group of youth is made up of teenagers who perform such duties as sweeping the village, repairing the paths and providing entertainment for the village or community. They anxiously look forward to the time when they will be promoted to the next rank of *Ighele*, warrior adults who perform more important prestige-enhancing duties. The Ighele group long for the period when they will reach the top of the social ladder when they become members of the *edion* (elders). Except in rare cases of bravery in war, or the death of an elder who is replaced in the Council of Elders by his minor child (where he has no surviving elder child), the passage from one group to the next senior group is strictly according to the criterion of age.

The elders are the focus of the society and in Bini outlying villages, the power-base. As the group closest to the ancestors, they are particularly powerful as they share in the power that will be completely theirs when they are transformed at death. The Bini maintained an unmistaken correlation between age and wisdom and they record this in their proverb which maintains that "by the number of days one is senior to a child, by so many days one is wiser" (*Ede na ya dien ovbekhan ore a ya wan se ore*). The elder is a symbol of peace who reconciles people in the society. In this capacity, he is symbolically linked with the kolanut (*Cola acuminata*) which is the Bini symbol of friendship and peace. It is offered to visitors as a sign that they are welcome. The association of the elder to kolanut transcends the prestational value of kola. It also derives from the imagery of a stout kolanut tree well-laden with fruit. In this image the elder is a source of fertility, health and unity of the community. Thus as the Bini say "a load of kolanut is never too heavy for a senior person" (*Ihe evbee ikhua odion*). Young men are taught not to challenge elders or to argue with them. To argue with an elder is like challenging a bigger person to a wrestling match. Such a contest will bring disaster on the young man because "if a child bends down and attempts to overthrow a bigger person than he, the latter becomes a load of him" (*Ovbokan gha d'otoe mue no se ore o ghi khin ere ihe*). Respect, affection and care ought to characterize the relations of the young with the elderly.

The Yoruba too subscribe to the view of respect for elders. Since most areas of Yorubaland are not organized along the division of the society into these clearcut groups, little points of etiquette are meticulously observed between senior (*Ẹgbọ́n*) and junior (*àbúro*) members of the community. Children are taught that when they get up in the morning they should greet their elders. Boys prostrate while girls kneel down. A young man is taught that he should look down and not straight at any senior person who may be correcting him. When eating food together, elders take meat (*eran*) first before juniors. Seniors are allowed to eat meat during a meal while juniors are expected to keep their pieces of meat until after the meal is over.

The elders are the focus of respect and affection in Yoruba society. A young man is judged as matured and responsible to the extent to which he takes care of his elderly people. The Yoruba think it an obligation for the young to look after the aged as a little way of showing appreciation for the sacrifices that the parents make in one's youth. Thus, the Yoruba insist that the principle that "when the rabbit becomes old, it suckles from its young ones" (*Ti okété ba dagba ọmu ọmọ rẹ ni imu*) so also the young should take care of the elderly. There is a check on the possible excesses of the misuse of power by an elder. The extent to which he conforms to standards of mature behaviour expected of an elder is the extent to which he is judged to be deserving of respect, care and affection by the young. A difficult elder who causes discord between people in the society and shows no sign of affection for the young is called "a foolish elder" (*Àgbà'yà*). He forfeits all right to respect.[14]

A major aspect of the sociological significance of the relative context of truthfulness among the Yoruba and the Bini is the relevance of seniority on the expectation of speaking the truth or telling lies. The rule of seniority rigidly arranges people in society in terms of age. It serves as a control mechanism in the social organisation of the society. The obligations of seniority which are internalised in the process of socialisation obliges those junior to one in age to respect one, accept to be controlled by one and avoid argument with the elderly one. This obligation also empowers the senior to exert punishment, to some degree on a recalcitrant junior. The assumption underlying this expectation is that the senior person has more experience and therefore he is right and has to be obeyed. The tendency is that this seniority control forces those junior to one to tell lies to short-circuit the system or to keep either the face of the senior or protect themselves from punishment. The obligations of seniority by implication institutionalises telling lies in order to give the impression that the system works.

The seniority factor in the social organisation and socialisation processes of the Bini and the Yoruba has led to friction as the society gradually transforms from a traditional agrarian society characterised by mechanical solidarity to an industrialising society predicated on organic solidarity. While both tribal societies remained close-knit, performing mainly farming as a major preoccupation, each family unit was a productive, residential, reproductive economic unit of the society. Homogeneity and commonality of major preoccupations reduced differences, enforced expectations and emphasized seniority in the process of socialisation since the group interests predominated over individual interests. Birth into the family, ascription, was what regulated the life opportunities of the individual who ought to live as member of a group. Seniority was the immediate strategic principle of subordinating the individual will to that of the group.

The modernising tendencies of formal western education, Christianity, trading and other economic enterprises which became entrenched under colonialism dictated that activities be predicated on the Durkheimean principle of contact which emphasised individual merit. Ascription, important though it is, is not crucial to the individuals achievement. It was merit, that counted not seniority. The demands of seniority in the old order conflicts with the pragmatic employment of merit to fulfill contracts and achieve goals in the modern nation state. A situation arises when those who are junior to one in age become more qualified and knowledgable. This corrodes the credibility established on the sole fact of seniority. This situation has compounded the difficulties in patterns of interaction as the society advances in western development.

Conclusion: The Art of Restritio Mentis (Dissembling)

In this chapter, a review has been made of Bini and Yoruba conceptions of the qualities associated with the person in society. Since the Bini and Yoruba realize that men are not perfect and are prone to excess, a fact brought out in the conceptions of their gods as imperfect spiritual beings, the analysis did not show a simple presentation of each quality. Such a view, had it been taken, would not have been representative of the views of the Bini and the Yoruba. Thus, each quality has been seen on the Aristotelian paradigm of the mean and the extremes. A vital factor in distinguishing the mean from both extremes of each quality was to re-evaluate an expression of a quality by analyzing it in terms of its context as seen against the over-all aim of the society. This confirms the view of A. H. M. Kirk-Greene, when he claimed in discussing who constituted the good man (*mutumin kirkii*) in the Hausa conception, "the framework is exclusively the societal context" (1974:4).

The need to maintain an act of dissembling or an exercise of mental reservation (restriction) is in conformity with the over-all aim of the society, whose fundamental duty is to seek its own survival by ensuring that there is unity within the group. The harsh realities of the environment coupled with the unmechanized system of farming in an essentially agricultural society create the need for maintaining unity that can be expressed in group labour for farming, house-building and ritual activities. The need for protection against enemies in times of military campaigns make unity in the group and loyalty to group aims very important.

The priority therefore is in maintaining group unity and peaceful coexistence. The Bini and the Yoruba, like other groups of people, teach their members to be honest, truthful, brave and respectful and other such values, but adult members who know what is expected of them would behave otherwise if, to adhere to any of these, would endanger the high good of the society. If a strict adherence to a principle like truthfulness brings others into trouble, a mature person would be expected to maintain some reservation which may imply not telling the truth. The Ọba in his attempt to maintain a balance between competing lineages or groups may refuse to acknowledge that one lineage performs better than another. He may instead choose a weak lineage as the one which performs best. These are not instances of dishonesty as far as the Bini and the Yoruba are concerned. They are necessary official untruths that are perfectly permissible and advisable for the sake of peace and unity within the society.

Much reliance has been put on proverbs in analyzing these qualities because, to the Bini and the Yoruba proverbs are the indispensable vehicles of clarifying and confirming consensus on a particular topic. As the Yoruba say "proverbs are the vehicles of thought when appropriate words are difficult to find or when thoughts are slow in connecting. It is proverbs that we use to find and connect them" (*Owe lẹṣin ọ̀rọ̀ tí ọ̀rọ̀ basọnu, owe lafin nwa*). The Bini maintain that "it is in proverbs that a Benin City man is addressed, but to a rustic, one needs to be brutally plain" (*Itan a i ne Edo, edigbie agbe emwan eho ma*). Besides most informants employed proverbs to illuminate their points of view on any particular subject. This tendency to resort to proverbs confirms Ida Ward's succinct observation about the importance of proverbs to West African society:

> In law, it seems to classify a court-case, to provide a precedent, to generalize a particular action; in family life, it regulates the attitude of one member of the family to another; it helps in the education of children; and in social intercourse, it smooths out difficulties and adds pith to the well-known accomplishment and the African conversation. (Ward, 1952:IX).

Thus, proverbs proved indispensable to a discussion of the qualities of man among the Bini and Yoruba.

CHAPTER THREE

REFERENCES

1. Taken from the documents "Extracts from the Diary of Lagos Mission", 1918-1932 to be found in the society of African Missions, Irish Province Archive, Blackrock Road Cork, Ireland.

2. The Closest image in translating the word *fúfú* is that of an erupting volcano. The temperamental person like a sleeping volcano, is beautiful at rest, surrounded by verdant pastures, but when it smokes and erupts, it reveals its destructive inner power.

3. One of the three Bini Palace Associations, *Iwebo*, conducted the Affairs of trading with the Europeans on behalf of the Ọba. It also had the duty of looking after the royal wardrobe. Its leader, Uwangwe, was, on this account, a very important member of the royal household.

4. A. Ryder, the historian, attributed the origin of town chiefs to the fifteenth-century king, Ewuare, who brought them into being to reward them for their support during his struggle for the throne, to provide through them, a channel for the participation of the members of the town in government, and to act as a check on the palace chiefs (1969:89).

5. Historians of a dialectic persuasion have implied that things were very often not normal and that the history of the consolidation of Bini kingship of the post-Ogiso dynasty was one of frequent conflict between the autochthonous elements and the "foreign members of the royal class" See Ryder 1969:4-23.

6. Interview with Sir Augustine O. Emumwen (Papal Knight) of 27 Agbado Street, Benin City on 26.6.80.

7. For more reading on this trading enterprise, see Igbafe 1967:37. Akintoye 1969:54-55.

8. From this practice emerged the Owo-Yoruba proverb (he who kills a leopard is sending himself on a journey to Bini' (*Enití ó pa ekùn rán ara rè lona Ado*). The same practice obtained in Etsako area of Bendel State, Imokhai 1979.

9. This exposition of policy through the names of Ilari was obtained at the Palace, Aafin Ọ̀yọ́ during an interview with Chief Kudefu on 3.11.80. It confirms the main outline of Reverend Johnson's exposition of the same in his *History of the Yoruba* (1921:211).

10. One could interpret "the king is Chief" in various ways. It might have been meant to remind Governor Carter that the King of Ọ̀yọ́ does not take

instructions from anyone. It was capable of being interpreted at Lagos as meaning the King (or Queen of Britain as the case was then) was the Chief and so her representative, the Governor, was free to act as the one who stood for the power of the King.

11. Interview with Chief Kudefu, Aafin Ọ̀yọ́, 3rd November 1980.

12. Interview with Sir Augustine Emumwen (Papal Knight) of 27 Agbado Street Benin City.

13. Most Yoruba communities have a section of their market which is devoted to selling medicinal items. These range from heads of snakes, alligator pepper, different types of bats to a host of other things like sea-water stored in little gourds. This section of the market is a sort of local chemist where one obtains what the doctor prescribes. Oja Iba in Ibadan and Oja Itokun in Abeokuta are two of such markets which have a local chemist section.

14. Collected from Chief Ifatogun at Itesi, Abeokuta 19.x.80.

The Yoruba symbol of Orí

CHAPTER FOUR

BINI AND YORUBA NOTIONS OF THE HUMAN PERSONALITY

The Bini and Yoruba attitudes to human qualities reveal the inconsistencies between the theoretical expectations and the practical responses to different situations. R. Horton puts it as follows:

> Nearly every society shows inconsistencies in its attitudes to one or other of the universal human motives. In training its young and propagandizing its adults, it enforces pursuit of an aim with one side of its mouth, then mumbles discouragement of the same aim with the other side; and it is these inconsistencies of attitude on the part of the socializing agents that give rise to the divisions and oppositions within the individual personality. In the society inconsistency may be over sexual desires; in another it may be over aggression and competition; and in each case the way the self tends to get divided will vary accordingly. Ultimately, many of these inconsistencies can be shown to have structural or ecological determinations; and thus there is probably a systematic covariation of personality conflicts with aspects of social structure and environment (1961:114).[1]

The inconsistent expectations include such examples as the obligation on one to be truthful and yet not to offend anybody in the process; the insistence on one to be brave and yet not to be foolhardy. Even the importance of informing action by the dictates of the Golden Mean points to the impossibility of fulfilling all society's expectations. This gap between normative ideal pattern and the modifications in the behavioural pattern caused by situation constraints derive from the societies' ambivalent attitude to one or other universal human motive. It could lead to conflict within the individual who aspires to succeed by conforming to social expectations but finds out that practical considerations dictate a response that contravenes the expectations. Notions of destiny, among the Bini and the Yoruba, enable the individual to resolve, to some extent, the conflict and come to terms with his experience. These notions make up for, on the level of symbolism, the conflicts that arise on the existential plane.

The idea of destiny is central to the twofold classification of human personality among the Bini and the Yoruba. The human personality is made up of a metaphysical essence and a physical essence. The metaphysical part of man includes ideas of his spiritual origin (coming-into being) and the pre-ordained plan for the course of life of the individual on earth. The destiny of the individual is taken before the Supreme Deity who puts a seal on it and commissions the spirit half of the individual to keep a close watch in order to ensure that the individual lives according to his chosen destiny. Notions of the spiritual or non-physical part of man also embrace the souls of man, their relations with each other, and their functions.

The uniqueness of the individual member of the society is also, for the Bini and the Yoruba, given a physical basis. Certain aspects of the human personality are, just as in European pre-scientific thought, held to reside in specific parts of the body. Notions about the physical part of man touch on ideas about conception, the development of the foetus, the birth and the naming of the child. More significantly these notions serve to articulate new generations of human beings into the existing social order.

I shall now discuss them in this order:

1. Ideas about Individual destiny, as expressed in notions about the metaphysical components of the human personality.
2. Ideas about the physical seat of various aspects of the personality in the human body.
3. Notions of conception, the development of the foetus, birth and naming of the child insofar as they reflect socially determined aspects of the human person.

Bini Notions Of Individual Destiny

Among the Bini, the metaphysical essence of the living person (*omwa*), that is, his spirit half, is *Ehi Omwa.* It alternatives existence with his *Ehi* seven times, making a total of fourteen phases of existence to the full person (*omwa*). It is of interest to note that the same word, *omwa*, is used to described both the living half of the full person and the complete unity of the metaphysical and physical essences of the individual.

The Bini maintain that before existence on earth, the individual goes before *Osanobuwa*, the Supreme Deity, to make the main events of his life manifest. The *Ehi*, the spiritual component, is the active participant in this exercise of predestining the self. This individual-in-potency, in awe and reverence, tells *Osanobuwa*, the Creator, what kind of life he wishes to lead and what fortunes he wants to attend his efforts when he gets down to the world of the living, *agbon*. If he wants a life of comfort and wealth, he asks for all the material things that will make his life comfortable. If he intends to be a famous medicine man, he will wish to ensure that he is born into the ward of medicine men of the King, and ask for the power of medicinal expertise, so as to be an outstanding member. If he wants to be a thief he askes for powers to elude so as not to be caught and insists that he does not want to live on the sweat of his own brow, but to prey on other people's property.[2] This exercise of making clear what one wants to be is called *hi*, and once it is concluded, *Osanobuwa* the Deity puts a seal on the chosen wishes by banging his sacred staff on the ground. These prenatal wishes, therefore, codify the main outline of a person's life. They remain known only to the spirit double of the individual who is appointed as the custodian who ensures that the living double keeps to the intentions which he had made about his life.

When a living person works assiduously without having much profit to show for his efforts while others around him who work less, reap great rewards and become great, his lack of profit is interpreted as the result of his *hi*, the contents of his prenatal wishes. Again, when a man who brings shame to his family by stealing is severely punished and shows signs of genuine repentance, only to continue to steal afterwards, this tendency is explained with reference to his prenatal choice. The Bini manifest their understanding of this spectacle when they say that "the thief is being given advice but his spirit is stealing yams in the farm" (*A bu oyi ude ehiere r'ugbo fenma*). The notion of destiny (*Eh*i), in evaluating the individual qualities in relation to social norms enables his failure or success by social standards to be "explained in terms of the innate potentialities of the individual and the use made of them" (Bradbury, 1973:273).[3]

The Bini illustrate the idea of destiny through many stories. One such story is that of *Ai Sagbon Hi* (literal translation, "You do not predestine yourself on Earth").[4] Long ago, two brothers lived in a town called *Ivekorhiomwo*. It was a time when most people did things by themselves since age`sets did not help their members with group labour. It was important for a man to have a large household so that the people dependent on him could provide labour on his farm. But in order to have a large household, one has to have the means to attract them. This the Senior brother did not have. He was a very poor man and could not even maintain the wife that their father married for him and so she too had to go away. The Bini say "a woman is a hat; it does not accompany one through the thicket" (*Erhu Okhuo Khin; e ilele omuwan la eti*). So he was left to farm alone, and to do a woman's work as well as his own. He worked so hard on the farm that his excessive working habits became proverbial in the village. He was the first to get to his farm in the morning and the last to leave it in the evening, with only a brief spell of rest in the shade. Yet, he could scarcely feed himself. His junior brother was the byword for success. Not only did he marry thirty wives in addition to the one his father married for him, he had so many slaves he could scarcely keep count of them. His farm was so big it took three days to traverse it. His food was sumptuous and as varied in choice as the number of wives he had.[5]

In village matters, the junior brother - although young - was well respected. His views, often stubbornly expressed, were well taken, his age notwithstanding. As the Bini say:

> If a young man is too stubborn, he either has much money or he is initiated into wizardary. It may also be that he is having a wealthy woman as a concubine.[6]

Thus, with money, wives, a big following and respect he was qualified to become a decision-maker for his village. His senior brother had none of these, and even if he spoke, nobody listened to him. In frustration, the senior brother went to the house of a feared medicine-maker, to ask for help to kill his junior brother, since he was perpetually embarrassed by his junior brother's superior wealth and status. *Ogiobo* the medicine`maker prescribed the ingredients for a medicine to be used against the junior brother and sent him to find them. When the senior brother had found them, *Ogiobo* made a concoction, gave it to him, and told him that, to test the speed and efficacy of the medicine, he should rub the Calabash which contained it against the stomach of a pregnant woman before using it. *Ogiobo* also told him to pay careful attention to whatever he saw when he rubbed the calabash of medicine on the stomach.

On his way home, the senior brother was told that the village was in turmoil because a woman in the village was experiencing the longest labour ever known. She had lost a lot of blood and was on the verge of death despite all the services of the best medicine doctors. The senior brother took this as the greatest opportunity to test the efficacy of his medicine and asked to be taken to the house. His appearance baffled all the relatives present in the house of the woman in labour, because the senior brother was not known for anything but ungainful labour on his farm. He was shocked to see the child in the womb clutching at matchets, a calabash and a hoe, and strings of wire for snaring game. He shouted in fear and the people around him thought that he had seen that the case of the woman was beyond cure. He rubbed the calabash against the womb again and the child came forth. His fame rose as a deliverer of babies and he was in great demand to deliver children.

In some houses when he rubbed the calabash, he saw other children holding other items manifesting what they might become. In one house, he saw a child dressed in rich garments with many attendants around him and he knew he was born to be the king. In another, he saw a child holding different types of leaves and pieces of bark and knew that the child could be a great medicine maker. In yet another, he saw a child holding a single sword and knew he would be a great warrior.

After much thought, the senior brother realized that the fate of each person was not decided here but in the land of spirits, the abode of the Creator Deity (*erinmwin*). Each person was only living according to the pattern of existence that he had chosen. No one ought to hurt another person on account of the blessings in his life, and so he was wrong to want to injure his younger brother because he had been successful in life. He resolved to make amends and went back to *Ogiobo* the medicine maker, apologized to him for not realizing that destinies were fixed in the abode of the Creator Deity, and now that he did, he did not intend to injure his brother. He asked *Ogiobo* to help him to overcome his "bad" destiny which was responsible for his abject poverty. *Ogiobo* advised him to win his brother's friendship by going to provide free labour on his junior brothers farm. This was unheard of among the Bini who institutionalize seniority in the principle of primogeniture.

Next morning, the senior brother went early to his brother's farms and, before the arrival of the first batch of slaves, had worked so hard that those who saw him were not only astonished at finding him working in his brother's farm, but also at the amount of work he had already done. They sent urgently for their master who ran to the farm and asked his brother, "why are you doing this forbidden act? Do you wish to kill me?" The senior brother said that on the contrary he wanted to thank the ancestors for making his junior brother wealthy. He then told his junior brother everything that had happened, how he had become so jealous that he had planned to kill him and that he had come to know the real source of his brother's wealth and his own poverty. On hearing this story, the junior brother embraced his senior brother and commanded his slaves and wives to kill goats to venerate the head of their dead father and make a feast for the reconciliation. In appreciation of *Ogiobo's* role, he sent presents of two slaves and wives to him. He gave his senior brother fourteen wives, fourteen slaves and fourteen sets of traditional attire. Both brother's lived happily ever after.

An analysis of this Bini story of destiny and the unconscious reveals certain significant points about its sociological value, to individual psychology, political control and professional satisfaction. The story manifests poignantly the tendency for people to make up, on the plane of symbolism, what is lacking on the practical existential plane. The main outlines of the story reverse the order of things in the orthodox Bini traditional community. Contrary to the dictates of the rule of primogeniture, the junior brother has taken the position that would normally belong to his elder brother. The junior brother was wealthy; the senior brother was very poor. The junior brother had power reflected in the weight attached to his decisions in the society; the senior brother was powerless. The junior brother who, at the death of their father should have received his wives through the benevolence of his senior brother, was the one who gave his brother fourteen wives. In order to resolve the difficulties from this role reversal, the expert, *Ogiobo* - dragged out of the senior brother's subconscious the content of his destiny. This had come about because the senior brother had, in an earlier incarnation, suffered the hardship of keeping up with his responsibilities in the hope that he would reap the reward when his father died. As it happened, he outlived his father by only fourteen days, and at his death, all that should have belonged to him passed on (since he did not have a son) to the next surviving son of his father. In frustration he (*hi*) predestined himself, not to look forward or work for the post of inheriting from his father in the next incarnation. Bini custom specifies that only first sons who perform their filial duties, particularly the sacred duty of burying a father and observing all the obsequies, can inherit all the property and status of the deceased.

The revelation, through the guidance of the expert, of the cause of the senior brother's failure exonerated him from the feeling of guilt and shame at not living up to social expectations. He is released from his fate when he fulfills the expert's instructions for his integration into normal Bini society. This integration is given ancestral support by the fact that both brothers "killed goats on their father's shrine." They venerated their ancestors with sacrifices of goat, which provides meat for a subsequent communion meal of reconciliation and reaffirmation of peace within the family group. As the Bini maintain in their proverb:

> It is unnecessary to ask a Bini if he knows how to eat the flesh of a goat; with what does he worship his departed father's yearly?

Through the symbolic meal and sacrifice to the ancestors, the Bini senior brother is reintegrated fully into the society, exonerated from guilt of failure and given a new and positive start in life.

It is important to note the tripartite level of reparation, restitution and reconciliation which ought to be fulfilled before complete reintegration is made. The ritual sacrifice makes up for the reparation on the metaphysical plane and reverses the self-imposed pronouncement of destiny. This ritual effort came after the gesture of reparation at the individual level when the brother initiates reconciliation by providing unsolicited free labour on his junior brother's farm. Having satisfactorily sought reparation at those two levels - the *metaphysical*, the individual, then he is ready to be fully reintegrated into the society. The Bini story itself contradicts Bini traditional expectations and emphasizes that things need not take their expected course.

Yoruba Notions Of Individual Destiny

Destiny sets the main outline of a person's life and the Yoruba refer occurrences in the life of a person to his destiny. The Yoruba always associate destiny with the "inner essence" (literally "the inside of the head") of the individual. *Orí* is a complex notion and it will be looked at in greater detail below under the section on the physical seat and aspects of human personality. Meanwhile, it is enough to note that *Orí* (photo page 124a) represents the uniqueness of the individual so that the cult devoted to it is in a sense opposed to ancestor veneration. The two cults could be taken as expressing, respectively, the principles of achievement and ascription, both of which are important in Yoruba society (Lloyd, 1974:39).[7] It is the *Oríinú* or inner essence that is thought of as the metaphysical part of man which precedes human life, shares in the divine essence and lives after the termination of human life. It is the part of the individual responsible for choosing his destiny. Although it sheds part of itself which subsequently animates the physical part of man (see Yoruba notions of conception below) it remains behind with the Creator Deity to monitor the extent to which the activities of its living double conform to its destiny. However, only itself knows and remembers the main contents of the destiny. Significantly enough, one of the most common prayers of the Yoruba is *K í orí inú mába tòde jẹ fun ẹ*, which literally translated, means "may the inner self not frustrate the efforts of the outer self." Yoruba thought on the dichotomy in human personality is apparent in this prayerful wish.

The Counterpart of *Oríinú* is the living self, *enia*. This would be the conscious mind as it is the seat of all the feelings, desires, thoughts and aspirations which belong to the individual as a living conscious being. The Yoruba closely identify it with the heart and the head. The choice of destiny made by the "inner essence" (*Oríinú*) is unknown to it, and may be opposed to its own aspirations. It is concerning this anxiety that the desires of the two selves may be in conflict and so nullify the conscious effort of the individual that the Yoruba sing, in praise of the inner being, in order that it may help to bring success to the efforts of one's hands. An extract of such a song recorded throws an insight into the anxiety that the awareness causes in the Yoruba:

> My inner self, steer me to a good course,
> My director allocate a good place for me,
> I look up to you.
> My inner self, do not spoil my endeavours
> Come and make my life successful
> My inner self, please, my director,
> Hearken to my call.
> Because if I want to have money
> I ask it from you
> If I want many children
> I will plead for them through you
> My inner self, please do not frustrate my efforts
> I look up to you.

Thus, aware of its ignorance as to its choice of destiny, the living self constantly pleads with the "inner self," its spirit counterpart, to harmonize their wishes.

These ideas about destiny and the unconscious are further illustrated by the following story taken from the corpus of Ifa divination -

> Long ago the Supreme Deity (*Olódúmarè*) appointed the divinity of divination (*Orúnmìlà*) to take care of the world. He also appointed (*Ọbàtálà's*) to form the human image. He wanted both to cooperate with each other to produce a peaceful world of perfectly-formed, nice-looking Creatures. People came to recognize *Ọbàtálá's* adeptness in moulding the human body and therefore nicknamed him "the perfect moulder" (*asèkan mákù*). No sooner had he been given this name of honour than things started to go wrong with him. He found to his embarrassment that, although almost all that he moulded came out perfectly, there were occasional blemishes (*òpọ̀lọpò dára, sùgbọ́n ọkọọkan ku díè ki á to*). Malformed beings increased in the society, yet all still continued to call him "the perfect moulder." *Ọbàtálà* could no longer bear the shame caused by the gap between his performance and what was expected of him. In desperation, he decided to take his case to the Supreme Deity. Early next morning he put on the special magical dress that enabled him to go between the two worlds. When he reached the boundary of the earth and the heavens, he was confronted by the gate-keeper of the heaven, *Ájàlorun*, who witnesses to the choice of the human destiny and has to approve visits to the Supreme Deity. When he asked what he came for, Ọbàtálá said, It was *Olódumare* who with your knowledge, commissioned me to mould the physique of all living things and especially of man. He also told me that when things get difficult on earth, *Òrúnmílá* and I should solve them. Most of what I do appears well. The moulding looks great and people are happy. This is why they call me the "perfect moulder." However, a few of them come out badly-formed. How can I, the perfect maker, fail to make things to perfection? It is a disgrace. I want *Olódùmarè* to give me the power to mould only perfect figures. Then I shall have lived up to the standards implied in my name.'

Ájàlọrun laughed and kept on laughing until the unveiled displeasure of *Ọbàtálá* told him that *Ọbàtálá* was not treating the case as a joke.

Ájàlorun told *Ọbátàlá* that if he insisted in going to the Supreme Deity, he (Ọbàtálá) would be sent back to him (*Ájàlọrun*), so they should both try to find a solution to *Ọbàtálá's* problem. He reminded *Ọbàtálá* that neither he nor the Supreme Deity could provide any additional power that would enable Ọbàtálá to perform better. Ọbàtálá himself would soon enough gain an understanding of the problem. He hid his guest, *Ọbàtálá*, in the inner room of his abode and told him to pay attention to what was going on around him. Not long after *Ọbàtàlà* had hidden, the batch of those who wished to go down to live on earth came into *Ájàlọrun's* abode. They were many. Each one started to make a wish. Some said they wanted to live a short but eventful life and that they would die on the eve of their wedding. Others said they wanted to be blind men, and others still wanted to be malformed (*abìràn*) so that they would not have to do any work. Some said they would be kings and be very wealthy with many people to serve them. The list of wishes continued until all in the batch had made his, then *Âjàlọrun* banged his staff and by way of drawing Ọbàtálá's attention to the wishes, sang:

> You caretakers of the World listen attentively
> and you representatives of the Supreme Being.
> This is what they say when they are about to go
> You hidden behind the veil, listen
> You hidden behind the veil (i.e. *Ọbàtálá*)!

Different batches came and went and at the end of the day, *Ájàlọrun* called Ọbàtálá out of his hiding place and asked him to relate his experiences. *Ọbàtálá* said most of the wishes. *Ájàlọrun* confirmed them and told him that he was not the cause of the imperfections in his duty, the malformed persons had specifically chosen to be malformed. *Ọbàtálá* returned to earth, satisfied that he had nothing to be embarrassed about if he continued to do his best.

The story reveals the gap between theory and practice. It shows the crisis of loss of confidence created in the heart of one who is thought to be perfect but in actual fact is not perfect. Thus *Ọbàtálá* then concluded that the gap between the ideal pattern of expectation and his actual performance makes his nickname - "the perfect moulder" - a mockery. It leads to a crisis of confidence in himself. He sought a solution by taking recourse to the source of this power. His intention is that there can be only two lines of action. The first would be that the Supreme Deity restores perfection to his (*Ọbàtálá's*) creative ability. Barring this, he should be released of his post so that he could live with a measure of dignity in his society. The expert, *Ájàlọrun*, resolves the crisis by leading *Ọbàtálá* to a higher level of awareness, by permitting him the therapeutic exercise of witnessing the process of sealing the destiny of those to be born. *Ọbàtálá*, the moulder of human physique, realized that people coming to earth choose their destiny which may include a special plea that they be malformed. When these are subsequently subjected to his expertise as a moulder, no amount of moulding could see them perfectly formed on earth. To achieve perfection in their cases would be contrary to the intentions in their destiny. The resolution then was not in his moulding ability but in their chosen destiny. Conflict arose because people on earth behave and live up to a standard of expectation often quite contrary to their chosen destiny.

The expert's services in unravelling the content of the "pre-natal" chosen wishes constitute a major step in the resolution of problems having to do with inexplicable failures among the Yoruba. If an individual who had experienced, in a former existence, the disappointment of failure or rejection as candidate for chieftaincy, returns for another span of existence, his spirit double over-awed by the fear of failure, may choose a destiny that forbids all kinds of competition. The Yoruba express their confirmation of this tendency in the saying, "it is never so bad that two generations suffer from the same fate" (*Kii buru titi koburu fun iran meji*). This choice would obviously be unknown to the individual who may choose to compete doggedly for status and rank in Yoruba Society. Since his spirit double has predestined the self to abhor any such competition, the conflict that ensues from the opposed desires of destiny and the activities of the living counterpart perpetually frustrates the ambitions of the individual.

To understand the anthropological significance of these stories it is necessary to equate the Bini/Yoruba "prenatal" or destiny wishes with Freudian "unconscious" wishes. It is also important to refer to some of the features of Bini and Yoruba societies. Like Fortes (1959) and Horton

(1961)[8] I make, therefore, some linited use of Freudian insights, especially the idea of the unconscious, an idea to which I equate the notions of "prenatal wishes" in order to illustrate the social significance of these ideas on destiny and personality. These ideas will provide a meaningful base for appreciating the use of symbolism to palliate the individual's psyche. Subsequently, an analysis of features of Bini and Yoruba society and ideas of the person along the line of the Freudian idea of the unconscious would "show that the introduction of the Freudian model is something more than a mere anthropologist's whim" (Horton, 1961:113).

Sigmund Freud maintained that the individual was an embodiment of enforced association of many distinct and conflicting personalities. The conflicting desires of these opposed personalities were associated with two selves in the individual; the conscious *ego* and the unconscious self (Freud, 1933, 1949[9]). The unconscious self was a powerful purposeful force whose desires remain unknown to its counterpart, the conscious *ego*, and often in opposition to its own. The intense opposition between the conflicting desires of these two selves leads to schizophrenic feelings which undermine the efforts of the individual. This situation is claimed to be resolved when an expert retrieves and reveals to the individual the conflicting desires of his unconscious self.

As a case in point, Freud maintains that to cure an individual of neurosis, the expert ought to begin from the cause, that is, getting at a traumatic experience, presently outside the range of the individual's consciousness, which triggered off the attitude of fear against some desire, which has developed into an overpowering fear (and avoidance). This overpowering fear constantly frustrates the victim's efforts when they are contrary. Once the expert has manifested the traumatic experience and the individual has recognized it as such, he proceeds to cure himself by choosing between his warring desires in a way that allows him to be reintegrated into society. Having done this, the society is left to admit the individual into it on its own terms. That the Bini and Yoruba personality concepts appear similar to Freud's psychoanalytic ideas will be shown briefly.

In the Bini patrilineal society, the village is the basic political unit. Male population in the village is divided into three groups, the Elders, the

Adults and the Youths. Importance in the society is in the descending order with Elders being the authorities. Each family is administered by the father who has final authority over his children, and the relationship pattern between father and son is set on the master and servant pattern. In his early years, before the individual qualifies for admission into the first of the three associations, Youths (*iroghae*), an extension in circles of relationship are confined to ever-widening circles of relationship within patrilineal groups. This exclusivist tendency is counterbalanced by admission into the association which brings him into contact with those of his age-grade in the village. The village allocates land for farming and rights of ownership of such land are ultimately vested in the village. Although the young individual Bini advances in society to the extent to which he distinguishes himself as a member of his association, he still remains under the authority of his father. It is only at his father's death that he acquires freedom and the status of an adult in his own family. As long as his father is alive, he remains a minor.

The principle of primogeniture complicates the father/Son relationship among the Bini. It vests on the first son not only the right of succession to office or title, but also the right to ownership of all the property of the deceased. At their father's death, when a first-born has successfully performed the burial of his father and set up a shrine for his veneration, to the satisfaction of the elders, all right and ownership devolve on him. As the Ọba of Benin's testimony in the case of Chief Obasuyi versus Peter Imaruedore clearly specified:

> There is no such thing as family house or property in Bini custom. The eldest son inherits his father's house but other houses in different plots are distributed to the junior children. There is one proviso as regards the elder son, as he must have performed the funeral ceremonies for his father. If he dies before he has done so, the property devolves, on the next surviving son (Ọba of Benin, 1942)[10]

Since few could build another house away from the plot allocated to the family, it meant that the junior brothers were at the mercy of the elder brother. Thus, the feeling of conflict pervading the master/servant relationship of the Bini is extended, at death, logically to the first son who subsequently occupies the position of the father, not only in terms of property but also in terms of religious sanctions that are associated with the role of the first son as the spiritual head at the father's shrine.

Bini practices of child-rearing and etiquette of behaviour to other members of one's family are characterized by respect and affection. The son is socialized to be devoted to the father. This pattern of relationship is extended beyond life to characterize that between the living and their ancestors. The shrine to one's father constitutes the immediate focus and translation of this father-son relationship between the living and the dead. To that extent, activities within the patrilineal Bini society which are descent-oriented impose filial obedience and the obligation of cooperation within the family group. Within this group, the uniqueness of the individual is played down and his role as a member of his house emphasized. Yet, implied in the relationship, is the association of lack of freedom and the conflict generated by the master/servant relationship.

Opposed to this set of relationships is that based on notions of destiny which focus on the uniqueness of the individual and explain his success or failure in terms of his ability to exploit his innate potentialities. (His failure in this regard is explained, still in reference to his person, but in a way that absolves him of the guilt of failure.) The Bini symbolically represent the uniqueness of the individual by the worship of the hand, *Ikegobo*. The sets of opposition which emerge from relating the features of Bini society with certain aspects of its belief system will be discussed in the next section on ideas about the physical seat of the various aspects of the Personality.

The Yoruba patrilineal society is based on politically articulate corporate lineages. The father has the final authority over his children and their kinsmen junior to him who live within the family. Except among the Yoruba sub-groups of north-east Yorubaland who have been strongly influenced by the Bini Kingdom, with which they share a common border, age-group associations are not strong (Akintoye, 1971; Lloyd, 1960).[11] Where they occur, they do not weaken the political base of the lineage as a corporate interest group. Although the father-son relationship is characterized by filial obedience and respect, the absence of the rule of primogeniture reduces the level of conflict, both between father and son and between the first son and his junior brothers. The Yoruba rule of inheritance specifies what goes to the children of the deceased (Lloyd, 1959).[12] In addition to ascribed status the Yoruba also recognize a different sort of status which is wholly dependent on personal effort, achieved status. Status through achievement motivates the desire to work hard and out-pace others. Thus, another source of intense competition is introduced among the Yoruba.

Seen against the backdrop of these peculiar features of Bini and Yoruba societies it is to be expected that great differences of structural and cultural emphasis necessarily distinguish the Bini and Yoruba stories of destiny. These differences also affect the way in which the stories are applied to resolve the conflicts inherent in social expectations of either society. Among the Bini, the focus of conflict is in the father-son relationship and its transference to the first son, due to the principle of primogeniture, which invests the first son with all the rights and privileges of the deceased father at the expense of the other children. In the story, the unaggressive "unconscious" manifested in the conflict-avoidance orientation of the prenatal wish conflicts with the aggressive, conflict-prone tendency to replace the father and dominate the other children manifested in the rule of primogeniture.

Among the Yoruba, the focus of conflict is not centered on an individual but raises a big question mark to social expectation. Why does a "perfect moulder" fail to live up to the expectation of moulding perfectly? Why does he have to lose his prestige on account of a fault that is not his? The unaggressive unconscious symbolized in the Yoruba father-son relationship conflicts with the competitive conscious desire to achieve rank and status. It is a resolution of these inconsistencies between theory and practice, between what is expected and what transpires in reality that the stories about destiny attempt to effect (Horton, 1961:114). The individual, is able, because he can blame his failure or associate his success with a spoken destiny, to come to terms with himself. In the Bini instance, the integrating agent is the source of conflict, the ancestor - deceased father - whose sanctioned social norms are symbolized by the warring desires of the unconscious and the conscious parts of the individual. In the Yoruba case in point, the integrating agent is the custodian of the secret knowledge of the society. Thus the notions of destiny provide an acceptable palliative to the individual's feeling of guilt for misdemeanors in the same way as Freudian notions of personality were alleged to have assuaged similar guilt feelings in the contemporary European. As Horton noted:

> Here as with the European, the conscious ego can often largely get rid of his guilt feelings by attributing responsibility for his misdeeds to his unconscious, which he sees as one or more distinct personal entities opposed to his core self; and many people who make no use of Freudian therapists none the less use Freudian ideas to enable themselves to go on living with palliated guilt feelings in their own sick way (1961:112).

Thus, the simple stories of the Bini and the Yoruba about destiny provide useful means of understanding their concepts of the person. Besides, revealing the individual in his own worth in societies where the individual often tends to be seen only in relation to his inclusive group, the notions of destiny, along with others to be explored, enable the individual to explain success in terms of his own achievement and failure in terms other than his own making. The ability to indulge in this rather selective process of explanation is vital to the mental well-being of the individual especially in societies which exert strong pressures of conformity and expectations of success on the individual. This ability effects a balance in the tendency in such societies to explain an individual's success in terms of the cooperation and help provided by his kinsmen. However, the failure of an individual is explained in terms of his own lack of ability to exploit the potentialities and resources at his disposal.

The Physical Seat of the Various Aspects of the Personality

Besides the metaphysical essence of man both the Bini and Yoruba recognize the physical essences. More particularly, certain aspects of the human body are said to be the physical seat of important components of his personality. These various aspects of the personality include the hand, the head, the waist, the stomach - "the inside" - the knee. The simple comparative table below illustrates these areas of the body in their order of pre`eminence among the two peoples.

TABLE A

	BINI		YORUBA
1. Hand	Obo	Hand	Orí
2. Head	Uhunwu	Stomach "Inside"	Inú
3. Waist	Ekun	Knee of woman in labour	Ìkúnlé-abiamo

Of the four most important ideas about human personality among the Bini, only *ehi* which stands for that aspect of the individual which predestines him, as well as the spirit-double or counterpart of the living person (*omwa*) has been discussed. The other ideas are classified under the physical essence of man and include the head, *uhunwu*, the hand, *obọ* and the waist *ekun*.

The notions of the hand - *obọ* easily pre-eminent among all other physical seats of the personality complement those of the *ehi* to produce the traditional Bini image of the worth of the individual. To the extent to which these two notions stress either his innate potentialities or his success through the employment of his hand to succeed by exploiting his resources, the ideas about *ehi* - destiny and *obọ* - hand are opposed to those of the head which stress the worth of the individual as a member of the segment of his patrilineage.

As is characteristic of Bini attitudes to salient aspects of its environment or belief system, these notions of the parts of the self have been transferred into objects of veneration. There is a shrine to the *head - uhunwu* and there is an annual feast celebrating the head of the king - *Igue Ọba.* There is also a cult of the hand, *ikegobo* and the annual feast devoted to venerating the resourcefulness of the hand is called *ihieku*. An individual who has become an adult sets up a shrine for his own head at which he not only venerates all the heads of his children and wives but also his own destiny. If he has not achieved this independent status on account of limited wealth, or the fact that his father is alive, he venerates his head and destiny through the good offices of his father.

On a note of comparative interest, the Bini are not alone in making the hand a symbol of worship. As Talbot noted about the Ika a neighboring group to the Bini:

> The Ika pray to the Ikengga for success in trade, war, hunting and farming. The heads of the leopards and of every enemy killed in war are offered up before the symbol (1926:142-143, Vol. 11).

Meek, who stated categorically that it was prevalent among the Igbo, particularly of the Okigwe area, connected it with the practice of headhunting and maintained that it had diminished in importance at the time of his research due to the impact of *Pax Britannica* (1937:39).

More recent scholarly contribution on the symbol of the hand presents a different and, in terms of notions of the personality, more meaningful contribution. J. Boston (1977) whose work on Ikenga figures brings this scholarship to a point of interpretative excellence compares both western Igbo and Igala societies, two contiguous groups who have the figures of the hand and shows how their development relative to the society's social features differ. In the more egalitarian north-western Igbo society, the spirit is fiercely competitive. This competition to supercede others in achievement climaxes in the Igbo system of title-taking which is based on purchase (1977:10). Rank and status in the community increase as more titles are acquired, the recognition of rank being manifested in special names, the ownership of particular stools and staff and also in the right to wear anklets.

These titles are symbolic manifestations of illustriousness concretized in the *Ikenga* form, the veneration of which is equal to the veneration of the self.

Among the Igala, the presence of traditional forms of ascribed status limits the intense competition for such titles, as the condition of taking them is clear cut. Furthermore, within the kin group the principle of rotation of title within groups rather than equal share by any group which can purchase it, reduces the level of social and political competition which the Igbo egalitarian principle encourages. The Igala, use symbols such as *Ogwu* or *Ode* to explain personal success and individual achievement. Ikenga among the Igala, acquired on the principle of rotation, connects the individual with his progenitors. Ikenga as a manifestation of personal achievement acquired after fierce competition celebrates the achieving power of the individual. As Boston noted:

> To the first category of cults concerned with the individual, belongs the cult of Ikenga. Older studies of this cult...describe Ikenga as a god of success, or luck, or as a spirit associated with good fortunes in masculine pursuits such as warfare, hunting, title-taking and so on. My own view is that Ikenga symbolizes the person as a particular individual, contrasting his own personal achievements with those which can be ascribed to hereditary qualities, or to some other external source (1977:13-14).

It is along the lines suggested by Boston that the full significance of Bini Ikegobo lies.

Although R. C. Bradbury draws attention to the elements of warfare in the Bini songs on the cult of the hand (1973:264-265), he made a reservation when he noted that, in the Benin society:

> ...large scale farming (with slave labour), trade, medicine, craft specialization and especially political power and influence were, for most people, easier roads to prestige than skill in battle, though this last retained its glamour. Wealth, rank and political power, rather than personal daring, were the measures of social success and this fact must for long have modified any more exclusive connexion which martial art once had (1973:266).

The Bini take the hand as the seat of power and of achievement (Hamlyn, 1960:16). As the Bini proverb states, "Loquacity does not make a man, manhood lies in the palm of the hand" (*A iye unrru okpia: atatabo re eghele ye*). The hand is the symbol of a man's willingness to subdue his environment. If a man's farming efforts yield little, he is invited to "serve his hand" (*ru obo*) which he does, not only by having the wood`carvers make an ikegobo for him, but by intensifying his efforts on the farm.

Obọ is also a symbol of reciprocity. As an informant claimed, a clenched fist never takes more than what it is holding. It has reached the end of what can be derived. It has to loosen its grip and allow what it is holding to go. When it lets go, those who receive from its kindness would give in return a bigger share out of appreciation and a sense of obligation.[13] This is the reasoning which motivated the Bini to say "when this hand washes that hand, that hand washes this hand, the two become clean" (*Obọ na gha sa ame kpe obo na, obo na ghi sa ame kpe obo na, ore evua na huan*). The wise individual maximizes his profits through reciprocity.

As a complementary aspect to Bini ideas of *ehi* (destiny), Ikegobo - the Bini veneration of the hand - is a veneration of the achievement of the individual as a member of his society, not as a productive unit of his kin-group. It is a way of making up on the *level of symbolism what often gets overlooked on the existential level.* The message is that the individual can achieve on his own, and is respected for such achievement, rather than the less salutary achievement that comes as a result of kinship cooperation. *Ehi* is credited with failure, but not the hand. The hand is always seen in the positive context of personal achievement. In a society like that of the Bini where no achieved status ranks with the rank that derives from the king (often vested in wards or guilds) the tendency of reducing healthy competition implied in his system of ranking is counteracted by a glorification of personal achievement.

If the Bini manifest their respect for the achievement of the individual and his importance in the society as a unique person in the notions of *ehi*, and *obo*, they constantly draw attention to the need for the individual to identify his interests with those of his kinsmen. In the belief system of the

Bini, the focus of the interests of the wider group is the head, *uhunwu*. In the ever-widening group of the Bini social relations, from the family to the segment head and finally to the king, the emphasis on group unity in order to preserve group interests is transformed into the concrete quasi-religious symbol of the head. The head of the Ọba is an object of veneration. At the annual feast of the veneration of the Ọba's head, called *Igue Ọba*, the King blesses his head and thanks it for the blessings that he himself and all his subjects enjoyed. The head stands for the ability to order one's life and that of his dependents in order to achieve. It stands for the victory of the power of thought (*iroro*) over brutal force. It is what helps a person to make a good ancestor. Hence, at death, the senior son gets an altar to venerate the head of the deceased. In this sense, the parent/child relationship is extended beyond death. These obligations underlie this extension. Firstly, the duties of the parent to the child are extended beyond life as deceased parents are expected to look after the interests of their group in the spiritual world (*erinwin*) where the fate of the living is decided. Thus, according to the Bini notion of conception, it is the ancestors who petition Olókun to send children to their descendants. Therefore, the head constitutes a representation of the unbroken links between one's ancestors and one's progeny. It focuses on strengthening the bond within the family group since the rule of primogeniture tends to exacerbate the fission within the family group at each generation.

Bini notions of physiology also single out the waist, *ekun*, for veneration. *Ekun* represents the procreative power of the male. It was claimed that the waist bears the brunt of the "natural battle of creating a new life" at sexual intercourse. On this account, the *ekun* of one who has begotten many children, particularly sons, is venerated at his burial. This veneration consists in the slaughtering of a goat presented to the *egbee*, the elders of the group of the deceased, by the son of the deceased. It was observed that:

> This goat is "for the *ekun*" (the loins and buttocks) of the dead man for "it is the *ekun* that is used in begetting (bearing) a child." The immediate reference is to the movements of the *ekun* in coitus but *ekun* here stands for the reproductive organs and processes in general. Thus, ...the goat is killed to honour

the deceased as a begetter of progeny (Bradbury, 1973:217-218).

The salient aspects of physiology in the Bini understanding are those which represent the transformation into symbolism of the ideas important to the essential features of Bini society. The head, *uhunwu*, represents not only the individual as a conserver of sanctified customs passed on from one generation to the next, but also the will of the society to exploit its resources jointly, even when practices such as primogeniture and the rule of inheritance tends to heighten the individual's desire to achieve by himself. The head stands also for streamlining patterns of hierarchy and superiority within the group. In his own immediate family, the head of the family venerates his head and, by implication, the heads of all his dependents.

To effect a balance which will encourage individual achievement, notions of individuality are transformed in the Bini belief system into the ideas of the hand and *ikegobo*, the shrine of the hand. In this symbolism, the Bini desire to give credit to individual achievement. The ideas of the hand complement those of destiny, *ehi*, to present the Bini notions of the individual. While some measure of success is attributed to his person and some is linked to his group, his failure is explained in terms which absolve the group from blame. The notion of destiny ascribes misfortune or failure.

Yoruba Ideas of the Physical Parts of Personality

The Yoruba take the individual to be composed of the body (*ara*) and spirit essence (*ẹ̀mí*). They call the living person *ẹ̀da ẹlẹmi* (lit. "the breathing creature"). Of their many physiological notions, those that are of relevance to the concept of the person are the head, *ori*, the heart, *okan* and the stomach, *ikun* or *inu*. The head is the seat of wisdom (*Ọgbọ́n*) and thinking (*ìrò*). As the host of the senses *gbígbọ́ràn*, hearing, seeing (*riran*), smelling (*gbígbọ́ oorun*) and the power of eating (*jijẹ*) it controls the remaining part of the body. This control is due to the fact that it is the faculties of the head that allow the individual to organize his life and activities in a way that leads to success. Success does not depend solely on the choice of a good destiny (*orírere*) from heaven. A man who wishes to succeed and who has been predestined to succeed without his knowledge, must put an effort into life. Two types of efforts associated with the head are necessary for success. Firstly, he ought to employ the resources of his being, his faculties as well as the use of other parts of his body, such as hands and legs, to succeed. The head as the seat of wisdom is responsible for organizing his various components for the individual to succeed. The Yoruba teach the necessity of exploiting the reserves of one's energy to achieve success through stories which demonstrate the failure of those who do not use all their powers. One such story from a verse of the chapter (*Odù*) of Ifa divination is illustrative:

> Opebe, the Ifá priest of legs,
> Performed Ifá divination for legs
> On the day he was coming from heaven
> All heads called themselves together.
> But they did not invite legs.
> Èṣù (Yoruba trickster divinity) said:
> Since you do not invite Legs,
> We will see how you will bring your
> deliberations to success.
> Their meeting ended in a quarrel.
> They then sent for Legs.
> It was then that their deliberations became
> successful.
> They said that was exactly
> What their Ifá priests had predicted.
> Opebe, Ifá priest of legs
> Performed the Ifá divination for Legs
> On the day he was coming from heaven to earth.
> Opebe has surely come,
> Ifa priest of Legs
> No one deliberates
> Without reckoning with Legs
> Opebe has surely come
> Ifá priest of Legs (Abimbola 1976:148-149)

Although Abimbola interprets this to connote the Yoruba belief that "even if one is predestined to success by the choice of a good *ori*, one cannot actually achieve success without the use of one's *ese*, Leg, symbol of activity and power," Yoruba notions of the head suggest a different interpretation. The Yoruba certainly believe that the choice of a good destiny is not sufficient for success. In addition the individual must use all his faculties to realize his innate potentialities for success. He achieves this by ensuring that all the parts of his body are in agreement, since he needs their different services, and he cannot afford to ignore the contribution of any part. The Yoruba try to emphasize the need for such judicious cooperation between the parts for the smooth running of the whole when they say the head needs all other parts of the body to survive. They also insist that the weak should cooperate with the strong, the wise with the powerful. Hence, Yoruba belief associates Òrúnmìlà, the refraction of the omniscience of the Deity, with Èṣù, the trickster divinity of brute force. Through such associations they believe that the blending of wisdom with energy ensures success.

On a point of comparative interest, the notions associated with the head by the Bini and the Yoruba, as the seat of knowledge and, often, the source of success, differ from Azande notions of the head. For the Azande, it has been noted that:

> The head is not thought to be the seat of thinking and feeling and I have never heard of any function attributed to the brains (*dudu*). There is said to be a tiny channel running round the back of the head from ear to ear, also one linking nose and eyes. Thought and emotion are associated with the breast and stomach, although there is here a possibility of misunderstanding because Azande commonly use the expression *vuse yo*, in the belly, in the very general sense of inside (E.E. Evans-Pritchard, 1970:163).[14]

The Yoruba regard the stomach as the seat of emotions both good and bad. A person with a good character (*ìwà rere*) is said to have a "good inside" or stomach (*inu rere*). A person with a bad character, *oniwa burúkú* is said to have a "bad inside" or stomach (*iwa burúkú*). There is a connection between the heart, *ọkàn*, and the stomach, *inu*, such that the heart is also regarded as sharing in the source of food and bad emotion. In the same way as a person is called good or bad in terms of his "inside" or stomach, he is also called good or bad in terms of his heart. A good person has a clean heart. A bad person is supposed to have a murky, conniving heart, *ọkàn burúkú*. Both the stomach and the heart are said to be located in that area of the body to which the Yoruba generally refer as *inu* (inside). The breast, *aya*, is the symbol of strength, and honour, and when a man touches his heart, he implies that he would bring the reserves of his being to keep his word.

The Bini and Yoruba Notions Of Conception

The notions of destiny prevalent in both cultures influence the ideas of conception. These ideas seem so similar as to warrant a treatment, not in a comparative but complementary sense. The total human being is divided, in Bini understanding, into two. The first, and essentially spirit half of him, is *ehi*, the spirit counterpart. The living person is *omwa*. This part of man is essentially physical and is the seat of all the senses and the feelings. The *omwa* and the *ehi* alternate existence seven times to complete the Bini cycle of fourteen phases of existence due to the individual before he finally transforms into an ancestor. The *ehi* and the *omwa* exchange, in this process of reincarnational alternation, their modes of being such that an *ehi* in a phase of existence becomes an *omwa* in the next phase of existence, while its *omwa* becomes its *ehi*. This ability to interchange the modes of being is made possible by that aspect of the spiritual in *omwa* which the *ehi* sheds to infuse an aspect of the Supreme Creator, *Osanobuwa*, in the living counterpart. It is this spiritual element in the individual which makes him unique and enables him, through the extendable quality of the spirit, to change from the *omwa* living person into the *ehi* spiritual counterpart. Thus, both the *ehi* and the *omwa* of an individual participate in the spiritual and physical essences and through this participation are able, when in the state of *ehi*, to predestine the individual to avoid experiences which have frustrated activities in an earlier life, even when the *omwa* of the same individual, in ignorance, consciously aspires to the goals tabooed by the *ehi*. The notion of conception explains this.

The Yoruba also maintain that man is made of two important parts; the spiritual (*èmí*) and the physical (*ara*). The spirit essence in man, *èmí*, is part of his share in the divine essence of the Supreme Creator. This share in the divine essence sets a mark of uniqueness on him as an individual and is distinct from another spiritual element, the *Eléda*, "the ancestral spirit", which unites itself to the spiritual essence of the child to be born. The ancestral spirit, through that unity with the essence of the potential child, is able to reap the rewards of an earlier life of responsibility and success. Once united, it forms part of the total essence of the individual.

The *èmí* (spiritual essence) in the child and unique to the child, is itself part of the spiritual essence deriving from the Supreme Deity. The existence of this spiritual essence precedes the physical counterpart because it precedes conception. It is the spiritual counterpart (*orí-inú*) which sheds part of itself to unite with and put a stamp of uniqueness on the child at pregnancy. The part of this essence that remains behind constitutes the predestining half which monitors the performance of its living counterpart.

There is an essential difference between the Bini *ehi* and the Yoruba *orí-inú*. Like the *ehi*, orí-inú predestines the total individual and is the steersman of the living person (*enia*). Again, like the ehi, the orínú is essentially spiritual and constitutes what marks out an individual as unique. It is the metaphysic of the individuals that which makes him himself and no other. However, unlike the *ehi*, the *ori* does not engage in the process of exchanging modes of being with its living counterpart. It sheds part of itself to which an ancestral spirit unites, and both of which join with the physical body to form the child. At death the *èmí* joins its other essence, the spirit double, to await an opportunity for reincarnation - the reward for success in its earlier existence.

The Bini and the Yoruba are aware of the part parents play in the conception of the child, but they also - in line with their notions of destiny - insist that the final gift of the child does not rest solely on the act of sexual intercourse. Evidence is easily available by reference to couples who have no children.[15] As both the Bini and the Yoruba point out, these couples perform their sexual duties and so, if begetting children depends on sexual intercourse alone, why have the couples not begotten children? The Yoruba say that one who wants a child must receive the blessing of *Olódùmarè*, the Supreme Deity, as the condition. The Bini insist that pregnancy depends to a large extent on the blessing of *Olókun*, the god of wealth and fertility. Thus, the belief of both groups concerning pregnancy are overlaid by beliefs of a mystical nature. This overlay expresses the experience of both groups about the existential circumstances surrounding the conception of children; it also confirms for them the observation made by V. Ochendu about the Igbo of Nigeria that:

> ...the biological facts of conception are accepted but other factors are also involved in pregnancy and are much more important. These are the consent of the deities and the willingness of the dead lineage members and other friendly spirits to reincarnate themselves. The absence of these two agents renders conception impossible (1965:57).

The additional forces required in procreation according to the Bini are the blessing of *Osanobuwa*, the Supreme Deity, manifested in the more proximate blessing of *Olókun*, the divinity of wealth, fertility and the ruler of the rivers and the sea. After the spirit counterpart, *ehi*, has predestined the individual, it is ready to be born into the *agbọn*, the world of the living. The ancestors appeal to *Olókun* on behalf of their descendants. A successful appeal motivates *Olókun* to employ this delegated power to release the breath of life, part of the unique spiritual essence of the individual, on the descendant of the ancestors who have appealed. This spiritual essence invigorates the sperm. At intercourse, which the Bini described as "the natural fight for life",[16] the all-pervading power of the Supreme Being, *Osanobuwa*, reaches out and imparts the breath of life in the invigorated sperm.

The sperm itself has all the physical attributes of a person potentially. At the joining of the shed piece of the spiritual self, the invigorating power, the sperm, completes its potential qualities as a human with latent but not yet operative spiritual and physical powers. At conception, the breath of life from *Osanobuwa* sets in motion the development of these latent qualities. The womb of the mother then provides the necessary protection and moisture for its full development. By the time a man reaches puberty, *Oriole*, the divinity who moulds the human physique has worked on the sperm of the individual and determined the potential physical qualities of the sperm.

The Yoruba also insist that additional forces are required for procreation. These forces include the Supreme Being, *Olódúmarè*, the services of the divinity entrusted with the moulding of the physique, *Obàtálá*, and the ancestors (*awon baba ará órun*). The Supreme Being as the owner of breath imparts life in the semen (*àtò*). This constitutes the essence of man and the source of his vitality. It is the source of the individual's participation in the divine. The divinity moulds the physique. The ancestor gives the ancestral spirit, *Ẹlẹ̀da* (Bascom, 1956:9; Abimbola, 1971:74-75), the second Yoruba soul.[17] This is the reincarnated element in the child which forms his object of worship in the future. All these elements are in the semen of the man. Thus, in his semen is a miniature child. However, it is at the moment of sexual union that the sacred arm of the deity sets into operation the actualization of the potency in the semen so that it can, giving the conducive conditions of the womb, develop into a proper child.

Some ideas about religious belief, features of the society, and notions of personality, result from the Bini and Yoruba understanding of conception. Although the notions of conception appear similar, there are important differences which can be related to the subtle structural differences in the features of each society. The first idea resulting from the notions of conception analyzed is that the act of sexual union is sacred and the couple are participating in the creative power of the Supreme Being. The act involves divine intervention since it is the Deity who sets in motion the process of creation. Thus, there are the taboos about what time and place are suitable for sexual intercourse. Sex, therefore, cannot be casual. The act must be performed with the intention of participating in Divine creativity. The practical result of this interpretation of sexual union is that it makes the individual aware of his unique contribution to the survival of the family or the segment of the lineage. Here, then, symbolic notions of conception buttress the need for the individual to appreciate the quality of his contribution to the group. Along with this appreciation goes also the awareness that this procreative ability does not originate from an innate power in himself but from the initiative of the Creator and his own ancestors. Thus, rather than claim credit for his performance, and treating his children as members of his own nuclear family, he ought to thank the Supreme Being and his ancestors and put the services of his children at the disposal of the family group. Symbolic explanations of conception, therefore, constitute a charter for justifying the family or lineage-segments' claims to all its members and their services.

The second salient point that emerges from the notions of conception is that they allow the father, who was alleged to contribute much to the making of the child, to have the sole claim on the child. In other words, the notions support the patrilineal ideology that vests ownership of the child in the father. This manner of explaining conception has been given considerable attention in literature. Helen Callaway (1978) quoted J. Needham as saying that it amounts to the "denial of physiological maternity":

> Joseph Needham calls our attention to ideas held in Greece before the time of Aristotle, ideas which may have had their origin in Egypt, that the father alone was the "author of generation" while the mother provided only the "nidus and nourishment for the foetus" (J. Needham 1959, p. 43). He cites a passage from the *Eumenides* of Aeschylus when Appolo, defending Orestes during the trial from the charge of matricide, brings forward a philosophical argument. "The mother of what is called her child," Appolo makes his case, "is no parent of it, but nurse only of the young life that is sown in her. The parent is the male and she but a stranger, a friend who, if fate spares his plant, preserves it till it puts forth" (Callaway, 1978:167-168).[18]

This tendency to underplay, if not to ignore, the female contribution to procreation, was not the monopoly of the Greek, the Bini and the Yoruba societies with their clear-cut male orientation. The prevalence of this "denial of physiological maternity" has been recorded among the Asaba Igbo. As P. Isichei noted:

> A good way to think of man's sperm in order to capture accurately Asaba notions of it would be to regard it as a kind of seed ready to germinate in the fallow ground of a woman's womb. Accordingly, the sperm was a kind of "miniature babe" and all that a woman did was to develop it (1970:90).

Similar ideas have been noted among the Taita of Kenya (Harris, 1978:145-156) and the Zulu of South Africa.[19]

Such tendencies to underplay the contribution of one or the other parent to the conception of the child are not only characteristic of patrilineal societies. It has been observed in matrilineal societies. Among the matrilineal Ashanti there is the belief that "a human being is formed from the blood (*mogya*) of the mother and the spirit (*sumsum*) of the father" (Sarpong, 1977:4). The greater contribution of the mother to the work of creating the child forms the basis of the belief that the:

> ...biological link between one generation and another is provided by the blood transmitted through the mother, hence an Ashanti traces his descent through the female line (Sarpong, *ibid.*).

Yet, the Ashanti appreciate to some extent, the limited part played by the father, whose recognition, expressed in name giving, is highly essential.

Other comparisons may emerge from these examples. Among the Ashanti as well as among the Asaba Igbo, the parent who does not determine the descent of the child is credited with the "menial" task of moulding the child's personality, or kneading the rough stuff into refined form (Isichei, 1970).[20] Thus, for the patrilineal Asaba Igbo, the work of kneading devolves on women; for the matrilineal Ashanti it devolves on the father. As if to rob the mother of this contributive role in order to establish a stronger case for male ownership of the child, the Bini and the Yoruba credit the work of moulding the physical features of the child to the creative refraction of the Supreme Being which they call *Oriole* and *Obàtálá* respectively. Yet again, the Bini and Yoruba ideas of conception correspond, in their general outline, with that of the Gonja of northern Ghana who hold the view that:

> ...it is the man who places a child in the mother's womb for warmth and protection, during the early stages of growth - the woman nourishes it, but does not contribute to the actual formation of the foetus (Goody, 1962:20).

These observations suggest two comments. Firstly, such partial explanations are needed to establish the claim of the parent whose sex is relevant for tracing descent, for inheriting and for placement of the child. These claims are, therefore, likely to exist where unlinearity is overt. Thus, where there is a stress on strong patrilineages, there is likely to be such explanation of procreation that either underplays or ignores, where possible, the contribution of women to the child. Secondly, such explanations of procreation do not reflect the peoples' ignorance of physiological paternity or maternity as was suggested of the Trobriand Islanders by B. Malinowski (1929:179-185). Rather, they are symbolic statements which employ ideas about the relations between men and gods to justify the customary ideas which regulate relations in the society and claims which otherwise may appear unjustifiable (Leach, 1969:87).

Conclusion

In this chapter, an attempt has been made to present Yoruba and Bini notions of the individual. The earlier chapters have examined the individual only as a member of the group. The impression created then would have been that apart from the group, the individual Bini or Yoruba has nothing that sets him out as a unique individual. Although this impression would conform to the group's ideology of progress through unity within the group, the Bini and Yoruba recognize the worth of the individual.

The notions about the components of the individual presented here reveal both societies' ideas of the person as an individual. Over and above this, in order to discern the motivations behind those notions, the meaning they have and the function they perform in reference to the individual in the society, they were analyzed in relation to certain salient aspects of Bini and Yoruba belief systems and certain features of the society. To analyze the wealth of meaning behind the symbolic association, some reference was made, in broad outline, to Freudian ideas of the unconscious.

In sum, through the review we are presented with the collective representations of the society as to who a good person is, and an attempt was made to reveal the individual's perspective of the "good person." In so doing man is seen in his worth as an individual as well as a member of the society. The extent to which the individuating notes set him apart in his uniqueness is the extent to which it cannot be claimed that:

> like flies to wanton boys,
> Are we to the gods (Society)
> They kill us for their sport (King Lear).

CHAPTER FOUR

REFERENCES

1. R. Horton, "Destiny and the Unconscious in West Africa," *Africa*, Vol. XXXI, No. 2; 1961, p. 114.

2. This was collected during an interview with Chief Priest Ebohon, 21, Igbinadolo Street, Benin City, 3rd of Septermber 1980.

3. *See* R.E. Bradbury Benin Studies (London: O.U.P., 1973), p. 273.

4. This was collected durning an interview with Chief Priest Ebohon, 21, Igbinadolo Street, Benin City, Bradbury recorded a variant of it.

5. Wives try to improve thier standing in the affections of their husbands through cooking choice dishes, so that wives tried to out-do one another.

6. "Ovbokhan gha ze vb" *udu gbe a ghi ren ighe to miven igho, oma ghi gha re rio a ghi ren ighe to ri azen ra okpuhe ro ru.*

7. *See* P.C. Lloyd, Power and Independence: *Urban African's Perception of Social Mobility* (London: Routledge and Kegan Paul, 1974), p. 39.

8. *See* M. Fortes, *Oedipus and Job in West African Religion*. (Cambridge: O.U.P., 1959), Robin Horton's analysis of the Kalabari idea of *destiny*was meant in the main as correction of Meyer Fortes' idea of Oedipal Complex in West Africa.

9. *See* S. Freud, An Outline of Psychoanalysis (New York: W.W. Norton and Co., 1949).

10. Evidence given in the case of Chief Obasuyi and Peter Imaruedore, Appeal No. 61942, Ref. No. Prof., 93, 12, p. 11.

11. S.A. Akintoye, *Revolution and Power Politics in Yoruba-land 1840-1873* (London: Longman, 1971): P.D. Lloyd, "Sacred Kingship and Government among the Yoruba," *Africa* XXX, No. 3, 1960, pp. 221-237.

12. *See* P.C. Lloyd, *Some Notes on Yoruba Rules of Succession and on Family Property*, *Journal of African Law* III, i, 1959, pp. 7-32.

13. Interview with Mr. M.A. Uhomoibhi of Uselu Quarters, Ewatto-Ishan, 15th July, 1980.

14. E.E. Evans-Pritchard, "A Note on Some Zande Physiological Notions," *Sudan Notes and Records*, LI, 1970, pp. 162-165.

15. In terms of priority between the consequences of not having children at all, or having them through adultery, it would appear that the Bini woman will be better off breaking the rule of marital fidelity to beget children, if this proves necessary. A woman without children is always regarded as junior in the house (Aigbe, 1960:43). The Bini seem to confirm the wisdom in this action in the proverb: "Emwiokun will remain barren for long; her husband is impotent, and she does not take an evening stroll" (*O ghai kpee Emwiokun vb 'agan odo re itie okhyu ren iye ele ota*).

16. Recorded at an interview with Chief Priest Ebohon, Native Medicine Specialist in Witchcraft and Delivery of Babies, on the 10th of July, 1980.

17. W.R. Bascom, 1956, "Yoruba Concept of the Soul," 5th *International Congress of Anthropology and Ethnological Sciences* (Philadelphia: University of Pennsylvania Press); W. Abimbola, "The Yoruba Concept of Human Personality," in *La Notion de la Recherche, Scientique*, Paris. Although Bascom has mentiioned that there is a third Yoruba soul, Ojiji, a shadow which becomes activated at the moment of death when it makes an appearance to relatives, data collected from different parts of Yorubaland from among the Ketu, Oyo and Ekiti give a different interpretation. This appearance, made just before death forms the last activity of the spiritual breath. It is, therefore, a function of the soul rather than an action carried out by a distinct soul.

18. *See*, H. Callaway, 1978, "The most Essentially female Function of all: Giving Birth," in s. Ardener, *Defining Females* (London: Groom Helm.)

19. *See* M. Fortes (ed.), Marriage in Tribal Societies (Cambridge: C.U.P.)

20. P.K. Sarpong, 1977, *Nubility Rites in Ashanti* (Accrs Tema: Ghana Publ. Corp).

Papa David Adepoju Adeniji Adeniyi. He died in 1986.

CHAPTER FIVE

A CASE STUDY OF DAVID ADEPOJU A. ADENIYI: LIFE HISTORY AS AN CHRONOLOGICAL DOCUMENT

Family Background

My father's name is Popoola Adeniji Laniran. He was the first son of the titled chief Olukotun of Iwo town near Ibadan. He was born, as I was told, during the upheaval caused between the Ekiti on the one hand and the Ọ̀yọ̀ and Ibadan on the other at the later part of the nineteenth century. He, my father, was actually born in the war camp close to the battle front, hence he was named *Abidogun*, 'one born in battle'. Our house is called Ile Olukotun after our line's chieftaincy title right and our house is located near the main market of Iwo town.

My father's mother, Tinuola, was the daughter of Látóṣìṣà, a reputed Ibadan warrior. She accompanied her father in his campaigns since she traded in war equipment such as bullets, cutlasses and little guns. She was said to have met my grandfather, Omọ́gbẹ́bẹ̀, during the long campaign and they got married and lived together as husband and wife in the war camp where, eventually she gave birth to Abidogun, my father.

My father, Adéníji Adéniyì Abidogun married Sègilolá, my mother, in the proper manner and with all festivities (*níṣu lọ́kà*). I am the second child of that marriage. It was claimed that I was born in the fifth month of 1904. Although there is no certainty as to the exact date, there is unanimity on the fact that it was in the fifth European month because it was the month of that year when the extension of the railway line inland reached Ile Igbo near our town. My mother was engaged in the petty trade of selling both cooked food and uncooked foodstuff such as yam flour (*èlùbọ iṣu*) cassava flour (*èlùbọ*), yams (*iṣu*), and plantains to the railway labourers. It was on one of her trading trips that the pangs of birth throes seized her. She mentioned her condition to her co-traders who tried to convince her to take refuge in a near-by hut and deliver her baby there. She refused and insisted on proceeding to her husband's house to deliver her baby. In those days it was important that a child be born in his father's house so that his father could perform his special duty of disposing of the placenta (*ibi ọmọ*) by himself. In exceptional cases, wives delivered in their own father's house. To ensure that she did not deliver her baby on the way to our village, my mother was alleged to have cut some fresh banana leaves and knotted them. She placed the knot on her load. The Yoruba believe that if a woman who is on a journey begins to have birth pangs and she does this, she will not deliver until she reaches her destination, that is her husband's house, where she would loosen the knot and the baby would be delivered. As I was told, she just managed to get to her father's house before giving birth to me. Naturally, I lived with my parents in my grandfather's house.

When my father's mother, Tinúolá, the trader in war implements (*Ohun Ogun*) died, her relatives came from distant places to give her a befitting burial, the type that the Yoruba think is necessary to turn the deceased into ancestors. The group of visiting mourners was large since the deceased came from a very famous Ibadan warring family, her brother being the *Are Latoṣìṣà*, while her father was the paramount chief of Oya Latòṣà of Ibadan originated from Ibadan. My father's sister subsequently got married to an Ibadan man from the house of Apena not far from Idi Ọmọ at Ibadan. I left Iwo to live in her husband's house in 1911 when I was seven.

My father's sister, with whom I was staying, used to sell European-made clothes to the outlying villages north of Ibadan as far as Akanran village. She used to buy a big bulk of cloth from a firm called the Miller Brothers' Company whose chief retailer in distributing in our area was a man called Adebisi. We would carry bundles of cloth around the villages especially during annual festivals such as *Odun Egún*, 'Egungun's festival' or *Odun awọn Onigbagbọ*, 'Christian feastdays', or *Ileya* (the Muslim feast celebrating the return of pilgrims to Mecca). This was the free way of upbringing that I had when I was with my brother (FZ) in Ibadan until I was taken away in 1917 by my father. The Oracle of Ifa had divined that if I was not taken away from Ibadan, that I would not do any farming and I would become a truant. Farming was then the most prestigious occupation, and success at farming made it possible to marry many wives and to be admitted into the group of elders. In order to prevent the oracle's prophecy coming true, my father hastened to Ibadan and took me away in August of 1917.

The style of my upbringing during the seven years spent in Ibadan did not prepare me at all for the farming which my father strongly had in mind for me. Since I found farming very difficult, I tried assiduously to avoid going often to the farm with my father. Ordinarily, this would not have been difficult to manage as it is part of Yoruba child-rearing practice for grandparents to bring up some of their grandchildren. Two things, however, prevented me from taking advantage of this practice. Firstly, my grandmother was dead and so the all-round attention I would have received was reduced. Besides, people cooked for our grandfather and looked after him. It would have been difficult to saddle him with me. Secondly, the gap in my traditional education symbolized by my stay in Ibadan put an obligation on my parents to force me to make up for it. My grandfather loved me very much and was in favour of my staying with him at home, but every other person in our house was opposed to the idea. The other ally I would have found was my mother but she had left my father in 1913 in order to pursue her trading profession at Paraku in Dahomey (Republic of Benin). So I had no option but to apply myself to farming.

Something sticks in my mind very clearly concerning my stay with my mother (FZ) in Ibadan. At such times when I had to carry bundles of cloth to sell around the villages, in the advent of some festival or celebration, my mother (FZ) settles in her husband's village and uses it as a base from which to launch her trade in cloth to all nearby villages. The village is called Ope-Ifá. It is seven miles from Ibadan. I remember that during the War of Adubi (local name for the First World War) young, able-bodied men used to be seized and put in the army. Not all young men were forced as some volunteered. In the villages, children were saddled with the duty of standing as sentries to warn against the arrival of the fearful conscriptors called *Akọda*. The Akọda wore a uniform of black shirt and shorts with a read sash around their waist. At their approach, we would shout such sentences as 'the partridge has entered the farm' (*Àparò Jáko*), or 'the chimpanzee is coming (*Akiti mbọ lọnà*). On hearing these sentences, able-bodied young men would put a respectable distance between themselves and the village. In a few cases, those who wanted to volunteer would remain with the aged people in the villages. One of such volunteers was my father (FZHB) called Ojo, who went and came back safe and sound. When the Akọda left the village we would allow a period of time to pass before we gave the all-clear signal. When any young man had been unkind to us children we used to take our own revenge by giving occasional false alarms especially during the course of the afternoon meal. It was a spectacle to see able-bodied men who had been eating contentedly, one moment, scramble to their feet and make for the forest. We had a field-day with the meals. To return to the main outline of the story, my farming training commenced in earnest when I was brought back from Ibadan. It continued until it was halted by the terrible epidemic of 1918. This affected my life so much later on that one has to look into the ravages of this influenza and its effects on me.

The 1918 Influenza Epidemic (Lùkúlùkú) and the Local Understanding of Its Cause

The 1918 epidemic was a fearful experience. May God not allow such a thing to happen again (*ki Ọlọ́run majẹ ki arírú rẹ mọ*). It was during that year that I first came in contact with a corpse. There was sickness in every household. We, my father, my father's new wife (step- mother) and her son and myself were at the farmhouse of our farm that was farthest away from our town (Oko Igbo). We had our supper (*onjẹ alẹ́*) and went to bed. We all slept in the same open area of the farmhouse. There was nothing unusual that evening. Deep into the night, before the first cock-crow, my father woke up to find that he was feeling weak and ill. Then he woke me up and I felt ill myself. Then his younger wife, Àwèró, a very kind woman (*obìnrin onónú rere*) who, then, was nursing a son called Àmòó was ill. Her child, too, was ill. After sometime when my father did not hear the sound of our moaning, he feared that something must have happened to us. He called out to me, 'Adépòjù, Adépòjù'. When he did not hear an answer immediately, he feared the worst had happened and he exclaimed, 'what a dreadful calamity has befallen me' (*irú ogun nla wo ni mo kàn yi*). It was then that I had mustered sufficient strength to answer him that, 'my father, no calamity has befallen you' (*Bàbá mi kò sí ogun kan tí okàn yín*). He asked about Àwèró the younger wife, and I said she was sleeping close to me. He then said that since she did not answer his call, I should shake her. I shook Àwèró three times and called "Àwèró, Àwèró, Àwèró, my father is calling you". There was no answer. Then I told my father that it appears her body was a little cold. Then my father said I should move away from her side. Then I tried to move but I could not move away. That was my first contact with a corpse. Àmòó, the little child, also died shortly after his mother's death.

The epidemic (*lùkúlùkú*) was a dreadful disease. It comes on one suddenly and gently weakens one completely. It can catch hold of one at any time and in any circumstance. It could catch one while eating or in one's sleep. The surest signs of its presence were an enervating sleepiness and the desire in one's waking moments, to drink water inordinately. If it catches one at sleep, one sleeps until one slowly passes away. This spectacle often makes it difficult for relatives to know when a victim has died, as they often think that one was just asleep. This was what happened to my father (FB) called Bankole, in whose compound Àwèró, my father's younger wife and her child, were buried. After their burial, we went into the hut to greet Baba Bankole, only to find out that he was dead and had died at least a day previous. That was an unforgettable period in my life.

At the peak of this dreadful experience, my grandfather, Omobẹ́gbẹ̀, the great warrior and farmer became disillusioned about all that was happening around him. He felt that the world had suddenly taken a turn for the worse and his understanding of the cause of the change was typical of those of his age-group as their discussions in our household conveyed. He felt that the dreadful experience was a result of the white-man's intervention in the traditional working of things. The white men had prevented, they, the warriors and leaders, from fighting and had imposed taxation, 'money for the head' (*owoori*) which was taboo to the Yoruba since nobody could put a price on man but Olórun (the Deity) himself. To avoid trouble, we had broken our taboo and paid it. Secondly, the white men had set up court-houses to judge palaver and made some of themselves the final judges and instead of allowing cases to be settled before the assembly of the king and elders, amicably. My grandfather was the first chairman of the first native court set up in Iwo in 1904. Thus, people who were, in the native courts, pronounced guilty were duly disgraced by being sent to prison as most people were too poor to pay the fines. Instead of helping the society to live together in peace, whether guilty or not-guilty, as our forefathers did, the court only sowed the seed of discontent and enmity. It was on account of these transgressions that the ancestors sent the epidemic as the most violent sign of their disapproval of what was going on. Since the solution of returning to the past was beyond the control of the old warriors like my grandfather, the world of the Yoruba having come under the white man, my grandfather decided that if he could not do anything else he would save himself the indignity of continued existence. Subsequently, he resigned from the post of chairman of the native court. He then went to the Ọba to tell him that he had had enough and would soon join his ancestors. In the olden days, you did not take laws into your hands. You had to consult the king. The reigning king then was Ọba Abimbola, the grandfather of the incumbent King of Iwo. He the king told my grandfather not to give up yet but to come back for an answer.

Not long after the epidemic subsided, as if to confirm my grandfather's views, the tax- collectors intensified their campaign and shifted the principle of taxation to a more demanding one. Formerly, 'the money for the head' (*owo-ori*) - taxation - affected only the heads of the families. Each head paid five shillings. But in October of 1918 the principle of taxation changed from taxing family heads to taxing people on the basis of the number of rooms in their house. Thus, some people who would have, under the old system paid five shillings (*ọ̀kẹ́ kọn*) now had to pay twenty-five shillings (*ọkẹ marun*) or more. You know that in the olden days, people lived together in wide circular compounds with many rooms. A head who was just recovering from the epidemic had to find, if he had a house with ten rooms, fifty shillings or stand the risk of going to prison. If a householder explains that the rooms in his house belong to his wives, who were not liable for taxation, the tax collectors or room-counters' (*kalé-kalé*) as they were now called, countered that no single person has the right to marry that number of wives. Matters became so difficult that many elders thought that my grandfather's views were the only sensible alternative.

In February of 1919, my grandfather died. Thereafter, I no longer had my time divided between periods of hardship on the farm and pleasure in the town. After his burial, an elder brother of my father was installed as Chief Olukotun or Iwo, our lineage's chieftaincy title. Unfortunately, he died within seven months of his installation. Then rumours circulated in the town that the spectacle of sudden deaths has come back into our family. As if to confirm this dreadful rumour, in August 1919, my own father died. I begged an educated man called Agogoìjà, living with us, to record the date of the sad event for me. Since that time until God (Ọlọ́run) established me as a responsible man in society, with a steady employment and a family of my own, life was a series of periods of loneliness and want. Things changed suddenly so that I, the son of a chief, had to accept to be a pawn.

I Entered into Debt-bondage (mo singba)

As things turned more difficult in our house, I decided to go and stay with my mother's people (*àwon iyèkan mi*). They were kind to me. While I was with them, it happened that my mother's brother, Maliki Olarewaju was of age to marry, but he could not because he did not have the means. This brought a lot of shame to the household as people in the town made terrible jokes about him. They hinted that he was either impotent (*òkóbó*) or that he belonged to a wretched household which could not perform its duties to its members. He was not considered a real person in society until he had married. To put an end to the public embarrassment which this situation caused the family, I was approached and consented to become a pawn in order to raise money for the marriage of my father (MB) Maliki Olarewaju.

In this system of debt-bondage, I provided the man who loaned us money free labour to pay back the debt. Since every effort was made to get from the pawn a service that would justify the exchange, this system is little improvement on slavery. I must mention, in fairness to the man I served, that I was treated kindly. Through the service I provided, my father (MB) was able to marry a wife, Taiwo Omolẹ̀ye, to the joy of the household. They gave birth to five children. Of the five children, the successful one is Rafiu. Not only has he gone on holy pilgrimage to Mecca, but he became a successful businessman with many wives and children. He owns five houses at Iwo town and some in Ibadan. Before Rafiu opted for Muslim arabic education, I had taken him to live with me so that he could attend Christian school. He opted out of that plan and went back to the arabic school. As the successes in his life show, the Muslim school suited his destiny much more than other venture.

I Became a Christian

Towards the end of my debt-bondage in 1928, I came in contact with the Baptist Christians. They were erecting school buildings in Iwo and provided some employment for unskilled labourers like myself. I liked their ways of doing things and, with the permission of my master, I used to go and watch them at religious service. When my period of debt-bondage ended, I enrolled as a member of their labour force. A certain man called Abayomi acted as the foreman for them and he employed me. I continued to work for them and save money. It was while I was at this employment that the foreman's brother, Labande, advised me to go to school. It should be remembered that I was not a small boy then as I was already twenty-four years old.

Until 1928, I did not have any inclination to go to school. As an important chief's son, school was not the popular choice of profession. Farming was what made a man great. Only the poor in our own area of Yorubaland sent their children to school. But as time went on, I began to think seriously about learning to read and write. So I took up Labande's advice and divided my day in such a way that I could attend school without losing my gainful employment. As soon as it was dawn, I would go the building site and carry my own volume of building sand to the site. I would leave shortly before school commenced (8:00 a.m.) and head for the school where I would be from 8:00 a.m. till two o'clock in the afternoon. Being a mature student, I followed the lessons closely. Often after the school closed for the day, if I had not done sufficient work at the building site, I would go back to continue. If I had done enough, I would spend some part of the evening fetching and selling firewood in order to have some pocket money to spend on books so that I did not need to touch the money I was saving. This was how I struggled through to complete my standard six education.

In my standard one, our class had the privilege of being taught by a very kind (*omolúwàbí*) person. He was called *Ọmọ́biyi*. He was a capable teacher (*afinju oluko*). He taught us so well that at the end of our year, the education officer, a white man called Mr. Cliff - you know how honest and appreciative of hard work these white people are - came on his annual inspection tour and having tested us, instructed that thirteen of us should be given double promotion to Standard III, since reading Standard II would be a waste of time for us. We continued to make progress in the school and completed our course in 1934. But that year did not see the end of my course since, of all the students in my class who were to take the Standard Six examination that year, I alone was asked to stay behind.

Unfortunately, in 1934, the white missionaries went home and the running of the school was left to the native teachers. Students in the senior year were assigned to stay with and provide domestic services to the teachers, most of whom were unmarried then. I served my teacher so well that he got used to my service and did not want to part with it. At the end of the year, before our examinations, during the teachers' meeting (so I was told later), my teacher- master (*Olukọni Ọgami*) moved that I should be delayed another year. I know that if the missionaries were there, this sad event would not have overtaken me. I also wondered that if I stayed another year, I might not be delayed again. So I left school since I was not allowed to take examinations with the other students. It was a tortuous experience as I did not have a certificate. All my fellow students who took the examination passed. The teacher who put me in the situation is till alive today and still living in our town, Iwo. Maybe if I give his name, his children may take offence. Yet, this thing ought to be made known, at least, for the sake of my own children too. He is called Awujọ́olá.

When I left school in 1934 without a certificate, there was little else I could do. Early in 1935, I left Iwo and went to stay with my mother at Badagry. She had become established in this coastal town from where she goes to outlying places to trade. Although she was happy to see me and wanted me to stay in her house, she said it would be against our custom because a child belongs to his father and his father's people and should live with them. So she arranged that I should go and live with my father (FFBS) who was a policeman based at Ilaro. He was called Couple Ojo and his area of supervision extended to most areas of Egbado Division from Ilaro to Imẹkọ, Aiyetoro and Ijana. He was glad to have me and bought a bicycle for me so that I accompanied him during his tours. People liked him. I remember that he had two great friends, one at Imeko and another at Ijana. They had a reputation as the most powerful medicine men in Egbado. My father (FFBS) told me that they were, like himself, powerful men and since powerful men should work together, he thought it worthwhile to make friends with them. I left my cousin for Ibadan at the end of 1935. It was when I got to Ibadan that the new Education Officer, a certain Mr. Adelakun, gave me the chance to take my Standard Six examination with the promise that if I passed, I would be employed. I sat for the examinations and passed and I was employed. I had become a Christian in my Standard One, having been given the name David (Photo page 160a).

I Became a Man

When I was employed as a teacher, I knew I was gradually taking on the responsibilities of manhood. I had to prepare myself. A man without a steady gainful employment would not be called a proper man as he has not got the means with which to discharge his responsibilities which include taking care of and sending relatives to school. There was, therefore, a pressure on us to become well-established and you could not be established on the Standard Six teacher's salary then £3. 10s. In any case, going as I did into an untraditional profession, the pressure was even greater on me to prove myself. To this end, I took on a few other things with my teaching profession.

I enrolled as a student of a certain Mr. Adebayo, Accountant and Auditor in order to learn elementary bookkeeping, accountancy and commercial laws. Mr. Adebayo also taught us journalism. I was engaged in these activities between 1936 and 1937. By October 1937, Mr. Adebayo who had admitted more students for the same courses, employed me as their instructor. While I was getting settled into these roles, N. Azikwe (later the first President of Nigeria) spread his nationalist movement to Ibadan. The main organ of this movement was the daily newspaper called *The Pilot*. Subsequently, my father (MB) Mr. J.L. Oyesina, founder and owner of Ibadan Grammar School, advised me to become a distributor and journalist for *The Pilot*. He paid the then exorbitant amount of £55 as guarantee on my behalf. Thus, I became the Chief Yoruba Representative for the *Pilot* in Ibadan. The Chief Igbo representatives was Mr. N. Onwuka. I had a daily allocation of 100 copies of *The Pilot* and each sold for two pence. It was this position with *The Pilot* that brought me in contact with the important men of the day, such as the Resident, the Colonial Officers, the heads of religious bodies, Azikwe's paper, was so popular and interesting to read that it almost stood next to the Bible to those Nigerians who could read and write.

I Became Secretary to the King of Iwo and Representative of UAC

In 1938, on account of the reputation that I had as the representative of *The Pilot*, it was decided by the Iwo town elders that the contacts I had would prove useful to leaders of the town in doing business with the Europeans. Consequently, the then reigning King of Iwo, Ọba Amida Akande Magoibon, sent a delegation to me in Ibadan. The delegation stated in proverbial language suitable to the occasion that 'when the ship sails the ocean and the lagoons, it eventually returns to its port of embarkation' (*Ti ọkọ̀ ba rokun ti oba rọ̀sà apadà sílé*). It was a simple request that I come back home to serve my town. I had no option but to go back home. Although I would have preferred to pursue my profession in Ibadan, it would have been unpardonable offence to turn down the request of the king. Besides, that king had progressive ideas and sought to bring back all the natives of the town who could contribute to its progress. He was a very good man. Unfortunately, his reign did not last long. He died in 1939. His successor was of quite a different disposition. He scandalized the population in many ways, particularly those of us who worked in the palace. He refused to give us our salaries on the pretence that he had opened up accounts for each worker into which he was paying our salaries (that was the time the local government authorities encouraged the payment of salaries into accounts). This state of affairs was endured until 1942, when quite a few of the workers, I inclusive, resigned - not without the approval of some elders.

In 1943, Mr. J. O. Adebayo, who taught me book-keeping, accountancy and journalism, recommended me to the Mac-Iver Representative (a branch of the United Africa Company) as the produce-buyer of cocoa attached to the Iwo Railway Station. While working for Mac-Iver, I took up photography between 1945-1947. I bought a typewriter in 1948, and after learning how to type, I became a letter-writer. About 1948, the Europeans who ruled Nigeria made moves to hand over the government to Nigerians. Towards the end of that same year, an effort was made to involve Nigerians in government work and prepare them for the end of European rule. It was on this account that I was appointed a Counsellor in 1948. The Europeans also insisted in 1950 that political parties be formed. At that time, Chief O. Awolowo founded the *Ẹgbẹ Afẹ́nifẹ́re* (Party of those who want Progress) known as Action Group (AG). I was subsequently appointed as the first Secretary and Initiator of the A. G. in Iwo. I contested as an Action Group candidate in our constituency and I lost to the candidate of the National Council of Nigeria and the Cameroons (N.C.N.C.) formed by Azikwe with its power base among the Igbo.

Contrary to the traditional underlying principle that all competitions among members of the town should, in the long run, contribute to peace and progress of the town, the climate in which the election campaigns were conducted was belligerent. It appeared that opponents did not want to stop at anything to win. At the end of it all, I was glad to be out of office because the new way of getting into office was completely different from what we were used to and I knew that if that was the way things were to be done in the future, it would bring a lot of trouble. As a matter of fact, the man who defeated me fell out , shortly afterwards, with the king. It was rumoured that he had not observed the traditional etiquette of respect, reverence and caution that ought to characterize people's behaviour to the king. It was alleged that the king got angry with him and cursed him. He died shortly afterwards.

Involvement in Research

In 1957, the Yoruba Research Scheme was established under the inspiration of Dr. S.O. Biobaku, in order to keep a record of the important contributions of Yoruba people which were destined to be forgotten. I was recommended as a member of this Research Group. The first assignment I was given was to take the members of the scheme to explore the riches of Ifa, the Yoruba process of divination. I took the group to Iwo and Ikire to speak to the specialists in divination - Babaláwo. The research proved so successful that I became a permanent member of the group. However, the break-through came with another research.

Following the success of the research on the process of divination, I was consulted as to what next important feature of Yoruba contribution the group should look into. After much thought, I suggested that they look into the traditional methods of iron-smelting (*Irun-sísun*). In the olden days, the use of iron gave the Yoruba a lot of power over their neighbours. Members did not believe that the Yoruba smelted iron, and some asked me whether I believed seriously that the Yoruba used Iron before they were introduced from European sources. I told them in confirmation that the ward of my ancestral line was noted for iron-smelting as we were known as *Ile Asunrin*, 'the house of iron-burning'. Some of the group members asked in jest whether the Yoruba mixed liquid substances to form their iron like they make their corn porridge (*ẹ̀kọ*). I told them that the Yoruba burnt different types of stones under great volume of fire. I was asked to take the group to the spots where this was done.

During my tour to prepare for the research visit to iron-smelting centres, I found that in the whole of northern Ọ̀yọ̀ where iron-burning was a flourishing profession, only one melting-pit remained. The pits connected with the Fatuke ancestral line were no longer operation. The pit that our ancestral line operated at the village of Ìporin (lit. 'where iron is mixed) had been closed. Then I got scared that people might think I had lied to them. While I was thinking what to do, I discussed it with a relative of mine who immediately mentioned that the pit at Isundunrin (lit. 'burning until it becomes iron') was still in operation. I went there and spoke to the iron-burners in the village and they agreed to give us a trial run. The members, subsequently, visited Isundunrin and were delighted to see how different special stones were burnt together under great fires to make iron. The research proved so interesting that when the Yoruba Research Scheme, formerly based at Eléyẹlé area of Ibadan was transformed into the Institute of African Studies, University of Ibadan, I was taken on its staff. I was also commissioned to write all I knew about the traditional Yoruba way of smelting iron.

Pa Adeniji's Opinions on Yoruba Personality and Human Characteristics

When the Yoruba say that a person is good, it has nothing to do with his is appearance. It does not mean that one is so beautiful that we have not seen his type before. A good person (*enia rere*) has a good character (*ìwà rere*). A good character is built on respect and love (*ìteriba ati ife*). Respect and love summarize all the qualities desirable in a person. The Yoruba believe that if a leper has both qualities, he will not be abandoned in loneliness. People will flock to him because his inner qualities have outweighed his external or outward appearance. I will illustrate that all the qualities the Yoruba envy in a man are summarized by *Iteriba* and *Ife*. Let us examine the quality of illustriousness (*akíkanjú*).

In the corpus of Ifá divination, illustriousness is highly regarded and many verses stress the need to cultivate this quality in children. A verse that comes to my mind now is the Odù Odun. Ifá tells the story of the illustrious Odun who wanted to succeed where others had failed. He wanted to become the king of Ado Ibini (a mythological place not connected to Benin City) and survive. The process of enthronement of a new king in Ado Ibini specifies that the first stranger who enters the town after the death of the reigning king is installed as the mock king (*Ọba ẹgẹrẹmùtì*) for a brief spell. He will be showered with gifts and property and given the insignia of office, horse tail (*iru-esin*); that same night, while he was still rejoicing, the mock king would be taken out and killed as the important sacrifice that precedes the installation of the rightful heir to the throne of Ado Ibini.

Odin decided to go to Ado Ibini immediately after the death of the king of that town. He decided to arm himself with all the protective charms he could get. He also had the good sense to consult the Ifá oracle. It was the custom that people first consulted the oracle before embarking on an important project. The Ifá oracle told him to make a sacrifice of water yam (*iṣu ewùrà*) and electric fish (*ẹja òjíjí*). He was instructed that while on his journey, if he wished to succeed, he should put good character, love and respect before reliance on physical and magical power. Kindness rather than the sword ensure the success of his journey.

Odin set out for Ado Ibini. On entering the town, he saw a huge crowd of its inhabitants who burst into spontaneous jubilation at seeing him. He ignored the great attention he had attracted and proceeded to the market place with his heavy load of yams. He set down his yam for sale. The market of Ado Ibini was noted as a rendezvous for different types of beings who transform themselves into human appearance to mingle with human beings and buy from the market. Unbeknown to Odin, his first group of customers were elephants who had transformed themselves into human beings. They asked for the price of the biggest yam, and after some haggling, they settled on paying six cowries (*owó ẹyọ méfà*). To Odin's surprise, his customers said they had not a single cowry but that they wanted to take the yam away. Then Odin remembered the advice of the Oracle. He told his customers that they could take the yam without paying but that they would have to pay next time. The elephants-transformed-to-men took away the yam.

Meanwhile, the people of Ado Ibini came to pay homage to Odin calling him "Our king" (*Ọba wa*). They gave him costly treasures and great property knowing that, come nightfall when Odin was killed, they would retrieve their belongings. They even brought the symbols of kingship, the crown (*Adé*) and the white horse-tail (*ìrukẹ̀rẹ̀ funfun*). They placed the crown on his head and placed the horse-tail in his hand. When there was a lull in the homage-paying, the six customers of Odin came back. They thanked Odin for his kindness. They told him that they had not eaten for seven days but that through his act of kindness they had overcome their hunger. They told him that that act of kindness would save him from imminent death. They instructed Odin neither to be taken in by the homage-paying nor to attempt to sleep in the town of Ado Ibini because he would be killed at night by the people of the town, who would then recover their gifts and install the rightful heir to the throne. Odin then asked what he would do to escape. His customers (elephants-transformed-to-men) told him not to worry and that his kindness would save him. They would repay kindness by ensuring that he escaped with all his gifts.

In the evening, the town people with the king-maker (*afiọbajẹ*) at their head proceeded from the palace to the market place on a ritual dance of 'enthronement'. It was their custom to make seven such ritual dancing trips. At the completion of the seventh trip, the mock king, in this case, Odin, was to be killed. At each of the first six trips, more gifts were to be showered on the mock king. The ritual dance group continued and after its departure for the palace at the end of the sixth and final trip, Odin to his surprise, saw six hugh elephants rush out and head for him. When they reached his place the elephants opened their anus' which led to big open spaces within them. Yoruba folklore states that the inside of an elephant was like a little town with a lot of space. He, Odin, quickly got to work assisted by the elephants in turn and all the goods were packed inside them. Odin was asked, just as the crowd was returning to the market place, to get into the biggest of them. Then, the six elephants made straight for the crowd which dispersed in turmoil. It was only then that he realized the meaning of the instruction of the Oracle, that on his journey he must put good character built on love and kindness before brutal strength for kindness is more rewarding than the sword. Then, in confirmation he burst into a song of thanksgiving:

Elephants climb the forbidden mountain
Elephants climb the forbidden mountain
Good character made Odin to climb the forbidden mountain, good character is the medicine.

CHAPTER FIVE

REFERENCES

1. *Mefa* comes from 'efa' which means six. The Yoruba use this numeral as the symbol of love (*Ife*). Hence, they say that one who loves draws all to himself (*fa enia mora*).

The possessed priestess of Olókun prophesying to an attentive audience which provides a gentle rhythm of music as a background to the priestess's ritual act.

The first daughter of heir-apparent to the chief-priestess of Olókun, Grace Ovbiohon, standing in front of the shrine of Olókun at Iyowe with her uncle Uyiekpen Bas Eweka.

Olókun devotees admitted into the inner area of worship. They are all dressed in white, the colour of Olókun which symbolizes ritual purity and coolness.

Olókun devotees kept out of the inner circle of worship on acccount of menstuation. Only female worshippers who have reached menopause or are not menustrating are admitted as pure enough to worship.

Singing and dancing Olókun devotees who slowly work on the chief priestess to become possessed by Olókun.

CHAPTER SIX

BINI AND YORUBA WOMEN: FEMALE ROLE IN PATRILINEAL SOCIETIES

Introducing the Paradox

Much of the foregoing discussion on religion and the human person in Bini and Yoruba societies has concentrated on views on social, religious and political features mainly about men and provided by men. Since the dominant features of both societies are male-oriented, this tendency is, to some extent, inevitable. Although inevitable, the approach needs to be extended to include female roles which throw into relief the status of women in both societies. The roles of women in marriage provide an insight into the social expectations about women. In marriage, women are represented as subordinate to men, but in certain contexts their prominence is emphasized. I take as examples the worship of Olókun among the Bini and the Gẹ̀lẹ̀dẹ́ masked dance among the Yoruba. I do not suggest that Gẹ̀lẹ̀dẹ́ ritual dance enjoys the same popularity among all the Yoruba. Rather, it is claimed that in different areas of Yorubaland, women are predominant in certain areas of ritual, particularly those that are associated with the society's concern for procreation and fertility. The demands of female subordination associated with patrilineal ideology are counterbalanced by the prominence given to women in these rituals.

As in other societies, the Yoruba and the Bini, who transmit names, rights and statuses through the patriline, are dependent not merely on fertility but on the assumed fidelity of women outside the patriline.[1] More so in these societies where the awareness of possible infertility in potent males depends on sophisticated medical knowledge which is not available to most of the people, men are more obviously dependent on female fertility. Yet the female sex is not relevant for transmission of name, claims to traditional office and inheritance of property. The paradox becomes more acute since Bini and Yoruba patrilineages require (a) biological continuation through time made possible through the fertility of their wives, (b) legitimacy in descent assumed only through fidelity of their wives and, (c) an affinal linkage to other patrilineages in the society through the transfer of their daughters who, at first marriage are expected to be virgins, and therefore, "pure women." These needs require a supply of "decent" or "pure" women from outside the lineage.

In the absence of any system of male initiatory rites in most areas of Yorubaland, jural adulthood depends on achieving fatherhood. This is even more important among the Bini who associate jural adulthood, not independence, with the Ighele age-association. The minimum age of each of its members at admission, informants insist, was thirty years. At this age, Bini men ought to have become fathers. Therefore, Bini and Yoruba men are very dependent on their wives, that is, fertile non-lineage women. On the one hand, they get these women from other lineages in the society. Both the honour of the patrilineage and the need to ensure the supply remain constant dictates which place an obligation to the wife-getting lineage also to supply women who are both fertile and faithful from among its own maidens. On the other hand, in real life, Bini and Yoruba women are not simply tokens to be exchanged nor passive wombs for impregnation. On this level the patrilineage is dependent on the cooperation of the unrelated women themselves, especially as regards fidelity. To admit this dependence, however, would run clearly contrary to the patrilineal ideology. Ritual provides the forum whereby women are given prominence and thus express themselves.

Marriage constitutes the penultimate step to jural adulthood which is conferred at the birth of the first child. A consideration of the marital process and the types of marriage approved of is relevant to an appreciation of the ways by which women acquire maturity and are looked upon as responsible persons in both societies. This consideration also provides an insight into the characteristics and qualities desired in would-be wives. As the "go-between", *Alárena* or *osuonwan*, investigates the character of spouses, the reasons for her (or his) approval or disapproval, point to the characteristics and qualities approved or disapproved of in both societies.

The contents of this chapter are presented, therefore, in a dialectical perspective. The views and activities of males about women made manifest in the marital types and processes, stand for the thesis in these male-oriented societies. The views of women about what meaning they attach to female roles and activities provide the antithesis. The synthesis is achieved when it is realized that statements about the sexes in both societies cannot be made in simple clear-cut terms of "superiority" of males and "subordination" of the female. Complementarity of the sexes would be more appropriate as each sex enjoys prominence in specific areas. Each specific area of prominence of either sex is seen not in isolation but in relation to the whole system of spheres which compose the total area of male/female relations in both the Bini and Yoruba societies.

Bini Marriage: Irhioha[2]

(a) Marriage Types

The Bini recognize eight marriage types: marriage by betrothal called "infant marriage," *Omo N'Agayi*; forced marriage, *Namukhui*; adolescent marriage, *Idegbe*; widow inheritance, *Ibiotoma*; marriage by abduction, *Ilevba*; marriage of a widow, *Egbe*; and *Areuwa* marriage in which a female stays at her father's house to raise children to his name. *Adegbe* is yet another marriage type found primarilly among the Northern Edo, especially in the Fugar and Agenedobe area. Betrothal of "infant marriage" was called *Omo N'agayi* which translates as "the child for whom you serve." It commences at the birth of a new baby girl (*omokhuo*) when the friend of her father says that he will marry the baby by serving her parents. He subsequently confirms the seriousness of his intention through the giving of gifts such as bundles of firewood, portions of game and tubers of yam. Besides these gifts, he also gives services which may range from the provision of free labour for thatching the roads of houses in his friend's compound to planting yam seeds and, at times of harvest, harvesting the produce from the farm. These services, periodic though they may be, continue over a long period and tend to increase in intensity as the betrothed girl nears puberty. Shortly before puberty, the father of the girl may give her as a prospective wife to this friend in recognition of long and faithful service. It is only then that the other processes of marriage which remove the genetricial and uxorial rights of the daughter from her parents' jural control to that of her betrothed spouse are begun in earnest.

The consent of the daughter is not sought for marriages of betrothal. She is brought up to be obedient to her elders whose authority is sanctioned by the ancestors. A Bini adage confirms this expectation when it states that for "one to bear a child and betroth her to someone is not an unprecedented act of kindness in the world" (*A bie ya ne omwan ire ese na ma mien vb'agbon ede*). In other words, the father who gives his daughter in marriage without asking her for her opinion is not doing anything extraordinary because he does not owe his daughter an explanation. When such arrangements have been made and approved of by senior members of the lineage, the daughter cannot refuse.

As P.I. Igbafe noted:

> To refuse should imply drawing down the anger and antagonism of her parents and other members of the family upon herself. In a society where corporate life had not given way to individualism and where the deeply-rooted extended family system had not lost its cohesion, a girl could hardly afford the isolation into which a refusal to marry a family-chosen husband would plunge her (1970:77).[3]

Thus, this type of marriage arrangement did not give much consideration to the preference of the girl, one of the parties to the marriage.

A second marriage arrangement which did not give the girl much scope for choice is "forced" marriage, *Namukhui*, which literally translates "taken to." It often occurs in two situations; either to cement the friendship between two men well-disposed to each other or to encourage reconciliation and friendly relationships between two well-matched enemies. In this type of marriage, the arrangements are made solely by men and, often, it is alleged by informants, the girls and their mothers may not be aware of them. The process was simple. The husband-to-be was instructed by his partner or friend to stay in. The girl was then taken without her consent and made to stay. One of the informants, Chief Osado Edomwonyi was quick to add:

> That was when things were normal. Then, when a father spoke his children heeded. The children know their place in the home and they knew that their father's word was law, against which, in such matters, there was no appeal. Nowadays too much learning and the *Ebo's* freedom (white-man's freedom) has changed the manner of behaviour of children to their parents. Most girls have been known to refuse their father's choice of husband in recent times. When they refuse, nowadays, their fathers cannot do anything about it. That is the change that has overtaken the world (*agbọn*).[4]

The third type of marriage reverses the trend of the first two as it represents rebellion against the choice of parents. It is called *Ilevba* which literally means "escape to meet." It institutionalizes elopement as a form of union that eventually receives the recognition of parents. Since it commences as a contravention of customary practices, the partners in this marriage are at the onset regarded as marginal figures in the society. This anomalous situation creates tremendous strain on the *Ilevba* spouses as it cuts them off from the protection and help of their kinsmen. As an informant who gave me the taxonomy of Bini marriages noted:

> The *Ilevba* marriage was a most difficult marriage to contract. Not only were the spouses out of favour with their relatives, they were also in trouble with the community. Members of the young man's age-grade association who felt that their member's contract of *Ilevba* marriage had impugned their reputation made things difficult for the Young husband.

> Besides, in disobeying their parents, the spouses felt that they had cut themselves off from their ancestors protection. Furthermore, the King (Ọba) in a sensitive case of elopement, ordered the capture of the spouses. In such a situation, the spouses did not escape punishment since as we, the Bini say in our adage, "No forest can accommodate the King's enemy" (*Oha igua oghian Ọba*). For these reasons, the beginning of *Ilevba* marriage was most difficult (a translation). (Interview with Chief Osado Edomwonyi. Interview on 2 Jan. 1981 at 50, Mission Road, Benin.)[5]

In cases which did not attract the special attention of the king, resolute spouses who put sufficient distance between themselves and their age-grade associations exploited the wider kinship opportunities by seeking refuge with their maternal relatives. When they gave birth to children, efforts aimed at reconciliation of the spouses to their age-grade association and close kinship groups were intensified. These efforts usually led to legitimization of their marriage. *Idegbe*[6] marriage is yet another type. This involves a girl who was not betrothed to anyone before puberty. It literally means "I preserve myself" ("I hold myself"). It gives a wider space for choice as the girl is able, at her age, to indicate some preference for a particular spouse.

The marriage of a widow is in two categories; *Ibiotoma* and *Egbe*. In marriage in which the complete payment of bridwealth has transferred both the genetricial and uxorial rights over the wife to the husband, the death of the husband does not abrogate the rights of his lineage over the services of the wife. She remains an affinal member of the husband's group and she is inherited, if young, by a relative of the husband. Hence, the second marriage, or widow inheritance, is referred to as *Ibiotoma* - "those who remain within the floor of the kinship group." The *Egbe* marriage of a Bini widow occurs in the rare case when a young woman refuses to marry a kin of her dead husband and chooses to mourn for him for two years instead. At the completion of the official mourning period, she seeks to leave her husband's kinship group and get married to any young man of her choice outside it.

The two other types of Edo marriage are *Areuwa* and *Adegbe*.[7] These are exceptional types of marriage in terms of the Bini marital practices since they come into being in peculiar situations which dictate the method of determining the ownership of the children. *Areuwa* marriage prevails among the Bini and Esan (an Edo subgroup). *Areuwa* marriage occurs when a man who has lived a successful life by Bini standards dies without having begotten a son. Tradition enables the eldest daughter (Omokhuo) to "remain within the house" (uwa) and raise up children to her father's name.[8] *Areuwa* marriage, therefore, encourages an uxorilocal marital residence as the husband who may not be polygamous, may set up house with his wife in her father's house. The children of an Areuwa marriage are shared between parents so that the first son is incorporated into the patriclan of the mother and the second into the patriclan of the father. Thereafter, each son inherits property, accedes to office and traces descent from the patriclan of either parent into which he is integrated by the Areuwa practice.

Adegbe marriage[9] is one of the dominant types of marriage among the northern Edo. Unlike the *Amoya* marriage, more prevalent among the people in which the payment of bridewealth transfers both the genetricial and domestic services of the wife to her husband's family group, these rights are not fully transferred in the *Adegbe* marriage. Bridewealth payment is minimal and does not determine the right of ownership of the children. The practice is that in cases of *Adegbe* marriage, ownership of the children is open to competition between the patriclan of both parents. The customary way of claiming the children is for patriclan to perform the ceremony of taking *Okhe*[10] title for the child. The irony of the situation which the rules of child ownership peculiar to *Adegbe* marriage causes is that the competition for the child speeds up the process by which an *Adegbe* child becomes a titled person in society. The children of a regularized marriage have been integrated into their patrilineal groups and have their identify defined. There is, thus, no anxiety about performing the *Okhe* title-taking ceremony for them. *Okhe* title is the key to rank and status in these societies. Since the time of taking this title determines seniority, *Adegbe* children who would have been regarded as inferior to the children of *Amoya* marriage on account of the differential marriage payment, actually become both senior and superior to the children of the *Amoya* wife by taking the title which integrates them into their father's lineage. An informant[11] noted:

> The children of the Amoya wife are called freeborn (omoto). They cannot take Okhe title in the lifetime of their father and on that account cannot succeed to higher ranks like otsu easily. The sons of Adegbe, on the other hand, have to be claimed by the father or the mother's father by making Okhe title for them. When this is not made, children of Adegbe cannot inherit from their father or mother's father or brother. At this stage, they are said not to belong anywhere. They are neither here nor there. If their mother's people (MF, MB) make an Okhe title for them, the children are cut off from their father's property, status and other things that can be inherited. For this reason, fathers of Adegbe children struggle to claim their children for their own patriclan by speeding the process of taking title.

Thus, by this marriage type, children of *Adegbe* whose rights were not recognized and whose identities were not defined, have been confirmed and defined through the process of title-taking.

(b) <u>The Marriage Process</u>

Infant marriage (*Omo N'agayi*) and adolescent marriage, *Idegbe*, were the two popular Bini marriage types. Of these two, social change has made adolescent marriage the more common. There are seven important stages in the process that leads to this marriage. When a young girl meets a man who seems agreeable to the idea of marriage, she is obliged to inform her father who in turn informs the compound head, *Edionwan*. The *Edionwan*, in consultation with his *Egbee*, members of his age-group within the compound, select a male member of the compound as the go-between, *ibiegnae* or *osuomwan*. He is confirmed in his twin roles of finding out information about the compound of the man and maintaining as easy communication between the spouses through the ritual of presentation of kolanuts, a symbol of reconciliation and peace. His duties included, as J.U. Egharevba wrote, enquiring carefully about the groom's suitability:

> Is there insanity, or epilepsy or any other fearful disease in the family? Is he and his family free from debt, from crime, from witchcraft? (1946:15).

If answers are satisfactory, the *osuomwan* subsequently introduces the suitor to the mother of the girl. Then comes a formal introduction of the suitor to the father of the girl. This is an opportunity for reinforcing kinship links as the father's siblings (*ovbiye*) and his father's children or half-siblings (*ovbierha*) assemble together. The suitor himself is accompanied not only by some members of his own age-association but more importantly, by members of his father's *egbee*, who are junior to his father. The purpose is to make a clear statement of interest in the girl. This ceremony is set to take place on Ọba's market day. It is concluded by setting a date for ceremony of "solicitation for marriage" (*Ivbuoma*).

The *Ivbuoma* ceremony, "engagement," takes place in the evening when representatives of both families assemble in the house of the bride-to-be. The eldest man welcomes the suitor's entourage by presenting them with kola nuts. The kola nuts are presented to the most senior member of the suitor's family who splits them in the name of his ancestors and passes the plate of kola nuts around the assembly. At the completion of this Bini customary courtesy of peace and welcome, the elder of the suitor's family gets down to the main task of soliciting the hand of the spouse-to-be. The subtle manner of soliciting is itself a measure of the formality and diplomacy associated with such important duties, hence it is left to elders. Among the distinguishing marks of an elder is the ability to communicate an important message with tact and formality. A typical text of solicitation recorded in Bini manifests the importance of these expectations in an elder:

> We thank you, our elder, for the present of kola nuts. Did our fathers not say that a load of kola nuts is never too heavy for a senior person? It is unusual to see the Prime Minister running: if it happens it is needless to ask if there is peace in the country. We have run here, not because there is no peace, but because we want more peace and progress and blessing than we bring. We ourselves bring a message that is important and too difficult for young men to bring by themselves. Children should not plunge into serious matters by themselves. Serious

> matters are like big persons to children. If a child bends down and tries to overthrow a bigger person, then he, the latter, becomes a load for him.
>
> We have come here on our behalf and that of our son, who has become an adult. Like all adults, he needs a support so as to prosper. We all know that he whom a woman supports cannot fall. We want your daughter to be that support. We want her to provide that support amongst us forever because there is no retirement for the wife of a king. We ask you to give our desire a favourable consideration so that all of us, your family and our family, may prosper, for when this hand washes that hand, that hand washes this hand, the two hands become clean.

A select group of most senior members of the spouse's compound, along with her father, retire from the room to consider the offer. Their absence is prolonged to give a semblance of gravity to the decision that is to be reached. Meanwhile, members of the spouse's lineage who remain with the suitor's group, try to carry on light-hearted discussions on topics that have no relation to the purpose of the ceremony in progress. Eventually, the group re-emerges from the inner room. The decision is conveyed by the eldest member of the group. A typical response is:

> We thank you for coming. We have heard what you have said and given much thought to it. Nobody begets a child and marries her. It is true that our people say that it is not too much kindness to bear a child and betroth her to someone else. Yet, one should not, on that account, just throw out her daughter or give her away to anybody. Children are our pride now and our security in after-life. They are great and precious presents. To make a present of any of them to a people who cannot appreciate is too much kindness, and when kindness becomes too much, it turns into foolishness. Ingratitude makes one to regret an act of kindness. You have shown that you have gratitude and now you are showing that you value good things, otherwise we would not be here. No one seeing you and people of your quality, will deny you your heart's desire. On this account I accept to give you my daughter.

The suitor's groups brings out more gourds of palm wine. The ceremony is concluded by a shared meal of pounded yam after which the assembly disperses to reassemble after seven market days for the ceremony of *Iwanio-Omo*.

The ceremony of *Iwanio-Omo*, "second engagement," takes place in the evening in the compound of the espoused girl. It is the ceremony of formal betrothal. Up till now, thetransaction has been conducted by men from both families to the total exclusion of females, particularly the wife-to-be. In this ceremony, the espoused girl and her mother are brought in after the exchange of pleasantries and the splitting of kola nuts. The father of the girl, if he is not the *Ediomwan*, the head of the compound, is called to give his consent to the decision of the head and his group of elders. He subsequently tells his wife about the decisions that have been made concerning their daughter. She answers:

> I am with you my husband, do as you please, I agree. *Nu ye ri gue ye odo, mwen, ru ube no ye rue, ikue yo.*

The other female attendants who belong to the girl's family would be asked if they agree to the request that their daughter should marry the suitor. They respond: *Ima kue yo*, "we agree." Subsequently a senior member of the wife's compound calls the prospective bridegroom loudly six times at intervals. He remains silent. The father of the wife-to-be then calls the bridegroom-to-be the seventh time when he answers enthusiastically, *"E yo".* Then the father shouts, "I give you my daughter." At this solemn declaration, all the followers of the suitor kneel down to thank the lineage members of the girl.

The ceremony of the *Imomo* comes after the giving of thanks and it concerns the prestations[12] which form the bridewealth. The gifts that change hands in the ceremony of *Imomo* belong to the category of prime prestations and they include twenty-one pieces of kola nut, twenty pieces of coconut, fourteen yams in two bundles, a big gourd of palm wine, three legs of antelope meat and the sum of one guinea. These items *must* be handed over to legalize the transfer of the wife from her own family to that of the groom. Prestations occasionally made at important periods reaffirm the husband's indebtedness to his wife's lineage. The *Imomo* ceremony ends with an agreement on a date on which the actual transfer of the girl to her husband's compound should be made. It is usually set for the period of seven Bini traditional weeks hence.[13]

On the evening of the appointed day for *Irhiohe*, the equivalent of Yoruba *Igbeyawo*, "to carry the wife," the bride is taken to her ancestral shrine where a goat is sacrificed to the Olókun, the Bini divinity of fertility, to ensure her fertility.[14] The ancestors intercede on her behalf with Olókun, so that she may bear children. A typical Bini prayer at the departure of the bride from her patrilineal compound was recorded from an informant as follows:

> We thank you our fathers for the blessings of the past. You taught us that a grateful person commands another kindness. We shall continue to show our gratitude to you. Your daughter who gives you this goat has become an adult. She is leaving us for her husband's place. We ask you to escort her there and to make the place a home for her. Do not let her come across enemies in her husband's house. We ask you to let the owner of all riches and of children to look favourably on her. Do not let her be barren. A barren woman is always a junior, never an adult. Make her truly an adult. Soon enough, let us be thanking you for more blessings and asking you to let *Obienwen* give her safe delivery. Let her life be peaceful and fresh as the fresh water from the river, so that the 'rope and the vessel may not fall into the well' (that is, the daughter, when she becomes pregnant may not die). Grant our prayer, Ise.[15]

The blood of the sacrificed goat is sprinkled on the symbols within the ancestral shrine. The bride's property neatly arrayed in local tin boxes are carried in a long row by followers who then proceed by the longest route possible to show off the wealth of their family.

The eldest wife at the bridegroom's house receives the bridal group and washes the legs of the bride with fresh water from the river.[16] The bride is then led to, or left in an inner chamber for the supposed first ritual of breaking her virginity. This is called the ritual of *Oha tuo vbu 'kpo* "first time in bed with the husband." If she is a virgin, the cloth showing the proof of her virginity will be preserved until the seventh night when the bride's mother pays a visit to her. Although there is no formal announcement as to the state of virginity, the amount of quality or presents manifest clearly to all the state of the bride. Information concerning the subsequent role and status of the new bride confirm J.U. Egharevba's observation that:

> The new bride is now put under the care of one of her husband's senior wives, who is now her mistress. She sees that the new bride attends to sweeping and rubbing the house, drawing water, getting firewood and doing any other ordinary domestic duty (1946:18).

Since seniority among wives is measured in terms of the time of incorporation into the lineage group as wife, and since the youngest members do the most menial tasks, the bride as the newest member and the youngest wife, performs the menial duties as a mark of her junior position. The exception to the rule of the seven stages of marriage occurs at the marriage of princesses. Theoretically, the Ọba as the "god of the land" owns everything and everybody on earth. He did not need therefore, the political advantages of alliance that marriages of ordinary citizens and minor chiefs of Bini bring. Besides, being particularly bound to any family indebted to him through the payment of bridewealth would seriously compromise his non-aligned "father-of-all" image in Bini society. Finally, the goods and services of bridewealth which come under the categories of prime and secondary prestations belong theoretically to him as king; to take some of these to him to marry his daughter or to find wives for his children would be superfluous as it would mean exchanging what belonged to him for what was naturally his. A corollary of his situation as king is that it would be presumptuous of any Bini man, chief or commoner, who already assumed his inferiority to the king, suddenly to become his superior or equal at marriage. The king, therefore, receives no bridewealth for his daughters and enriches those who are considered privileged to marry his children.

In practice, the marriage of the daughters of the king was highly regulated as their choice of partner was restricted to very important chiefs, particularly warrior-chiefs, Edohen and Iyase, the distinguished chiefly class of the Uzama, and the leading chiefs of the palace and town chiefly associations, *Eghaevbon' Ogbe* and *Eghaevbo n'ore* respectively. The royal marriages were motivated for the political reasons deemed unnecessary under the theoretical consideration of royal Bini marriages.[17] The simple form that the marriage of a princess takes, stated that it was customary for the Ọba to give his daughter in marriage not only to the important chiefs such as the Uzama, but also to some powerful rivals such as the head of Udo, the rival to the King of Bini.[18] The simple form the marriage of a king's daughter takes, was described by J.U. Egharevba:

> ...the Ọba places the Princess, his daughter, on his lap and addresses the crowds saying: I am marrying my daughter Aduwa to the Iyase (Bini Prime Minister) today and wishing her good health and fruitfulness in her husband's house. The people then answer "Amen." After the blessing of the Ọba on her, the Princess would then proceed with the escorts to the husband's house (1962:8).

The choice of marriage partner widened, eventually, to include commoners as the demands of empire-building, particularly in the seventeenth century, gave more scope for acts of heroic patriotism. These were often rewarded by being given the daughter of the king to marry.

The general thrust of the argument in relation to Bini marriage so far, has been to present women as items of exchange between different families and powerful chiefly groups. The business of transferring women seems to be an all-male affair; men make the enquiries that lead to the commencement of the process of marriage; men exchange the prime and secondary prestations of bridewealth for the girl and the girl is removed from the jural authority of one male-group to another. The restricted focus of female participation in this apparently all-male affair was manifested in the act of seeking the agreement of the mother of the bride-to-be. As was to be expected in a society with patrilineal ideology, the agreement or consent of the mother is expressed in terms structured to give the impression that male-views were the dominant and relevant views. Thus, she fulfilled the image of the "well-behaved" (socialized) female in a male-oriented society by saying "I am with you my husband, do as you please, I agree" (*Nu ye yi gue ye odo, mwen, ru ube no ye rue, ikue yo*).[19]

Bini female views, in reality, are not often a reproduction of Bini male views. In fact, the Bini show that they recognize a unique and different female view in such adages as "he whom a woman backs up cannot fall" (*Ne okhuo mu vbovbo ide*) and more particularly since it celebrates the support of a female as one of the vital elements for continued success of a male:

> If a young man is too stubborn, he either has much money or he is initiated into wizardry. It may be that he is having a wealthy woman as concubine.
>
> *Ocbokhangha ze ub'udu gbe a ghi ren ighe to mwen igho, oma ghi gha re rio a ghi ren ighe to ri azen ra okpuhe ro ru.*

Although recognition is given to female contribution and importance to Bini society, it cannot be given in an overt and unrestricted manner so that it does not jeopardize the partrilineal ideology. Yet some amount of recognition ought to be given to Bini women who perform such vital roles in the society both as the encouragement and assurance that these female contributions will continue. This recognition ought to be made in a way that will prove effective without weakening the patrilineal ideology. Ritual constitutes a safe forum for the expression of such a recognition. Thus the predominant roles of women in rituals of male gods contradict the accustomed roles of women in Bini society. In so doing, Bini culture compensates, on the level of symbolism, for what it refuses to recognize at the level of existential reality of day-to-day dealings between the sexes. The observation by one informant, Chief Ebohon, who was pressed to explain the reason for the unusual predominance of women in Olókun rituals is instructive for its political overtones. He observed that:

> It is safe to give women important roles in religion when you deny them such roles in political dealings, because there are no queries and questions and answers during religious worship.[20]

This may be illustrated by a consideration of the role of women in ritual with particular reference to the Olókun ritual (Photo page 178a).

The Olókun Ritual and the Status of Bini Women

Olókun, the first son of the Supreme Deity, Osanobua, is the Bini god of wealth, fertility and success in human endeavours. He rules over the waters which in Bini symbolism constitute the gateway to the world of the spirits (*erinmwin*). He is a positive "god as he does not cause death, illness or bad luck, but is responsible for life, health, good fortune and all the aspects of fertility." On this account he is regarded as a cool and clean god, in contrast to the Bini god of death, *Ugiuwu*, and Ogun the enforcer of the will of the gods.

Since he is a male "god" in a male-oriented society in charge of a domain - fertility - which is most crucial to the continuation of Bini male-oriented institutions, it might have been expected that the important figures in his worship would be men. On the contrary, women take predominant roles in Olókun ritual, in which men accept secondary or auxiliary roles. The explanations for this role allocation between the sexes provide an insight into the divergence of views between the sexes. Chief Ebohon, a male native doctor and expert in witchcraft treatment, observed that:

> Although Olókun is male, most of his votaries are women. It is women who are over-anxious about begetting children and who on this account go to the source of fertility to have their wishes granted. Potent men have no such worries. Hence, the number of men who are votaries of Olókun is small compared to those of women, and hence, also, women are allowed to play the important roles in that ritual.[21]

From a typically male-oriented point of view, therefore, this specialist thinks that it is women's duty to worry about their infertility[22] and this worry is what qualifies women for their predominant role in Olókun ritual. Since some other religious rituals, particularly those concerned with methods of divination, do not give predominance and prominence to women, even though the anxieties of meeting male expectations make women more prone to use services of the diviner, the prominence of women in Olókun is still not solved by Ebohon's opinion. The Chief Priestess of Olókun shrine at Iyowe noted that:

> Women are more prominent than men in Olókun ritual. That is how it should be because Olókun is a cool, and peaceful god. He should be served by the more cool and peaceful part of the human race. We women are the cool ones. We do not go to war. We do not hunt. We bring new lives into the world. We are as cool as the fresh water from the river and as fertile as the fish in the river. Olókun is not only cool but owns the river, that is why we women are more suited to worship Olókun and that is why we are more important in his worship than men (a translation).[23]

Thus, the views reveal that as men think that the prominance of women in Olókun ritual was due to the natural anxieties of motherhood, the women, on the other hand, think that their prominence was a reflection of the similarities in their nature to the god which they serve. The implication is that the inauspicious qualities of manhood reflected in brute force and hotness of spirit disqualify men as the sex more suited to occupy the priestly office of the cool and clean Olókun. Another informant and devotee, Grace Ovbiahon (photo page 178b), maintained that:

> Olókun rules the seas and the waters. Fishes live in the seas and the rivers. They beget children in plenty. Men need many children to feel important in society so they depend on us women to make them important by giving birth to many children. That is why it is only ourselves who give birth to children who need to be the important people in this ritual in order to help men.[24]

This view seems to have been confirmed by the observation of one of the male devotees, Samuel Aghedo of Ehor, who noted, when asked why he had come to consult Olókun, that:

My brother's wife no born	My sister-in-law could not give birth to a child.

We want make he born	We want her to give birth.
We try everywhere and everything	We tried all known medicine.
He still no born	She still could not give birth.
Then I bring am all the way here	I brought her all the way to this place.
Make Olókun make am born	So that Olókun can help her to give birth.

In Samuel's case, therefore, the anxiety was not solely that of the wife but of the family of the husband.

It was not only those who sought to have children that were clients at the Olókun shrine. The clientele, wide-ranging and diverse, included not only young women and men but also old men of high achievement in Western education. The different purposes of worship included not only the desire for children, but wanting to make profits from a dwindling trade or wanting promotion in government service, or wanting to be cured of illnesses which Western medicine had failed to cure. Mr. Uyiekpen Bas Eweka expresses this as follows:

> Until seven years ago, I was very healthy. I thank god that until then I had always been very healthy. On that fateful day seven years ago, I became ill suddenly in the office. It was a dreadful experience as I was semiconscious. Being an educated Christian, I tried one hospital after another, and one house of prayer after another, in search of healing. But it was all in vain. Then, one day, a relative of mine who had been worshipping at the Olókun shrine at Iyowe informed me that the priestess of Olókun had prophesied that health and salvation would be mine; that the healing may be slow but eventually it would be complete. I then became a regular devotee and gradually my sickness left me. Now, after three years of regular attendance at Olókun rituals, I have become normal and healthy again.[25]

It would appear then, that male views which explain female prominence in rituals of Olókun in terms of anxieties associated with motherhood do not grasp the full importance of this worship to other features of Bini society.

It ought to be noted that although the paramount shrine of Olókun was Ughorton, the traditional port from which the Bini kingdom centered its trade with European powers since the fifteenth century,[26] other Olókun shrines besides those set up for newly married women in their houses have arisen and overtaken, in popularity and number of adherents, the reputed ancient one. Some of the reasons which led to the decline of Ughorton as the main Olókun center of worship include the loss of Bini trade with Europeans which led to a disassociation of wealth from across the waters through Ughorton. Although trade with Europeans through this port brought considerable wealth which was associated with Olókun it alienated the more conservative elements who felt that Olókun worship at Ughorton was no longer pure and who moved away to start shrines run along what they considered to be the pure, traditional lines.[27] However, over and above Olókun factions, the Olókun shrine at Iyowe was chosen because of its unique aspect in relation to Bini cosmology with reference to the traditional opposition between the King of the land (Ọba) and the King of the waters, Olókun.

An important preoccupation of the symbolism of Bini kingship and religion is the attempt to seek a reconciliation between the dichotomy and opposition of Olókun and the Ọba. The Ọba could not be as cool nor as clean or opposed to the use of force as Olókun because:

> ...hostility within the framework of order and control is a metaphor for leadership, while hostility which violates order is an embodiment of extraordinary power (Ben-Amos, 1976:246).

The Oba, as leader, needed to employ hostility (the use of force to evoke fear) in different contexts in order to enhance his leadership role. However, this aspect of leadership needed to be balanced by an image of the king as a benevolent father with the power not only to take life but to give it and whose well-being influences that of the society (Beattie, 1965:136). Thus, Bini myths resolve this contradiction by representing the Ọba as possessing some of the benevolent powers of the "god" of wealth and fertility. One such story tells of how a magically powerful Bini warrior king in the fifteenth century, Ewuare,

> ...went down to the river at Ughorton village and stole the beads belonging to Olókun, god of the waters; he brought them back to Bini and thereby established the palace of the Oba, King of dry land, as the earthly counterpart of the palace of Olókun, King of the waters (Ben-Amos, 1980:23).[28]

Thus, symbolically, the king became credited with some of the powers of Olókun.

The climax of the success of attempts at symbolism to associate the life-giving powers of Olókun with the Bini King (feared as one who takes life) appears to have been achieved in the case of the Olókun shrine at Iyowe. The chief priestess of this shrine, Iduzemwogie Eweka,[29] is the aunt of the reigning Ọba of Benin. Thus, the powers of leadership in religion and politics have been concentrated in the royal lineage.

The shrine of Olókun is divided into two parts; an inner section which houses the figures of Olókun, Osanobua and Ogun, and an outer section reserved for devotees who are not in a state of ritual purity. The alter is located at the north end of a rectangular inner section, and has behind it a large sculpture of Olókun, a smaller one of the Supreme Deity, Osanobua,[30] and an even smaller one of Ogun, the god of war (photo page 178c). White is the predominant colour, not only of Olókun and Osanobua, but of the devotees who smear their foreheads with powdered chalk as they approach the shrine for worship. Devotees sit in rows of pews facing each other with a large space in the middle for the chief priestess and her assistants who lead the liturgy.

There is a central and marginal dimension to the spatial arrangement of the Olókun shrine. The central focus at the onset of worship is the alter before which sits the chief priestess as she gradually becomes worked up into being possessed by Olókun, where she becomes an instrument of divination and healing of the god. The margin of this inner shrine is the space very close to the entrance which is mostly taken up by men. Women sit on the pews clad in white according to their importance to the Olókun congregation, either as senior devotees or as assistants. The outer precincts of the Olókun shrine contains pews for women who are menstruating and are, on that account, considered impure and are kept away from the center of ritual. The Bini used to isolate a menstruating woman in a room built for that purpose at the back of the house adjacent to the kitchen (Aigbe, 196:38-39). (Photo page 178d).

The ceremony begins when the congregation of devotees call, all together, not on Olókun but on his wife, Ora, seven times. [31] Ora O! Ora O! Ora O! Ora O! Ora O! Ora O! Ora O!. She is believed to mediate on their behalf before her husband who then hastens his descent on and possession of his priestess. At the seventh call on Ora, the chief priestess comes out from a sacred location where all the aspects of ritual regalia are kept. Her ritual vestments include a lighter, inner, white linen cloth and an outer garment bedecked with cowries. She sits in front of the altar while the songs are sung with a monotonous regularity which drives her into a frenzy (photo page 178e). On either side of her, her assistants hold up her arms in the classical position of Bini royalty, when the Ọba appears with his arms carried on either side by Esomo, one of the two paramount Bini warrior chiefs and Edaiken, the first son and heir apparent or successor to the throne.[32]

In relation to human personality, the songs recorded are of vital interest because their constant repetition is said to produce a change in the personality of the chief priestess. Some of them are:

(a) A boy is warned not to reveal secrets and he says he will reveal the secrets
He is told that if he reveals the secret
He will not live as long as Osanobua has appointed him to

(b) Olókun is the greatest
Olókun is the most kind
Olókun has no evil in him
No one but Olókun can prevent evil

(c) I will always thank Olókun
I will always thank Osanobua
I will always thank the mothers
I will always thank the ancestors

(d) The mother is the living guardian
The mother is the counsellor
The mother is the support
May the spirit of the mothers not lead you astray.

(e) Glory, glory, glory, glory

Praise, praise, praise, praise
I will always praise Olókun
I will always praise Osanobua
I will always praise the ancestors

When these songs have been repeated often, with each repetition rising in intensity, signs of frenzy show on the chief priestess as her body appears rocked by paroxysms. The rhythm increases in speed and intensity until the now possessed priestess begins to rock violently in her seat and then go limp in the chair as if in a coma. At this stage, she is taken to be completely possessed and devotees come forward making confessions about misbehaviour in the recent past and asking for forgiveness. This is followed by the giving of thanks by those who have been blessed by Olókun with health and success in business, the birth of children and examples of good fortune attributed to the blessing of Olókun. The chief priestess then calls on names of people in the crowd and makes prophecies about the imminence of a solution to their problems and the need for them to exercise patience and believe that Olókun will settle their problems. The session ends with a repetition of the songs that effected the possession of the priestess and as she gradually appears to gain better control of herself, the songs change to those of thanksgiving.

The main outlines of the ceremony exhibit the features of a rite of passage. The priestess is taken from her ordinary mundane exercises and made to enter a liminal stage of possession when she becomes not only dangerous but mystically powerful (Van Gennep, 1909; Douglas, 1966). At this transitional stage, she reverses the role of the sexes in ordinary Bini society as she becomes a symbol of power as the instrument of Olókun. She gives orders, not only to women but also to men, who see her as the source of solutions to their problems. At this time, she becomes the symbol of female power dispensing blessings of fertility to enhance the prospect of Bini men, the symbol of healing to such men and women and, as the earthly representative of Olókun, the cool god who has no evil and knows no danger, her services ensure a much-needed soothing refuge for men known for their hotness of spirit and the violence of their gods such as Ogun, the god of war. The subsidiary place of Ogun in the Olókun shrine testifies that Olókun predominates over him.

The contents of the songs in Olókun ritual appear to confirm the reversal of roles that action represents. It is uniquely noteworthy that the Supreme Deity Osanobua has been pushed into a secondary role next in importance to his first-born, Olókun, as the ordering in the songs suggest. What is more germane to the point here is the fact that the mothers come before the ancestors. Thus, here at last, the power of the mothers and their contributions are praised over and above those of the fathers. When this is added to the fact that succession to the office of the chief priestess, particularly in the Iyowe Olókun shrine and some others, is through the mother down to the daughter, then the structure of kinship and inheritance in ritual reverses that in Bini society. This establishes the argument that what the Bini society refuses to accept - on account of its strong patrilineal ideology - it makes up for on the level of symbolism.

Yoruba Marital Procedure

Among the Yoruba as among the Bini, the formalities of the process that leads to marriage would appear to an observer as an all`male affair. The impression is given that it is a man who initiates the process; that it is a man who takes the woman's transfer. Furthermore, the negotiations for a woman's transfer from one lineage to another are said to be mainly carried on by males representing the interests of the two lineages that are to be united in marriage. In actual fact, and as far as the ideas of personality are concerned, the roles that women are expected to play in the marriage process are very important.

In most areas of Yorubaland, the "evening market" (*Ojà alẹ́*) provides the meeting place for young men and young girls. After a meeting there, flirtations may lead eventually to marriage. The age when young boys and girls become meticulous about their appearance and frequently pay visits to the evening market is known in various parts of Yorubaland as Ìgbà *Ìfojúsóde*, "the time of being on the look`out," *Ìgbà Ìfojúṣóna*, "the period for being anxious" or *Igba afẹ́fẹ́yẹ̀yẹ̀* "the time for bluffing" or "showing off."[33]

When a young man meets a young woman who seems agreeable to the idea of marriage, he is obliged to tell his father who in turn informs the lineage head. His father and the other elders appoint a go-between, or *Alárenà*, who runs errands between the two households involved.

The "Go-Between" (Alárenà)

The chosen "go-between" is often an affinal member of the lineage group who has distinguished herself as a good wife and successful mother, and the duties of the "go-between," vital to marriage all over Yorubaland, show the important contributions of females to the marital procedure. The *Alárenà* must be a cheerful person, known for her ability to make strangers and visitors comfortable, and with a firm loyalty to the lineage.

The position of the *Alárenà* can be interpreted in many ways. As one chosen from another lineage to represent the interests of the lineage on such an important issue as marriage, she holds out to the one being wooed the attractive possibility that she may one day play this role herself. Her choice (as a co-opted "outsider") to represent the lineage group of "insiders" reveals the trust that the lineage reposes in those women whom its members have taken as wives. It also reminds the girl that such responsibilities await her if she acquiesces and comes into the lineage as a wife. The fact that the Alárena is also a senior wife on the compound creates in the girl feelings of attachment and companionship, which cushion the shock of moving to her husband's home. The *Alárenà*, therefore, serves as a means of integrating the wife smoothly into the polygynous system,[34] guaranteeing that the new wife is not companionless, but has an ally and confidante in her senior wife. The Spindlers brought out this point clearly when they wrote about the *Alárenà* that:

> One of the mechanisms for integrating a new wife into the compound lay in appointing one of the established wives in the

> compound as an intermediary and "senior wife" of the fiance, thus ensuring her co-operation. She carried installments of bridewealth to the fiance's house, carried messages back and forth, and often gave presents of her own to the fiancee. Until she had a child, the bride lived with the senior wife, who often furnished consolation and support for her (Bascom, 1969:vii).

The *Alárenà*, as a wife, and therefore, an "outsider" to the lineage of her husband, is a neutral person suitable to conduct investigations into the background and upbringing of the wife-to-be. On this account, she is immune from giving offence in the discharge of her duty. It would be looked upon as grossly improper for an agnatic kinsman of the suitor to conduct an enquiry into the history and background of the lineage of the girl, because what is accepted from the *Alárenà* would not be accepted from a man or woman of the suitor's lineage. The aims of the enquiries, appear, to some extent, identical with those of the Bini. As has been observed:

> When we find out through enquiries that debt is an endemic vice of her lineage members, or that leprosy is rife among members of her lineage, or that insanity is common in the lineage, or even that the girl is a notorious fighter and hater of harmony, it is right that the young man forgets the affair and looks elsewhere (Daramola and Jeje, 1968:26 - my translation).

When enquiries are positive, the *Alárenà* gives her approval which sets in motion the process of betrothal by the first ritual of consulting the oracle called "the oracle approves" *Ifá Fọ're*.[35]

The oracle is consulted in the ritual of *Ifá Fọ're* with the consultation fees of pairs of goats, hens, pigeons, tortoises and snails. Each ritual item presented to the priest has been chosen for a special quality. The goats are docile; the hen produces profusely and is reputed for its protective and motherly qualities as it protects its chicks from hawks; the pigeons are symbols of permanence among the Yoruba; the tortoises are reputed in Yoruba folklore for wisdom, and snails have the capacity to remain cool. The imagery of marriage is an imagery of the snail and the shell, the husband and the wife staying together at all times no matter how difficult, hence the

Yoruba say "when the snail moves, the shell follows in obedience" (*Bí ìgbín bá fa, ìkarahun atèle*).

If the oracle gives a positive answer (*Ifá Fọ're*)[36] the couple become espoused through the payment of *Isihun* which constitutes the next important step in the betrothal process.

The *Ishihun* ceremony between the spouse and the suitor is a process of allowing a dialogue between them when they meet. Although they could meet regularly after the ritual of *Ifá Fọ're*, until this *Isihun* payment is made, such meetings are characterized by a monologue, as the suitor does all the talking while the spouse stays silent, looking down or away from the suitor. Informants explained that:

> The approved fiancee may be likened to a queen, resplendent, sacred, and precious. Her voice is the symbolic expression of her precious personality. Precious things are not to be given away free, otherwise their worth will not be appreciated. Custom, therefore, makes the suitor recognize the pricelessness of his "queen" by insisting that he makes a payment to get the spouse to talk. Hence the spouse shows through such actions and antics as searching aimlessly on the wall in reply to questions, that she has much to say, but that the importance of what she has to say should be appreciated before she speaks. (Maria Asiwaju. My translation.)

This Yoruba spouse-suitor ethic socializes the fiancee to accept, in the context of the new relationship, the domination of her husband who ceremonially permits her to speak through the payment of the "money for releasing the voice" (*owo isihun*); just as the payment of ten shillings as the "virginity price" announces that it was the husband who set in motion her female procreative activities. As a male informant noted:

Ọmọ tí abí ire án í ìbọ̀wọ̀	A well brought-up child has respect
Ọmọbìnrin sì gbọ́dọ̀ fi ìbọ̀wọ̀ fún ọkọrè	A good girl should always have respect for her husband.
Àpẹrẹ omolúwàbí ati oníbọ̀wọ̀ niyi	This is a sign of good character
Nitorina obìnrin fi ma ndákẹ́	That is why the girl remains silent
Títí ọkọ rè fi nṣíi lóhùn	Until her husband releases her voice.[37]

The next ceremony after that of "releasing the voice" is the "pleading for the girl's hand in marriage" (*Ìtọro*).

When the young man has informed his father that the girl in question is willing, his father discusses the issue with the elder members of his lineage group who send a delegation to pay the spouse's father a surprise visit. Members of the delegation state their intention to the spouse's father, who responds cautiously but with warmth, informing them that the decision on his daughter's marriage is not his but that of his elders to make. He gives them another appointment.

On the appointed day, very early in the morning, elders of both family groups meet in the house of the spouse's father. The suitor and the spouse are also present. A female elder of the spouse's family group is detailed to take both into an inner room and ascertain that both desire to marry each other. When this is confirmed, there is some merriment and a date is set for the engagement, called "creating the affines" (*Ìdána*).

The *Ìdána* ceremony centers around the payment of bride-wealth called *owó-orí* (lit. "money for the head") and concerns in particular, the transfer of items which fall into the category of prime prestations. These necessary items, which also figure positionally in other rituals of Yoruba life crises where they retain the same symbolic functions, form that part of the bride-wealth which transfers genetricial and sexual rights in the spouse to the suitor's family group. With local variations, the Yoruba ritual items consist of honey (*oyin*), salt (*iyò*), palm oil (*epo*), and kola nut (*obí*). The quality of these items is used to compose prayers for the success of the impending marital union, in a way similar to their use in prayers at the naming ceremony of a newborn child. The qualities the Yoruba consider to represent success in life and their notions of what constitutes a good character are shown in the following[38]:

(1) This is honey,
although it is made by bees that sting, it is sweet,
May your life be sweet (i.e. happy) as honey.

Oyin nì yi,
Bóti jè wípé ágbón tí ontani lónse e, ódùn púpò
Kí aiyé yín ládùn bí oyin.

(2) Salt puts flavour into the stew
May your union be flavoured with happiness

Iyọ̀ ámá mu obè dùn
Kí igbépọ̀ yín dùn

(3) Palm oil brings a cooling effect on stew
May your life be cool

Epo lẹlẹ́rọ̀ obè
Kí aiyé yín rọ̀

(4) This is kola nut which produces profusely
May you increase and multiply

Obì niyi abí èso jẹ̀gbẹ̀nnẹ̀
Ki ẹbí si ki ẹrẹ si.

The Yoruba hope that each of these items will communicate its quality, homeopathically, to the union of husband and wife.

The prayers referring to honey and salt express similar wishes deriving from a common quality of "sweetness".[39] It is hoped that the life of the couple will be happy. Furthermore, the preservative quality of salt is evoked and made to express the wish that the couple should live to a ripe old age. When the prayers are finished, a date is set for the ceremony of the transfer of the bride to her husband's compound.[40] Often, the date is fixed for a month, or seven Yoruba weeks away.[41] The ceremony is called "carrying" the wife - *Ìgbèyáwó*.

The *Ìgbéyàwó* ceremony provides an insight into Yoruba values and assumptions about human personality and success within the family. Although the actual ceremony of transferring the bride to her husband's compound does not begin until about midnight, at about noon, the belongings of the bride are neatly stacked into tin boxes (*bembe*) and set at a conspicuous place in the compound to attract admiration and praise. There is merriment in the compound throughout most of the day and night.

At midnight a bridal group arrives from the wife-taker's lineage group to take away the bride. This is the first of three attempts. The first two attempts meet with failure as the bridal group is received with all cordiality and given in the end a girl who pretends to be the bride. Each time the bridal group gently rejects the impostor and in patience goes back to their compound to return about two and a half hours later. However, at the third attempt and after deliberate delay[42] the real bride is brought forward and handed over to the leader of the bridal group (ìjọ-Ìyàwó) at the first cock-crow (about five in the morning). The bridal group proceed to the husband's house amidst singing and jubilation. The bride remains veiled and silent in their midst. When the group is very close to the husband's house, she is carried by senior wives in her husband's compound. It is this act that gave the name Ìgbéyàwó to the marital process. At the door of the house, she is put down and her feet are washed with fresh water from the flowing stream. An informant's explanation of this ritual is as follows:

> We wash the feet of a new wife with fresh water because fresh water from the river stored in pots (amù; ìkòkò) is cool and we want the wife's life to be as cool and peaceful as well. We also use fresh water from the river because it is the environment of fishes. Fishes have many children; we want our wife to have as many children as fishes in the river (Àbẹ̀jẹ́ Babatunde; my translation).

The first official ceremony of the bride in her husband's home, therefore, points to the aims of marriage which, if realized, distinguish the successful couple and the "proper man" of high rank in the society.

The Yoruba marital procedure, but for the vital role of the *Alárenà* (often a female) gives the impression that women are silent partners in marriage. They are transferred from one family group to another through a business procedure that appears to give them little say. However, the Yoruba acknowledge their indebtedness to their women whose importance is made most manifest in economic spheres in Yoruba markets (Surdarka, 1973; Little, 1970; Hoch-Smith, 1978; Karanja, 1981). More important for the evaluation of human personality and characteristics among the Yoruba, the importance of women is celebrated and demonstrated more clearly at the level of symbolism. At this level, the prominence of females reverses the usual order of things in Yoruba society. An example is the role of women in the Gẹ̀lẹ̀dẹ́ masked dance of Western Yorubaland.[43]

Gẹ̀lẹ̀dẹ́ Masked Ritual Dance and Yoruba Women's Prominence

The Gẹ̀lẹ̀dẹ́ cult of Western Yorubaland performs ritual activities primarily concerned with enhancing fertility in the society (Beier, 1958:5; Harper, 1970:67; Drewal, 1974a:26, 1974c:62; Asiwaju, 1976:272, 1975:200). These ritual activities are directed to the worship of the Yoruba goddess of fertility variously called, in different areas of Yorubaland, "the Great Mother" *(Ìyánlá)*, "the owner of the Earth" *(Onílẹ̀,)* who is, as discussed earlier in chapter three, taken in some areas to be the co-eval counterpart of the Deity *(Olódùmarè)* (Verger, 1970; Odugbesan 1969:99). The climax of the ritual activities of her worship is the Gẹ̀lẹ̀dẹ́ ritual dance which is performed to induce the Great Mother to ensure her blessings for fertility to the land, the animals and human beings.

The crux of the matter is that although the ritual dance is aimed ultimately at the "Great Mother," women in society constitute the proximate object. In this intensely patrilineal society where residence at marriage is virilocal and where the relevant sex for the transfer of status, inheritance of property and succession to office is male, and where institutions have a decidedly male orientation, men often dress up as females to perform the Gẹ̀lẹ̀dẹ́ dance in order to placate powerful women. The belief is that the performance will induce these powerful females to employ the mystical power attributed to them for the good of the society.

The need to placate women is linked to the Yoruba belief that every woman beyond the age of menopause has dangerous mystical powers and is potentially a witch (Beier, 1958:7; Morton-Williams, 160:34-35). The characteristics of the Yorubaland witch are peculiar in that they are neither wholly good nor bad but a witch may be bad if not kept entertained and constantly pleased. Thus, while the Yoruba witch shares some traits with the medieval European witch and her Azande counterpart, she *(Âjẹ́)*[44] has some peculiar positive features which make her indispensable to the society.

Yoruba belief holds that there is a special link between the witches and the earth goddess. It is this alleged link that explains the abilities of witches to act as the proximate forces controlling fertility in the society. One who petitions for fertility does so in vain unless the witches are placated.

This point was well brought out in the statement of an informant related by Beier:

> ...no orisha can do good without the mothers (Aje). The mothers could spoil any good action if they wanted to, therefore, Shango himself cannot help his worshippers without permission of the mothers. The prophecies of the Babalawo will come to nought, if he has not appeased the mothers (1958:7).

It is in order to induce women to use their talents that the Gẹ̀lẹ̀dẹ́ Masked Dance is performed. As Harper noted:

> Gẹ̀lẹ̀dẹ́ is essentially a fertility cult which stresses the mystical powers of womanhood and together with the other masquerade underlines the structure of the society by mounting performances which voice moral precepts in repetitive poetic incantation and song, and express ideal social mimetic performance (1970:68).

The main outline of the ritual dance will now be narrated and analyzed to show the prominence of women, not only within the cult group but as a reflection of their prominence in certain areas of Yoruba social life.

(a) <u>The Gẹ̀lẹ̀dẹ́ Cult Group</u>

The Gẹ̀lẹ̀dẹ́ cult covers most towns of Western Yorubaland. For instance, the Ketu town of Imeko has three Gẹ̀lẹ̀dẹ́ associations all belonging to the town Gẹ̀lẹ̀dẹ́ cult group.[45] The *Òkè-Òdo* (up-stream) the *Ìsà-Odò* (down-stream) and Èkété Ọ̀wun-- (a thicket rabbit), names that remind one of the forest and symbolize social marginality. Each association has its own masks which appear at the annual Gẹ̀lẹ̀dẹ́ ceremony. In each town all the groups or associations of Gẹ̀lẹ̀dẹ́ come under the authority of the "mother of power" (*Iyálàse*), the priestess of the earth goddess. The highest and the most powerful group within the Gẹ̀lẹ̀dẹ́ cult groups is that of *Iyálàse* and her council of six elderly women. The second group is that of the "father of power" (*Babaláse*) and his council of six men. *Babaláse* is the male counterpart of the *Iyáláse* (Harper,1970:79) and takes orders from her. The third group headed by Alayande includes all Gẹ̀lẹ̀dẹ́ drummers and their families. The different family groups of dancers and composers form the fourth group. Everyone who wants protection from the witches or blessings from them joins the Gẹ̀lẹ̀dẹ́ ritual cult as a devotee.

The Gẹ̀lẹ̀dẹ́ ritual masked dance itself commences on the first night of the four`day Yoruba week, "the day of enterprise" (*Ọjọ́-Ajé*) which is also the market day. It takes place in the market area. Women dominate the Yoruba market (Suradarka, 1973; Karanja-Diejomaoh, 1981). It is danced by men chosen by the Gẹ̀lẹ̀dẹ́ who also approves the wooden mask that each important dancer is to put on. The ritual of counteracting the destructive powers of those witches who would not use their talents for the service of society takes place during that night. The masquerader who performs this ritual is *Ẹ̀fẹ̀*, whose wife is Gẹ̀lẹ̀dẹ́.

The crowd which builds up gradually during the evening is entertained and kept in suspense by the performance of the drummers and singers. About bedtime for Ketu elders, around ten o'clock, the suspense of the crowd is heightened by the appearance of the masked *Ògbàgbà* who represents *Ẹ̀ṣù*, the Yoruba divinity of good luck and fate. He, as the representative of *Ẹ̀ṣú* (the trickster divinity who enjoys introducing confusion among friends), tries to raise controversy about his appearance by making two appearances, first as a boy wearing a white cap and raffia skirt of banana leaves and then with iron rings on his ankles.

The masked dancer called "fire-carrier" (*Agbéná*) next appears carrying a pot of fire on his head. He is greeted with the song:

> Farmers of Èkété Òwún come quickly,
> Fire destroys your farms, fire is destroying your farms.
>
> Àgbẹ̀ Èkété Òwún etete wa,
> Iná njó loko, ina njó lókò yin.

His exit is followed by the appearance of another mask called "the fire extinguisher" (*Apaná*) who is greeted:

Owner of the fire, kill your fire, the hoopee is coming,
put down your load.
Because one does not carry fires
To behold the bird of night (i.e. witch).

With the exit of *Apaná*, the ritual of propitiation, appeasement and/or counteraction begins in earnest.

Tètède is the wife of the chief mask *Ẹ̀fẹ̀*. She is welcomed to the assembly. It is danced by a man dressed as a woman with

> ...formalized wooden breasts, which thrust aggressively forward to end in metal nipples and two sticks, *Bebe*, which are tied across the back of the hips under the wrapper to exaggerate the size and provocative swinging movements of the buttocks (Harper, 1970:80).

When she has performed the dual roles of praising the mothers and summoning *Ẹ̀fẹ̀*, she sings a final song of exit, in praise of witches. Beier records a Ketu version of this song which is quite illuminating:

All powerful mother, mother of the night bird,
Mother who kills animals without striking
We are three whom the mother has born and placed in the world.
The first one inherited the cloth (*Egúngún*)
The second one inherited the bloody buba (*Ajẹ́*)
the third one looks in the house,
and looks on the road, but finds nothing to inherit.
That is why he has inherited the voice and the dance (*Gẹ̀lẹ̀dẹ́*)
My mother kills quickly without a cry.
To prick our memory suddenly,
Quick as the woodpecker pecks the tree on the farm
The woodpecker who hammers the tree, while words rush forth from his mouth,
Great Mother with whom we dare not cohabit...
Mother who kills the husband yet pities him
(Beier, 1958:10-11).

This song explains that the *Gẹ̀lẹ̀dẹ́* cult, the Egúngún cult of the ancestors and the witches (i.e. women credited with mystical power) originate from the same sources. Besides the divinities, these three groups, the Egúngún, the Aje Witches and the *Gẹ̀lẹ̀dẹ́*, form three basic angles in the triangle of Yoruba metaphysical beliefs. The ancestors are presented as the elders. The witches come next in importance. The *Gẹ̀lẹ̀dẹ́* cult which placates the witches and persuades them to employ their services for the good of society come last.

Ẹ̀fẹ̀ answers the call of his wife *Tètède* by sending out a virgin dressed in white carrying a calabash. She goes to the center of the arena and kneels down. The pot which she carries contains a bird which is alleged to be the heart of *Iyálàse*. The ominous bird is said to give protection to the *Ẹ̀fẹ̀*, the chief mask of the ritual dance.

Ẹ̀fẹ̀ comes into the crowd singing the praises of all those who played the role in his association. He, too, praises the name of the witches. On the pain of death he must not break off the ceremony and the young virgin must remain kneeling for as long as his performance lasts. He sings incantations which are thought to neutralize the power of the destructive witches. Not unexpectedly, some of the songs are neither in praise of women nor aimed at neutralizing the destructive powers of witchcraft. They simply show social disapproval of certain trends of behaviour among youths, especially girls, or simply reinforce social mores. Other songs show the resentment of the people against certain unpopular colonial policies. Two songs recorded in the Ketu area of Western Yorubaland, under French influence, will serve as cases in point. The first of these, allegedly dated as having been composed by an *Ẹ̀fẹ̀* between 1911 and 1919 when the French colonial authority deliberately taunted this intensely patrilineal people by installing a woman, Ida Alaba as head of the town, resents the French lack of respect for indigenous culture. The inversion, which the people felt that the appointment of Ida Alaba constituted, was unmistakably brought out in the song:

> Father, if note were to be taken of Ida,
> Yamseed planted would germinate into a Maize plant
> Ilikimu People! Please come back home.
> We beg you.
> We invoke all departed ancestors to beg you

Afin, please come back home.
We beg you.
Ida expelled us into the forest hideouts.
And brought smallpox epidemics on the community,
And this led to the death of several persons,
Many were kidnapped and sold into slavery.
All in the reign of Oyengen Asakaisa.
Things have become upside down (the world is in turmoil).
(Asiwaju, 1975:221)

Thus, strange happenings accompanied the strange and untraditional appointment of the woman, Ida. The *Ẹ̀fẹ̀* songs also record resistance against other unpopular French colonial policies. Thus, when the French, in an attempt to check tax defaulting, introduced metal tags to be worn around the neck as proof of tax payment (taxpayers who did not wear these tags were either beaten up or imprisoned, Asiwaju, 1975:221), an *Ẹ̀fẹ̀* song criticized the practice. The song itself, drawing on the consolation that no condition was permanent recalled the passing of the periods of the Dahomey and Hausa invaders and cautioned that the French phase would soon pass. An extract from the song notes that:

We are now subjects of Europeans/French rule,
We have not rejected this;
We have accepted to be paying tax.
Hark! You elderly one!
Look at the bead I bought for a pound from Dadi-oku
Father/Mother! What is this that shines frightfully on your chest!
It is Kange (the metal tag) bead.
Isn't it all for tax
Which we have been paying since...
We never had to fasten it around our necks
But please hasten to fasten it.
For you cannot move freely in Ketu
If you do not fasten...it properly. (Asiwaju, 1975:221)[46]

At cock-crow, the performance of the *Ẹ̀fẹ̀* ends and he moves back to the preparatory ground accompanied by *Arugbá*, the virgin. The crowd soon disperses to convene again later in the day for the entertainment provided by masked dancers who dance in pairs to entertain the crowd. In this crowd, the important seats are reserved for and taken by elderly women.

The symbolism of the virgin is important to the Yoruba evaluation of the proper woman. The symbol of the virgin as the pure, inaccessible female contrasts with the tenets of the society which socializes its women to be readily available to their menfolk. The power that this inaccessibility gives her is paralleled by the figure of the powerful female who, on reaching menopause, is alleged to be able to control fertility in others. These two extreme expressions of female power fuse together as a personification flying out of the reach of men like a bird (the Yoruba image of the witch is a bird). At these two phases of the female life cycle, the woman comes into her own and makes her presence felt.

In the person of *Iyálàse*, the personification of female power, the females become dominant in the political scene as well. If the *Iyálàse* refuses to propitiate her goddess, she undermines the institutions of the society which aim at survival through the continuation of fertility. If she refuses to support a king-elect, by declining to hand over the ritual portion to him (a role tradition assigns to her) she raises a constitutional crisis because no other king-elect can be chosen while another is alive, yet the one chosen cannot be enthroned. If she refuses permission to the devotees of other divinities, they cannot worship without infringing an important dogma of Yoruba religion.

Structurally, therefore, the position of *Iyálàse* is most vital to the society because of the relations between her post and other institutions which her post guarantees. In her person, the importance of Ketu women is symbolized. Such importance is not restricted to the domain of the domestic, important though it is, but touches on procreation, the highest good of Yoruba life. It is on this point that the male ideology is at its weakest. The Yoruba need children to keep the group in existence. The physiological impossibility of men giving birth to children on their own is compounded by the social rule of exogamy which forbids the group's females from providing the genetricial services to their own kin. This rule necessitates going out of the group to find females who will help by giving birth to the children. The Yoruba does not need just any unrelated female but those whose fidelity will help to keep the blood of the lineage pure by not bringing into the group foreign "seeds."

The Yoruba man is, on the foregoing points, totally dependent on the female. Yet, it is this dependence that the patrilineal ideology cannot afford to admit openly in daily activities. It tries to deny this dependence by its notion of procreation, which reduces the contribution of the mother to the minimum of providing the conducive atmosphere for the seed that already has its potency to being. This denial is necessary because, try hard as man may to claim complete ownership, the Yoruba woman, like most mothers, naturally feels a strong sense of union with her children in a way men cannot, for although

> ...in this patrilineal society children belong to the father's and not the mother's lineage...the mother has experienced both the continuity of her own identity (in spite of changes of residences) and also the recurrence of motherhood, however many begetters her several children may have had (Morton`Williams, 1960:37).

It is suggested, therefore, that the Gẹ̀lẹ̀dẹ́ (or other ritual forms in which women predominate) serves to redress the imbalance, at least in the sphere of symbolism, by drawing attention to the significance of female contribution.

<u>**Conclusion: Ìwà (Good Character)**</u>

In this chapter, the roles of women have been explored with a view to throwing into relief social expectations about the female in these patrilineal societies. The approach has taken the dual perspective of first looking at how men treat women in the Bini and Yoruba marital processes and then looking at distinctive areas of female prominence in rituals. The argument was that given the patrilineal ideology which has put a definitive male-oriented stamp on the social features of Bini society, both societies, if they want the main orientation of their traditional institutions to continue, cannot afford to give an overt recognition to females in their daily activities. Yet, the importance of females in these societies is both great and clear`cut.

How, then, do both societies manifest their indebtedness to the female (whose sex is not relevant for transmission of inheritance and accession to office) without compromising the their "ideology."

It is suggested that this recognition is achieved at the level of symbolism. In ritual, women who are normally withdrawn and muted become rather conspicuous and assertive. In looking at both the *Olókun* and the *Gẹ̀lẹ̀dẹ́* rituals and highlighting the prominence of females in them, the intention was to claim that what both cultures deny or ignore at the existential level, they recognize at the metaphysical level; that what they deny at the level of daily activities, they own up to at the level of symbolism.

It is not by coincidence, therefore, that a poem of the authoritative divination verses of Ifá conceptualizes "good character" (*Ìwà*) as a woman.[47] Ìwà was herself the daughter of Suuru (patience) the first-born of Olódùmarè, the Supreme Deity. Òrúnmìlà, the oracle divinity proposed to Ìwà. Ìwà the granddaughter of the Supreme Deity agreed on condition that Òrúnmílà would observe certain rules. She was not to be sent away from her matrimonial home due to ill-treatment without compromising the ideological base of their societies. She was not to be treated like a slave. She was not to be punished, especially beaten, unnecessarily. Òrúnmìlà, the refraction of the omniscience of the Supreme Deity, gave his word that he would observe all these rules. He pledged in a loud voice that:

Oun a tọju ẹ	He would take care of her
Oun a kẹe	He would treat her with love
Oun a gẹ e	He would treat her with kindness
Oun O ni ṣee ṣiboṣibo	He will not treat her without affection.

Orúnmìlà paid the traditional courtesies and they got married. The marriage was marked by pomp and pageantry because of the noble pedigree of the bride. Opinion was unanimous that the marriage would succeed almost effortlessly due to the sterling qualities of the bride and the all-knowing ability of the bridegroom. For a long time, things went very well and all the people said "we have said so" (*a ti sọ bẹ̀ẹ́*).

After a long time however, Òrúnmìlà became fed up with Ìwà and started to make life impossible for her. When she cooked, Òrúnmìlà would complain about the "frightful cooking prowess of badly brought up wives." When she sang to entertain guests, *Òrúnmìlà* would announce to all that they had had enough of her croaking. When she corrected the children, Òrúnmìlà would shout that she was too harsh on them. Even when Ìwà slept peacefully in her corner of the house, he would occasionally go up to her and rudely wake her and tell her to stop snoring. The disgrace was too much for Ìwà to bear. After a long time, she went back to her father's house.[48]

Òrúnmìlà searched for her everywhere but could not find her. Finally he went to the diviners and they told him that Ìwà had gone back to "the abode of the spirits" (*orun*) the house of his father. He was also told that, if he wanted to get in touch with her, he would offer a sacrifice of a net and honey to Ẹ̀sù, the trickster divinity, and messenger of the gods. When he did, he was given the Egúngún costume.[49] When Òrúnmìlà and Ẹ̀sù got to "heavenly abode" (*orun*) Ẹ̀sù tricked Ìwà to come out of her hiding place and speak to Òrúnmìlà. He embraced her and asked her to come back to earth with him. Ìwà refused and said the rules had been contravened. It was no use. Since she still loved him, she would help him. She would abide with him, not in the visible form of a wife, but in the invisible form of a helper. She cautioned him that he would succeed in life if he took her advice and abided by it. She said that:

Ki omaa see daradara laye	You should behave well on earth
Niwa ti Odara	Have a good character
Tọju àwon ọmọ rẹ	Take care of your children
Tọju àwon Ìyàwo rẹ	Take care of your wives
Latoni lọ, oni fi oju ri emi Ìwà	I, Ìwà shall become invisible to you from today
Sugbon Màa wà pélu rẹ	But I will be with you
Isowo huwasi rẹ simi	And it is according to how you treat me
Ni àwọn ọmọ araiye a fi mọ	That will show how good
bi otiṣe dara to	and successful you are.

The poem lists the order of qualities that the Yoruba approve as important to success in life. It personifies them and sets them out as the basis of a good character, Ìwà. The epitome of good character is the Supreme Deity, the Creator. His first son is Patience (Suuru), the father of good character. A person manifests good character in his life when he treats his wives with kindness and affection, takes care of his children and does what is good. Ìwà abides with such person and he will succeed in life. The irony in Òrúnmìlà's case was that, as the oracle divinity, he symbolizes the omniscience of the Supreme Deity. He who is all-knowing forgot his promises. Hence Òrúnmìlà submits through his treatment of Ìwà to the overall image of the Yoruba and Bini divinities whose closeness to perfection is impugned by a flaw. Through this flaw, they are made to experience the human condition. In and through that experience, the Yoruba and the Bini are able to identify with their divinities.

Furthermore, the poem stipulates the customary rules that should regulate a husband's dealings with his wives. The extent to which he carries out his obligations and fulfills his promises is the extent to which he succeeds as a "good peson: (*Eniti oni Ìwà rere*). It is not surprising that the imagery of a woman is used to symbolize good character. The "cool" qualities of patience, kindness, and endurance are associated with Yoruba and Bini women. "Hot" qualities of impatience, frequent outbursts of anger are associated with men. Thus, the Yoruba who say "When we use the right hand to beat the child, we use the left to make him comfortable" (*Ti aba fi owo òtúa na omo à fi òsin fàá mora*), identify men with their hot temper with the right hand, and women with their cool spirit of reconcilation with the left hand. The auspicious left-hand women repairs the injury done by the right-hand men.

CHAPTER SIX

REFERENCES

1. The Danish writer Isak Dinesen's description of North European aristocracy illustrates this point. She wrote:

> The Ladies...carried the future of the name in their lap and were, like dignified and debonair caryatids, holding up the houses....For how free were they not, how powerful! Their Lords might rule, the country, and allow themselves many liberties which was the vital principle of their world, the centre of gravitation lay with them (1942:231-232)

Hence, the paradox: the overt power of the Lord and the muted but, in social terms, tremendous, and, in some sense negative power of the Ladies. It is negative because it lies with their power to destroy legitimacy, the "future of the name."

2. The main sources of the information on Bini marriage are Chief Osado Edomwonijii, 50, Mission Road, Benin City; Chief Ebohon, 21, Igbinadolo Street, Benin City; Sir Augustine Emumwen, 27, Agabdo Street, Benin City; Papa Azali Iredia, Iselu Quarters, Ewatto and Chief Onwude, Agenebode.

3. Professor P. Igbafe, of History, University of Benin, first drew my attention to this type of marriage during a discussion. Subsequent interviews revealed that it had a wide recognition and was regarded in the circumstances which necessitated it as a customary obligation.

4. Chief Osado Edomwonyi. Interview on 2 Jan. 1981 at 50, Mission Road, Benin. He also gave me the taxonomy of Bini marriages about which there was considerable unanimity.

5. Chief Jacob Egharevba. Interview at 1, Lagos Street, Benin on 17 July 1980.

6. The term *Idegbe* is used to cover different patterns of relationships among the Bini proper and the Northern Edo, particularly at Eme Ora and Ora. *Idegbe* is used as a term for daughters of the lineage who, having married out, have for some reason come back to their family house, where they acquire the status of men, and would be allowed to speak in gatherings which women are not normally allowed to do. Interview with Joseph Eborime, Asst. Curator, Benin Museum, native of Ora.

7. These two categories are illustrated by the northern Edo marriage types of *Amoya* and *Adegbe*. *Amoya* has all her bridewealth paid and remains a member of the husband's family. *Adegbe* is described as more casual and involves a part payment of bridewealth. Ownership over children of such marriages is competed for by the patriclan of both parents through the performance of Okhe title for the children. The children become members of the patriclan which performs Okhe title for them. Chief O. Owunde, Auchi Road, Agenebode, 1 Aug. 1980.

8. N.W. Thomas who first drew attention to this type of marriage, misunderstood it as a form of loose-living in which the daughter takes on as many lovers as she can to get children to the memory of her father. Thomas noted:

> under certain circumstances, a girl remains in her father's house unmarried; the house is her property and she is free to receive as many lovers as she pleases; if she leaves a son, he is the heir to the house (1910:8).

It is difficult to see why the Areuwa marriage was presented in this casual manner. Perhaps, realizing the importance of the patrilineal principle in descent and inheritance rules, Thomas sought to explain the exception to the rule by presenting the marriage as casual. Informants insisted that since the daughter's role was sacred, she was well-behaved.

9. N.W. Thomas called this marriage type Isomi (1910:5).

10. *Okhe* title-taking is most important among the Weppa-Wanno of northern Edo. It is taken normally by groups of *otsu* age-grades, now at a three-year interval. It is the key to other titles in society. It guarantees the right to a proper burial and a right to be heard in the community. It integrates the son, the *Adegbe*, to either the patrilineal group or his father or his mother. The time of taking it confirms seniority in the society. Each *otsu* "age-group" performs it, is sponsored by an *Ifotu*, "father of the brotherhood," who is also called *Anawu*, "father of children."

11. Chief Charles Onwude, Auchi Road, Agenbode, interview, 25 July 1980.

12. These prestations are periodic in nature; they include the provision of free labour and the economic support provided to make the wife's father's burial meet the required standard.

13. A Bini traditional week, like that of the Yoruba, is four days. Unlike the Yoruba days which are associated with an important divinity, the Bini days take their name from the four corners of the earth. The first day, *Eken* (east) is the day of rest. The second day, *Orie* (the west), the third *Aho* (the south) and the fourth, *Okuo* (the north) are working days except at the palace when

it is given over wholly to the performance of important sacrifices to the ancestors of the king. Interview with Chief Jacob Egharevba 1, Lagos Road, Benin City, 24 July 1980.

14. This is one of the two goats to be sacrificed on the bride's behalf to ensure her fertility. This is provided by the bride's father and is sacrificed at the father's ancestral shrine to symbolize the activation of the power of fertility which the lineage ancestors have given their daughter. The ancestors also intercede for her with Olókun. The second goat is sacrificed at her first pregnancy and is provided by the husband, but sacrificed at the father's ancestral shrine. Chief Edomwonyi, Benin.

15. Chief Edonwoyin, 50, Mission Road, Benin City. *Klri kuuva defi uhae*, "the rope and the vessel may not fall into the well" is a euphemism for the death of a pregnant woman.

16. As will we see later, references to the river are references to Olókun, the god of fertility. Fresh river water is put daily in special containers in the little shrine to Olókun which all married women ought to have and which symbolizes the constant presence of Olókun with the devotee.

17. Chief J. Egharevba who confirmed in an interview in July 1980 the main outlines of the simple form that the marriage of a princess takes, stated that it was customary for the Oba to give his daughter in marriage not only to the important chiefs such as the Uzama, but also to some powerful rivals such as the head of Udo, the rival of the King of Bini.

18. Interview in Pa. A. Emumwen at 27, Agbado Street, Benin on 4 January 1981.

19. This tendency has been remarked by scholars as typical of the relationship between muted and dominant groups in most societies. The two groups have their opinions about any particular issue in society. The views of the dominant people are often heard as this group has more resources at its power to make itself heard. Those who belong to the less dominant group will have to use the resources of the dominant group if they wish to be heard (Ardener, 1972; S.Ardener, 1978, 1979).

20. Interview with Chief Ebohon on 10 July 1980.

21. Interview with Chief Ebohon, 17 July 1980.

22. In most areas where there is no sophisticated knowledge of fertility, a distinction is not made between potency (as the ability to achieve erection) and fertility in males.

23. Interview with the Chief Priestess of Olókun, Iduzemwongi Eweka, at Iyowa Village, 14 kilometres from Benin, 5 January 1981.

24. Interview at Iyowa before the commencement of the Olókun ritual worship, 5 January 1981.

25. Interview with Uyiekpen Bas Eweka, uncle to the present Oba of Benin, brother of the Olókun priestess, Iduzemwongie Eweka. He is an officer at the Nigerian Institute for Oil Research.

26. Egherevba, 1946; Ryder, 1969:7; ben-Amos, 1908:23.

27. Aspects of the syncretism of Christianity and traditional worship still manifests themselves in Olókun art symbolism. The sign of a white cross forms the central focus in front of the shrine at Iwoya.

28. The main outlines of this story were confirmed in an interview with the traditional Bini historian, J.U. Egharevba in July 1980.

29. Iduzemwongie, literally translated, means "god makes me laugh."

30. Making the sculpture of Olókun bigger than that of Osanobua is deliberate as it is believed that Olókun, the first-born of Osanobua has superseded him.

31. Opinion is divided as to the number of times Ora is called upon. Egharevba, in an interview, insisted on four times; the chief priestess at Iwoya mentioned seven times, which was the actual number of times she was called by the congregation at the commencement of the ritual.

32. This similarity is strengthened by the fact that at Iwoya one of the two women who support the arms of the chief priestess as she is slowly worked up into possession by Olókun was her daughter and would-be successor, Grace Oviabon. The other support was a member of the womenfolk of the village of some importance.

33. Interview with Baba Adesina at Ekiti, 5.1.81. Interview with Baba Augustinẹ Akanbi Bạbatunde at Imeko, 28.8.81. Interview with Chief Kudefu, Ọyọ̀ Palance, Ọyọ̀ 10.10.80.

34. N.A. Fadipe, whose ethnographic account of Yoruba marriage is outstanding and who rightly makes much of the traumatic experience that the spouse goes through due to change in residential arrangement at marriage, seems to have overlooked the vital integrating role of the *Alárenà* and her alleviating effect on the trauma caused by change of place at marriage.

35. The function of the *Alárenà* is not peculiar to Yoruba and, as already seen, the Bini. The existence of a similar intermediary institution has been highlighted by Laflesche (1912) and Imohkai (1979). The former studies this role among the Osage Indians who called it by the name of *nigka do he*, while later stated that the Etsako, an Edo subgroup called *okhiukhu*. Though the functionaries occupying both offices differ (the role is played by four old men among Osage Indians and by an adult male among the Etsako) the functions parallel those performed by the *Alárenà*.

36. This ritual draws the attention of the community to the commencement of the commitment between suitor and spouse, involves a redistribution of wealth and confirms the general statement of Evans-Pritchard about the social character of bridewealth as one of the "techniques which employ wealth, by a gift or payment, as a means of establishing, defining, expressing and evoking social cohesion" (1965:182).

37. Interview with Papa Adesina, Agbo-Ile Adesina, at Ado-Ekiti on 5 Jan. 1981.

38. These were collected at Ibonwon, near the Baale's Compound on 24 Aug 1977, while the author of this work was serving as the resident Catholic priest for Epe Division of Lagos State with Headquarters at Ibonwon.

39. In the African sense, "sweetness" connotes "flavoursome."

40. Location variations in some areas of Yorubaland account for the performance of some other rituals between the ceremony of Idana and that of transferring the woman to her husband's compound. Thus, among the Ketu subgroup, two important ceremonies come in between those of Idana and Igbeyawo. These are the ceremony of ritual excision or clitoridectomy and the dance of departure, Bolojo. This practice still survives among people of Yoruba descent in Sierra Leone (Bassir, 1954:252). In Ijeshaland, Igbeyawo is often termed Idans, the core ritual prestation that effects the transfer of rights at marriage.

41. The Yoruba, like the Bini, have four-day weeks. But unlike the Bini who name the days of their weeks after four cardinal points (informants statements, cf. Egharevba 1946:81) the Yoruba name the days of their week after their divinities.

42. Similar to that characterized among the Bunyoro as the privileged obstruction of marriage (Beattie, 1958).

43. In using the Gèlèdé as an illustration, there is no intention to claim that the Gèlèdé Masked Dance is performed all over Yorubaland. It belongs to the Ketu, the Sabe, the Ohori and the Nago Yoruba subgroups of Western Yorubaland (Beier, 1958:5; Harper, 1970:67). Rather the contention is that

it provides a paradigm applicable to most areas of Yorubaland, as each subgroup has a local variety of rituals which manifest the prominence of Yoruba women in ritual. It is beyond the scope of this work to explore them. Perhaps further localised research will; bring some of these rituals forward.

44. Àjé has been inadequately translated was witch, but it has to do with women who are said to possess mystical powers which may be used to the advantage or disadvantage of the society. The Yoruba Àjé can bilocate, communicate with her colleagues over long distances, operate in the dark and has a bird for a heart. She can also employ her talents and powers for the service of society. She can cause barren women to be pregnant, poor people to become rich and sick to become well. She can control the flow of menstrual blood and kill the foetus. She can control the earth's fertility by withholding rain. The image of the Yoruba witch does not correspond to the classical ideas of the witch as a personification of evil who works psychically without spells, rites and medicine (Evans-Pritchard, 1937). Modern dramas on Yoruba witchcraft have taken the view that the Yoruba witch is completely evil.

45. The word "caste" was used by Harper (1970). Since the concept of caste in sociological literature has rigid sets of associations which make it synonymous with class, I prefer to use the word "group."

46. My attention was first drawn to the existence of these songs by the historian, A.I. Isiwaju, during fieldwork interviews in Ketu confirmed the contents apart from a slight variation in interpretation.

47. The bare facts of this Ifápoem were collected from Babalawo Oguntegbe of Apogere Compound, Imeko, Egbado North. This variant of the story of the marriage of Òrúnmílà, the oracle divinity who symbolizes the omniscience of the Supreme Deity, Olódùmarè, to Ìwà, good character, is less well-developed than the variant of Modupe Alade (1969) and Wande Abimbola (1975). Since it throws into relief the qualities admired in men, it has been reproduced in poem form in the Appendix.

48. The Egúngún cult commemorates the ancestors. Egúngún Masquerades are said to represent the ancestors who visit their progeny. It is only as an ancestor that a human being can be admitted to the "abode of the spirit," Orúnmìlà, in his role of an earthly-dweller, had to borrow an Egúngún costume.

CHAPTER SEVEN

SOCIAL CHANGE AND THE SELF

This study of the characteristics of the human has focused on the cultural components in terms of attitudes, factors and social expectations that are present in those that the Bini and the Yoruba societies regard as "proper" and "successful." The definition of culture which served as a discriminating background to the study was provided by Clyde Klukhorn. He noted that:

> culture is an historically created design, for living, rational, irrational, non- rational, implicit, explicit- which serve as potential guides for the behavior of people at given periods of time (1945).

The components of culture - Ideas, Institutions and material technology (Chinoy, 1968:28-34) - peculiar to the people and determined by their ecology enable one to perceive the dimensions of change as cultures come in contact with others or as extraneous powerful factors impact on a culture. A significant change in any of the components of culture will necessarily effect a shift in all the other components. As a case in point, the internecine wars which took place in Yorubaland throughout most of the 19th century and abated as the effect of *Pax Britannica* was gradually felt in the hinterland of the Yoruba area, wars which Pa Adeniyi alluded to in chapter 5, effected a significant change in the attitudes of the Yoruba to their belief system and their perception of power. Hitherto, considerable reliance was put on people reputed to have medicinal powers that can be used both for productive purposes and in inflicting untold injury on the enemy in times of crisis. There was also a significant belief in the power and the ability of the divinities to deliver their devotees as well as conquer the enemies of their devotees. However, when conflict ensued between the Europeans and the Yorubas and their neighbours and the Europeans inflicted crushing defeat on their enemies, the faith of the Yoruba in the ability of their divinities shook considerably. When the French defeated the Dahomey at Bohicon in 1893 and the British defeated the Ijebu at Mọ́jọdá in 1894 and defeated the hitherto invincible Bini in 1897, the series of defeat inflicted such an injury on the psychological ego of the Yoruba that there was a consensus that if the Europeans could be so victorious then their divinity must be superior to the divinity of the Yorubas.

Research shows that during this period such names given to children at birth included "*Ogúntóyìnbó*" (the whiteman is an equivalent of the Yoruba divinity of war-Ogun), and Ifátóyìnbó (the whiteman is an equivalent of the Yoruba divinity of Wisdom and Knowledge). In other words, the introduction of extraneous power variables not only proved the inadequacy of traditional familiar aspects of material technology, but it also led to a shift in the significance that was placed formerly on the symbolic forces said to ensure the survival and protection of the Yoruba and the Bini.

At another level of abstraction, the analysis of the changes that have taken place in the concept of the person from what used to be to what is, now, must take into consideration the differences in the social structure of traditional life and its demands and on contemporary life and its expectations. Emile Durkheim in his influential contribution on societal taxonomy, in the *Division of Labour* has provided a paradigm of eliciting the differences between cultures in terms of their basic principle of mobilization. Those societies like the Yoruba and the Bini, traditionally, and to some extent, even in their present day practices, mobilized members in the group around the principle of kinship or filiation. The kinship group was the guarantor of security. The individual inherits nomenclature from the kinship group. He inherits land for farming also from the kinship group. It was, thus, important to be part of the group, to be loyal to the group and to protect the interests of the group because ultimately, one's interest was bound up with that of the group. Ascription, understood as the accident of birth into a kinship group was the primary determinant of the life chances and opportunities for the improvement of the individual. This kind of principle of mobilization was identified by Durkheim as mechanical solidarity.

In direct opposition to the principle of ascription was the principle of achievement. It is based on the concept of contract which specifies the conditions that qualify members of the given society to participate in given enterprises. The philosophy and intention of this specification is that whoever qualifies ought to be admitted. In otherwords, merit rather than the factor of birth ought to be the utmost determinant of participation. This implies that it is the worth of the individual that is of moment if he is to participate in the essential activities of the societies organized on the basis of organic principle. Therefore, although the individual is a product of his kinship group, he does not need the support of his kinship group to participate in a modern economy that is interested in his achievement as an individual. Mechanical principle of mobilization predicates the individual in his kinship group and considers success as achievable only through the joint efforts of kinsmen. Organic solidarity, on the other hand, emphasizes individualism. It has been argued that the mechanical/Organic solidarity taxonomy must not be seen to apply so rigidly such that non- industrialized societies are said to conform to the one while industrializing societies are said to conform to the other in all respects. Modern societies subscribe to certain practices which are dictated by the demands of mechanical solidarity.

The postulates of this taxonomy are crucial to the understanding of the impact of social change on the human person in societies, characterized as mechanical, which are undergoing transformation into industrializing communities. The demands of traditional life are quite different from those of modern life predicated on merit and success through individual effort. As the essays in chapter one reveal, people in those societies undergoing transformation from one form of economic mobilization to another are often under pressure to submit to the different dictates of the two systems. Participation in productive enterprises in modern societies ought to be on merit and not on the considerations of ascription. Yet the contemporary African employed by the state or in the private sector of the modern economy is expected to submit to the rules of modern production, during his official hours, and submit to the rules of traditional life, when he is not at work. Even when he is at work, he is expected to put the obligations to his kinship group first. This double cultural demands characterized as the demands of the Two Publics (Ekeh:1980) lead to a confusion in human behavior.

The Two Publics and the Human Personality

One of the enduring consequences of colonialism and the entrenchment of its value system in most areas of Sub-Saharan Africa, in general, and in Nigeria in particular is the creation of what is called "The Two Publics." It is replicated on the Durkheimean taxonomy of societies in terms of the mechanical and organic principles of mobilization. The African was reared on the merits of loyalty to kinship interests and responsibilities. He or she was nurtured on being sensitive to community concerns and the demands of extended family ties. Whether as male or female, the African socialization process drilled the individual on the necessity for one to be one's brothers' keeper. The African spent seven hours of the working day on terms specified by the principle of colonial value-system of organic solidarity. After his working days, he spent the rest of the day ensconced on the mores, expectations and values of kinship protection and support. He can mobilize kinship property for limited personal use. Although he submitted himself to the beliefs and practices of Euro-Judaic or Islamic cultural expectations at work, to the superficial extent needed for the approval of his European or Arabian superiors, once he leaves work, he came under the barrage of the socio - psychological pressures of African value system. Witchcraft fears dispelled by the established orthodox Christian Churches as non-existent become real concerns which might affect his progress in life. The scene was, therefore, set for the educated Africans to live in terms of two levels of expectations and differing dimensions of moral demands.

The primordial hold of kinship expectations supported with the frightening sanctions of the fiery power of the ancestors and the vengeful divinities made an offence against the injunctions of the kinship group more grave than that against the colonial injunctions. In fact a "booty-syndrome" type of orientation was adopted to the colonial resources, the civic public. The African endeavored to succeed and excel at the standards set by the Europeans for progress in the echelons of the modern society. Once the African was promoted to such exalted positions, he was expected to use the resources of the civic public, the colonial system to service the needs of his kinship interests, the primordial public.

Infringement of the injunctions, such as fraud money spent for one's relations was not condemned as fraud by ones's kinship group. On the other hand, fraud against one's own kinship group was regarded as thoroughly morally reprehensible. Such was the relative concept of the good person from the viewpoints of kinship groups and the colonial or civic public that the traits and characteristics of goodness in one disqualified one in the other. Within the kinship public, in matters related to the kinship interests, one was expected to be honest, hardworking and altruistic. For the colonial public, one was expected to do less and less work for more and more pay and to employ the benefits of one's positions to improve one's personal fortunes and those of one's relations. In this regard, Ekeh succinctly noted:

> a *good citizen* of the primordial (kinship) public gives out and asks nothing in return: a *lucky* citizen of the civic (Colonial) public gains from the civic public but enjoys escaping giving anything in return whenever he can. But such a lucky man would not be a good man were he to channel all his lucky gains to his private purse. He will only continue to be a good man if he channels part of the largeness from the civic public to the primordial public. This is the logic of the dialectics. The unwritten law of the dialectics is that it is legitimate to rob the civic public in order to strengthen the primordial public (Ekeh 1975:108).

The consequences of this peculiar phenomenon of working at two levels of value demands, and relative meaning of morality was keenly felt after Independence in the spheres of political process of democratic practice and in economic practice. Before patterns of performance at this two levels are examined, it is necessary to highlight the peculiar supportive structure of cash crop economy as against "oil boom" economy to the emergent value orientations.

The development of cash-crop economy fully integrated the economic activities of what became Nigeria, into the world economic system - the capitalist economy. It institutionalized dependency by firmly establishing the metropolis/periphery pattern of relationship between Europe with particular reference to Britain and Nigeria. Raw materials were grown, collected, bought at cheap rates and sent abroad to feed the industries of Europe. The processed or manufactured goods were packaged and distributed and sold at great profit in the satellite colonial enclaves such as Nigeria. This deprived Nigerian of jobs that would have been available had the industries been located in Nigeria.

A positive arrangement, however, in the colonial practice of economy based on cash-crops - was that since farmers grew the cash-crops, money currency necessarily percolated to the grass-roots of farmers. The farmers were protected from the fluctuations of prices in the world market by marketing boards, which bought the cash crops at great profit but kept some percentage of the money for the economic rainy day to cushion off the depressed prices when they occurred. The significant point is that distribution of money was wider and deeper than it became under the "oil boom" economy. As Fieldhouse noted:

> The supreme irony of Nigerian economic development, however, is that, despite the flow of oil wealth, by 1982 the country was more heavily burdened by debt than any previous time... Until the flow of oil money began, debt service stood at a conventional African level of about 4.0 per cent of export goods and services. In the 1970's the great expansion of exports allowed this burden to be substantially reduced, but, despite the second oil price increase of 1979, between then and 1982 external debts increased by about a third and the burden of debt service rose almost to its highest previous level. In 1979 Nigeria had a favourable trade balance of $1,429m. and gross international reserves of $5,870m. By 1982 she had a balance of payments deficit of $7,324 million and gross international reserves were down to $1,927 million about one month's coverage. While this position resulted largely from the drop in oil prices after 1980, it also reflects the excessive dependence of the economy on oil and the extraordinary lack of wisdom on the part of a federal government which had gambled on the continuation of high oil prices in undertaking huge foreign borrowing and committing itself to equally large imports (Fieldhouse 1986:159-160).

A major feature of the economic practice in the "oil boom" era was the abandonment of agriculture and the cash-crop base of the economy and the over dependence on oil money. There was an unwholesome transformation of the economic base from multidimensional agro - based economy to a monolithic economic trust based entirely on the proceeds of oil. Since oil funds went to the covers of the government, distribution to the grassroots level was neither as deep nor as all-embracing as it was with cash economy. The immediate consequences of this situation include:

(a) The unequal and unjust distribution of resources which did not get to the grassroots.

(b) The higher stakes of occupying responsible positions without the necessity for having the merit to serve effectively in those portions.

(c) The conversion from agro-based economic activities in preference for the contract syndication short lived ventures which attracted high profits.

(d) The establishment of an orientation to government as a machine of exploitation for personal aggrandizement which went hand in hand with the politicalization of crime such that criminal acts of non-accountability and graft were not dealt with decisively on account of what was regarded as political expediency.

(e) The subsequent institutionalization of amorality in dealings of public performance. This created the chain effect of perceiving that election to political offices provided the opportunity for easy wealth. This has in turn led to an inordinate rush for political office predicated not on the notion of service for the fatherland but rather on wealth that the fatherland would bestow on one who is in office. The only exception was the probe set up on the misdemeanors of Public Office holders under the Idiagbon - Buhari regime.

(f) The widening of the economic gap between a minority in the urban areas of the nation and the rest of the country compounded by a flamboyant show of ill-gotten gain to cause a shift in traditional value expectations in favor, no longer of morality, but the amoral maxim of the end, wealth, justifying the means, ill-gotten or 'easy come' syndicated contract money.

(g) The consequent institutionalization of *anomie*, a state of normlessness which enthroned the concepts of "might is right" and "Cobweb Theory" view of law. Law became effective when it dealt with the weak.

The first and major consequence of oil boom was the sudden expansion of the revenue base in the urban areas. This led, *inter alia* to changes in the consumption pattern and massive expansion of the aspirations of people. The Udoji award which sought to allow some cash-flow to the generality of people gave rise to conspicuous consumption patterns and inflation. Opinion varied on the longterm effects of the award although the view is strongly held that the money which financed the award would have been more profitably spent by raising the standard of living without encouraging a run-away inflation.

Another major shift was that since agriculture was not encouraged as poor prices were given for agricultural products until the structural adjustment programme of the Ibrahim Babangida Regime (1985-) and since the bulk of investment was set up in capital cities, both in the state and the nation, the impression was given that to participate in economic activities and have the benefits of petroleum economy, all one had to do was move into the state capitals and large cities. This situation led to the phenomenon of the "rural push" and "urban pull". The first massive wave of urbanization was immediately after the Nigerian Civil War in 1970. The second massive wave of unskilled laborers was in 1975 when the construction industry reached the peak of its expansion. This led to the population rise of shanty-town in the cities at a degree hitherto unrivaled. With little or no skills, the shanty-town dweller was at a disadvantage in the stiff competition for participation in highly remunerating economic enterprises. The gap between the desire to participate fully and the lack of skills coupled with the limitedness of opportunities available for full participation led to *anomie* and the transformation of the normally law-abiding compassionate and warm-hearted rural dweller to the disorderly, hard-hearted urban criminal.

Yet another area of value shift consequent upon massive injection of petroleum funds was the expansion of taste and a creation of a consumerist culture not supported by the level of industrialization attained. The two fundamental phases of primary production and processing to consolidate industrial growth were ignored. The third phase of industrial development, packaging was concentrated upon. Local industries, thus, lacked support mechanisms for consolidation. They were, with few exceptions assembly-plants and packaging centers of already manufactured goods. This was responsible for the highly inflated prices of locally "produced good".

Tastes became expanded and sophisticated but not satisfiable in terms of local industrial productive power. The Nigerian was exposed to international culture with expensive tastes. Before the oil boom, a few travelled abroad to pursue specific developmental objectives, for training or educational programmes to meet the manpower development needs of the country as codified in the Ashby Report. It was highly desirable then that one may be among the chosen few to participate in this international opportunity. It was then a foremost prayer on the lips of parents that their children be given the opportunity to study abroad. However, the sudden availability of resources, made international travels so common place and ordinary, enjoyed both by literate and illiterate Nigerian traders (euphemistically called businessmen and business-women) that it ceased to be a point of high desire and prayer. The net result of this was the acquisition of expensive tastes and habits that were not supportable by existential levels of productivity. The writing was already on the wall that when the legitimate sources of satisfying these expensive tastes, built on false values were no more, illegitimate sources would replace them.

The performance of the Nigerian elite in politics was predictable. Proximity to the colonial administrators exposed the Nigerian elite to the pleasures and influence that power conferred. In due time, the Nigerian elite closed ranks ostensibly for nationalistic obligation so as to wrest political power from the colonial masters. In reality if the hindsight of thirty years is anything to go by, their intention was to grasp power, enjoy the benefits that it proffers without actually performing the ultimate obligation of consolidating the nominal Independence that was granted on October 1, 1960. Wrestling political power from the European was one thing, sharing power among Africans was another. As it turned out:

> They (the elite) subsequently fissioned into ethnic groups. They travelled all over their area of origin to convince simple, unprejudiced, contented rural dwellers that they belonged to a tribe whose interest must be protected against the domineering

> tendencies of a contiguous people. They, the elite, were there to champion the progress of the tribe. Through this manipulative use of chicanery excitement of tribal antagonism, the Nigerian elite power brokers entrenched themselves at "Independence". With a few exceptions, they were all modernized tribal chiefs (Babatunde 1989:11).

Thus, instead of being national leaders who directed their energies into launching programmes of national redemption, programmes meant to liberate the nation from the exploited relationship of the periphery in relation to the European metropolitan centre, the Nigerian Political leaders were transformed, at Independence, to tribal leaders whose main mission was to promote the "interest of their own tribes" even when it conflicted with the over-all intention of maintaining the new nation, united and indivisible. This situation of expanded kinship base as a principle of organization, mobilization and exclusivity - tribalism - degenerated into civil strife. With civil disorder in the new nation, the law enforcement and security agencies came onto their own. As Professor Claude Ake noted:

> The military is what I call the organization for defence of the last resort, defence through violence. It is a fighting machine. The military comes into its own when our common humanity and sociability have disappeared in irreconcilable conflict. It comes into its own when two parties confront each other as executioners to kill or be killed (Ake 1982:21).

The army which had watched with interest the behavior of the Nigerian politicians noted that power and prestige attended the seizure of power. They prosecuted the civil war but decided to hold on to political power. The end of the civil war coincided with the peak of "oil boom". The availability of petroleum funds made the stakes of power acquisition higher and the spoils of power more exorbitant. Money rather than the humane philosophy become central to this emergent neo-African value system. The end of acquiring money justified the means which had gradually become unethical.

The civil war had other major areas of impact on the traditional value system. Life was considered sacred. Long life was a blessing. Every effort was made to prolong life and keep death away. Sickness in the family paralysed the daily activities of people as relations struggled to get healing for the sick. However, with the civil war, death became so common that life itself became cheap. Civil war had institutionalized killing as necessary for survival. In doing so, violence was institutionalized as a necessary fact of human existence. Instruments of death became common and illegal killing, that is, killing not officially sanctioned by the State, became, for some, a profession. Thus the phenomenon of hired assassins; armed-robbery, arson and riots confirm the entrenched factor of violence in the national psyche. Professor J. P. Clark, in his Inaugural lecture, *The Hero as the Villain* put the cause of this anomic situation very clearly. He noted:

> But the military vis-a-vis society, the soldier who in every society is a candidate for hero when he fights to defend the integrity of his country from without or, as in our tragic case, from within, has he together with society had purgation, has he had purification?
>
> It is my humble submission that we have our state of health as it is today largely because we have not done our duties to our soldier and to ourselves by cleansing him of the guilt of war. The armed robberies and public executions after seven years of peace, the running battles between police and gangs requiring curfews in several cities and states, the outbreak of fire in offices, factories, markets, and homes, all these incidents of violence are problems either directly deriving from our civil war or ones that have been compounded from civilian days by it (Clark 1978:15-16).

So the presence of other initial factors such as the violence-prone culture of the civil war was yet another remote contributor to the peculiar consequences identified with "oil boom".

The area in which the "oil boom" had its strongest impact was the family the most potent, basic social-engineering unit of the Nigerian society. Seeking contract awards to execute some of the unplanned and overambitious developmental programme of the government, was a ready method of getting good renumeration. It was common practice that the contract awards were made not on merit but as syndicated acts of collusion in which the award winner and the awarding body benefitted monetarily. Contract invoices were inflated to increase the profit margin that will accrue. It was then shared in different percentages between the award winner and members of the awarding body. In urban centres, the spouses, went in search of contract award and neglected the upbringing of children to secondary institutions like the "nannies" and "house help". Often, in order to pursue career opportunities spouses broke up family roles. Parental care was commuted to the buying of expensive gifts to children who were taken on elaborate holiday trips abroad. This cultivated, in *minors*, expensive tastes. Satisfying the acquired expensive tastes was not difficult as long as the "oil boom" lasted. Economic depression however unleashed, in the youth, the desire to satisfy their acquired tastes through any means, legal or illegal. This gave rise to heightened degree of juvenile delinquency expressed in such acts as armed-robbery, prostitution, arson, hired-killing or assassin and more recently hard drug trafficking.

Cultural Symbols And Social Engineering

A major concern of research into cultural phenomena, and for that matter other areas of knowledge articulation, in contemporary Sub-Saharan Africa is the point of relevance of research for social engineering. The new processes afoot at restructuring the World Order witnessed in the democratic movements in Eastern Europe has highlighted three relevant areas of power articulation; America, Japan and the New Europe embracing the Old Europe, Eastern Europe and Russia. Sub-Saharan Africa is regarded not only as irrelevant to this world ordering but a burden on it. The euphoria that began with the "Independence" of Ghana in 1957 and was sustained through the 1960's has been transformed, in the decade of 1980-1990 to the tragedy of recession, huge indebtness and consequent loss of confidence in the ability of the local leaders to govern without reducing the features of governance to a personality cult. A combination of natural and man-made calamities, flooding, drought, dissertification, ideological clashes and civil wars motivated by subgroup attempts to maintain exclusive interests within supposed inclusive nation communities and mismanagement have made instability, witnessed by rapid oscilation of government between military dictatorships and quasi-democratic or outright dictatorships, the only form of stability in contemporary Sub-Saharan Africa. The elementary consequences of governance; security to enable the citizens to engage in free, legimate occupation or leisure, equal access to justice, to educational opportunities for the enhancement of citizen's talents and potentialities, and access to health-care facilities, have or are becoming functions of relative wealth and status rather than the inalienable rights of the tax paying, law-abiding citizens.

A rethinking is necessary as Sub-Saharan Africa reaches the cross-roads in this last decade in the same way that Japan had to conduct a self-study after her defeat in the Second World War. The critical Japanese self-study concerned (a) the recognition of defeat, (b) the predication of defeat, not on superior culture, but on superior technology, (c) the recognition that in the components of Japanese culture with its yardsticks of loyalty, honour and hardwork as a measurement of human worth, the Japanese had the cultural will power to turn things around. A corollary of the pragmatic dictates of this belief in the self to rise from the prostrate posture of defeat was a refusal to romanticise the past. Rather the intention was to select the essential components and employ them to mobilise for a cultural economic and technological regeneration. Hence notions of loyalty to the kinship group was extended to the business corporation which entrenched the rights of the worker as an owner uniting both the employer and the employee in one single corporative exercise of pursuit of excellence in order to maximise profit. Hardwork ensured that the technology that was copied or borrowed after the Second World War was improved upon, perfected and employed to compete with other industrialised nations. In other words, since the technological advance of Japan after the 2nd World War had a cultural foundation, technological development need not lead to a destruction of the unique cultural life patterns of non-industrialised societies. Industrialisation and "Modernity" need not be antithetical to the cultural life if non-industrialised societies can take the responsibility to make the dynamic equivalent adaptations that will rearrange new extraneous influences meaningfully using old but equally dynamic cultural metaphors.

If kinship is a mobilizing priniciple, the family is the forum and unit of loyalty, mutual support and security. The loyalty arising from this principle is made to extend beyond the nuclear or compound family barriers of siblingships and biological or social fatherhood. Through the deliberate preference for classificatory kinship terms instead of specific kinship terms, groups achieve a stronger bonding which, if transferred into business and other areas, can stimulate greater cooperation that will lead to greater productivity and accountability. The necessity for groups to compliment others for survival should lead to the extention of the artifical social boundaries of the extended family to cover groups whose cooperation is necessary for survival. This should lead to successive stages of widening of narrow concentric circles of bonding. The family is naturally extended to cover the extended family. The extended family is further expanded to cover people formerly excluded but people whose contributions are now seen as crucial to survival. Then the tribal boundaries will be expanded to cover people of other tribes with whom cooperation ought to be maintained in order to survive and compete with other nation states. In order that these extentions of hitherto narrow boundaries be feasible across cultural boundaries there must be some common cultural categories and orientations which provide the context of rationality for the action. In order to establish this fact, the cultural archetypal symbols which serve as epitomes of cultural success and excellence and what is culturally expected will be closely analysed among the Bini and the Yoruba with some insights into those of the *Hausa* and the Igbo, some of the major sociolinguistic groups in modern day Nigeria.

Archetypal Cultural Symbols

The "good person" or the "successful self" among the Bini and the Yoruba, as indeed among the Hausa and the Igbo, epitomises the salient expectations, attitudes, and etiquette within the cultural group. Although the focus of this study is the Bini and the Yoruba, a comparative study of the two other major sociolinguistic groups in Nigeria should provide an insight into the shared values and norms and the differences about the self, work ethics and aspects of social expectations relevant to the study. This comparative approach will provide a rationale for the intention of employing cultural metaphors to stimulate cooperation across normally exclusive tribal boundaries. It should also provide a basis of ethical regeneration as it will draw attention to those salient cultural expectations that used to inform the actions, decision, manner of behavior of the self that is regarded as "good" or successful.

The patrilineal Bini who put great emphasis on primogeniture socialise their young to maintain the basic interests of their male-oriented culture. Primogeniture specifies that the first son occupies the position of the deceased father both in terms of status and obligations. The role of primogeniture evaluates children not only in terms of sex but also in terms of the order of birth. Male children are more relevant to primogeniture but the first son, has a lot of pressure on him to prepare for the role of the successor to his father. He must be hardworking, kind, and competitive. He must also take his responsibilities very seriously and apply himself to them with a zeal that impresses the group that, should the inevitable occur - the father dies - the family will not break up.

On account of this singular principle and the obligation it places on the first son, *Omorodion*, much attention is paid to the rearing of the first son in whom much is so expected. In addition to the demands of primogeniture, there is the special expectations arising from the peculiar features of stratification of the Bini village male community into the three distinct groupings of the Elders, *Edion*, the Adults, *Ighele* and the Youth, *Iroghae*. Culture assigns special roles, duties and expectations to each of these cultural phases of the developmental life cycle. The Youth are expected to be law-abiding, respectful to the seniors, competitive, not only in the farming responsibilities but in other exercises such as the provision of amusement for the village through wrestling matches and dance competitions. The Youth ought to develop a keen sense of community responsibilities. The Youth is expected to clean the house and organise the cleaning of the villages, the rivers from which the village community draw water.

The *Ighele*, before the consolidation of *Pax Britannica* used to be responsible for the defense of the community. They provided the soldiers from their ranks. They were expected to be brave, persistent, loyal to the group members and obedient to the elders, the *Edion*. In peace time, the adult group, *Ighele*, were judged in terms of how successful they carried out their responsibilities. These responsibilities were of two types, those to the family and to the larger community. Those to the larger community were subdivided into two kinds, those to the palace of the king either directly or indirectly through the representatives of the king. The responsibilities of the adult to his immediate community was equally important.

In his extended family relations the adult was expected to be caring, hardworking and benevolent. If he is a farmer, he had to have big barns of yam and many wives and children. Economic preoccupation dictated preference for polygamy. The level of material technology for farming was rudimentary using hoes and cutlasses. This labour intensive farming which produced little yield specified that many hands be employed for in the farm. The surest hands were those of one's children. The successful adult person was expected to be able to cater for his family, providing guidance and discipline. He was judged in the society as successful only to the extent to which he is a successful head of his family.

Responsibilities to the king varied as to the needs of the palace. Traditionally this group provided the conscripts to the army of the Bini King which up till the period of the entrenchment of British Colonial influence, was regarded as the most effective in Southern area of what came to be Nigeria. In peace times, the adult who is a member of a guild provided the services obligatory to his guild. Adults in the villages contributed victuals through the representative of the king to the palace of the king in Bini.

The elders articulated political order over their extended family units and in the *Edion* group. They adjudicated in conflicts, rewarded excellence and punished recalcitrance. The successful self among the Bini was the elder who was kind, truthful and who maintained peace. He was also a person who was known to be firm and persistent when the moment required it. He was the person who was accountable and fair minded.

Among the Yoruba, the "successful" "good person" *Omoluwabi* was cautious, respectful to elders and committed to and persistent in hardwork. He took family responsibilities seriously and understood that his obligations to the family included those to the extended family. In behavior to and treatment of the relations he operationalised the communitarian principle of shared responsibility inherent in the concept of classificatory kinship terms. He was loyal to relations, accountable to the members of the kinship group and a good father and husband. Whatever success attended his works in life;

be it success in the farming, trading, hunting, or in the artistic works; was subordinated to how he has proved himself as the head of his extended family. If he behaves in an exclusivist manner, treating his children with preference to those other children of the extended family, he was regarded as mean and unworthy of the responsibilities of success. If he accumulated resources and used them on himself and his immediate compound family, he forfeited having the group of dependents which was part of the consequences of success.

The successful person among the egalitarian Igbo of eastern Nigeria was the owner of Ikenga, the physical representation of success. The *Ikenga* symbol was not inherited or transferrable. It was attached to the peace. It was a symbol representing the social statement of success. The owner of the Ikenga was hardworking, fair and frank on issues. He was one who made it by the sheer dint of personal effort and against all odds. He displayed his wealth and success not only in the size of the yam barns and the member of his children and wives, but the extent to which he was an effective father and husband by the standard of Igbo culture. In moments of crisis he was tough, persistent and unyielding. He was accountable and loyal to kinship interest. He rose in ranks in the society by competing fairly with others, for gradations of chieftaincy titles which were a reflection of his achievement and mettle to compete rather than a patronising gift of some leader. The *Ikenga* symbol summarises all the levels of his excellence which led the society to recognise him as an achiever in the *Ikenga* form.

If *Ikenga* symbol epitomises the Igbo "successful self" or good person, and the *Omoluwabi* stands for the same among the Yoruba, Mutumin Kirki epitomises the "good man" or "successful self" among the Hausa of Northern Nigeria. As Professor A. Kirk-Greene noted:

> Every culture and every century has its own concept of the standards of good behavior, of what is to be admired and what is to be abhored. Yet by and large, within a single culture, the fundamentals of what is decent and decorous possess the elements of continuity (19:191).

The *Mutumin Kirki* has good *hali*, good character. Good character itself is summarised in being able to speak the truth *gaskiya*, in friendliness based on trust *Amana*, in generosity *Karamci* (not legislated by religious obligation) and in intense cordiality, *Karama*. The *Mutumin Kirki*, the "good person" must have patience, *hakuri* and good sense *hankali*. It is indispensable to the good person to have a sense of shame, *Kunya*. He ought to be accountable. The mutumin kirki was generous to the stranger, fair in competition and obliging to the benefactor. He must be hardworking when he is successful, he should use some of his wealth to assist the needy.

In briefly analysing the cultural content of these comparative archetypal symbols, *Ovbunoma, Omolumwabi, Ikenga* owner and *Mutumin Kirki*, the intention is to argue that given the meaning of each in its cultural context, there are shared values among the major sociolinguistic groups of Nigeria. For the purposes of social engineering, the similarities in the meaning generated by those symbols which have been selected for analysis on the principle of dynamic equivalence, offers an opportunity to employ cultural archetypal symbols as mobilising principles for national integration, and enhances self-identity and a recapture of traditional aspects of work ethics crucial to the regeneration of the society.

In contemporary Subsaharan Africa, tribalism, defined as a form of exclusivist preference for people of one's own tribe at the expense of others, has constituted one of the significant barriers to development into nationhood. Artificial international boundaries have brought people of different tribes together and have often divided people of same tribe and assigned segments of the division to separate nation states (Asiwaju, 1984, 1986). The tension and suspicion ensuing from this form of exclusion is often justified under the pretext that the tribes in their ways have very little in common. The argument, using the prinicple of dynamic equivalence in looking at the archetypal symbols that serve as key to the demands and obligations of success in different cultures is to establish that most of the tribes have more essential values in common. The tension and suspicion paralysing politics, economics and social life is not solely the function of irreconcilable differences between the tribes. A consistent indepth study of the essential correlates of the different tribes shows a refreshing similarity in expectations, norms and orientation with some variance in methods of approach. This reality could be employed to mobilise people of different groups to function together with less suspicion.

Among the Bini, Yoruba, Igbo and Hausa traditional expectations of the "successful person" are similar. He is expected to be hardworking, accountable and cordial. He is expected to treat strangers kindly and seek fairness. In addition, the greatest principle of evaluation of the worth of an individual is how effective he is as a husband and a father. Traditional work ethics specified that approval was to be given to hardwork and wealth that has been accumulated through ethical methods. Wealth whose source is unknown or suspicious brought social disapproval. Traditional leadership expectations specified that the leader was a symbol of the collective will and strength of the community. There was no other source of legitimation for leadership except in the community that produced it. Leadership could be alienated only at its own risk. Hence the leader was the distributive centre who looks out for the interests of all, in the understanding that to fail to do so will lead to its demise. Control mechanisms were not apparatuses distinct from the community and existing in their own right. They were vested in the community and provided by the community.

A cultural resurgence similar to the Japanese example after second World War is crucial to the rejuvenation of Nigeria. This will be based on a recognition of the fact that essential cultural similarities exist between all tribal groups. That each culture specifies hardwork and a sound work ethics. It is important to reestablish success in the family and at work as crucial to approval just as it is significant to disapprove of wealth whose sources are either not known or known to be unethical. The traditional expectations that go into the socialisation process that produces the "good self" or good person in the society are crucial to survival in a world of great qualitative competition. It is also useful to extend the boundaries of loyalty beyond the extended family or tribe to embrace all the people whose cooperation is necessary for survival. That was the motivating logic of keen kinship loyalty. Survival, protection of shared interests has also became the major reason for the transformation of the disparate tribes into a cooperative vibrant national polity in the contemporary world in which small groups are merging into bigger entities for survival. For groups to segment into exclusive tribes in Subsaharan nation states is for the groups to plot their own demise.

BIBLIOGRAPHY

Abimbola, W.
1971 The Yoruba Concept of Human Personality in *La Notion de Personne en Afrique Noire* (Colloques Internationaux de Centre National de la Recherche Scientifique, Paris).

________. 1975 wàpèlé: The Concept of Good Character in Ifá Literary Corpus in Wande, W. (ed.) *Yoruba Oral Literature: Selections from the Papers Presented at the Seminar on Yoruba Oral Tradition Poetry in Music, Dance and Drama*. Ibadan, I.U.P.

________. 1976 *Ifá: An Exposition of Ifá Literary Corpus*. Ibadan: O.U.P.

Abidodun, R.
1976 A Reconsideration of the Function of Ako, Second Burial Effigy in Owo, *Africa*, ILVI, No.1.

Abraham, R. C. 1958 *Dictionary of Modern Yoruba*. London: London University Press.

Adedji, Adebayo (ed.)
1966 *An Introducation to Western Nigeria: Its People, Culture and System of Government*. Inst. of Administration: University of Ife.

Adesanya, Adebayo
1958 Metaphysical Thinking, *ODU*, 5:36-41.

Adunni, Olorisa (Susanne Wenger)
1976 A Review of H. Courlander, *Tales of Yoruba Gods and Heroes*, New: Cown Publishers, in *R.A.L.* Vol. VII, n1. 1.

Afigbo, A. E. 1967 The Warrant Chief System in Eastern Nigeria: Direct or Indirect Rule? *J.H.S.N.*, CXI, 4:683-701.

Aigbe, E. 1960 *Itan Edo*. Lagos: Ribway Printers.

Ajayi, J. F. A. and Smith R.
1964 *Yoruba Warfare in the Nineteenth Century*. Cambridge: C.U.P.

Ajisafe, A. K. 1924 *The Laws and Customs of the Yoruba People*. London/Lagos: C.M.S. Bookshop.

Akinjogbin, I. A. 1966 Western Nigeria, its People and its Culture in Adebayo Adedeji, *An Introduction to Western Nigeria: Its People, Culture and System of Government*. Ile-Ife: University of Ife Press.

Akinola, G. A. 1976 The Origin of the Eweka Dynasty of Benin: A Study in the Use and Abuse of Oral Traditions. *J.H.S.N.*, Vol VIII, no. 3: 21-36.

Akinyele, 1952 Newly Discovered Stone Figures from the Yoruba Village of Ijara, Northern Nigeria, *Man*, LXIII, no. 115.

Ardener, E. 1962 *Divorce and Fertility: An African Study*. London: O.U.P./N.I.S.E.R.

________. 1972 Belief and the Problem of Women in La Fontaine (ed.) *Interpretation of Ritual*.

Ardener, S. 1973 Sexual Insult and Female Militancy, *Man*, Vol. 8, No. 3, p. 422.

________. (ed.) 1977 *Perceiving Women*. London: Dent and Sons.

________. (ed.) 1978 *Defining Females: The Nature of Women in Society*. London: Croom Helm.

Armstrong, R. 1964 *The Study of West African Languages*. Ibadan: I.U.P.

Asiwaju, A. I. 1974 Anti-French Resistance Movement in Okori-Ije (Dahomey) 1895-1960. *J.H.S.N.*, Vol. VIII, No. 2, June.

________. 1975 Gẹ̀lẹ̀dẹ́ Songs as Sources of Western Yoruba History in W. Abimbola (ed.) *Yoruba Oral Tradition*. Ibadan: I.U.P.

________. 1976 *Western Yorubaland under European Rule, 1889-1945*. London: Longman.

________. 1979 The Aja-speaking Peoples of Nigeria: a Note on their Origins, Settlement and Cultural Adaptation up to 1945. *Africa*, Vol. 29: 15-28.

Atanda, J. A. 1973a *The New Ọ̀yọ́ Empire*. London: Longman.

________. 1973b Government of Yorubaland in the Pre-Colonial Period, *Tarikh*, Vol. 4, No. 2.

________. 1979 The History of Ọ̀yọ́ Empire, *Gangan, A Magazine of Ọ̀yọ́ State of Nigeria*, Issue No. 8, October.

Awe, B. 1967 Ibadan, Its Early Beginners in P.C. Lloyd A.L. Mabogunje and B. Awe (eds.) *The City of Ibadan.* Cambridge: C.U.P.

________. 1975 Notes on Oriki and Warfare in Yorubaland in W. Abimbola (ed.), *Yoruba Oral Tradition*. Ibadan: I.U.P.

________. 1977 The Iyalode in the Traditional Political System in A. Schegel (ed.) *Sexual Stratification : A Cross-Cultural View.* New York: Columbia University Press.

________. 1979 The Yoruba Woman in Traditional Society. *Gangan: A Magazine of Ọ̀yọ̀ State of Nigeria*. Ibadan: The Sketch Publishing Co.

Awolalu, J. O.
1970a The Yoruba Philosophy of Life, *Presence Africaine*, 73 (1).

________. 1970b The African View of Man, *Orita. Ibadan University Journal of Religious Studies*, Vol. IV, 11 June, pp. 101-7.

________. 1973 Yoruba Sacrificial Practice. *Journal of Religion in Africa*, V, 2:81-93.

________. 1979 *Yoruba Sacrifices and Sacrificial Rites.* London: Longman.

Awoniyi, T. A.
1975 Omoluwabi: The Fundamental Basis of Yoruba Education in W. Abimbola (ed.), *Yoruba Oral Tradition.* Ibadan: I.U.P.

Babalola, S. A. 1966 *The Content and Form of Ijala.* Oxford: Clarendon Press.

________. 1975 The Delights of Ijala in W. Abimbola (ed.) *Yoruba Oral Tradition.* Ibadan: I.U.P.

Babatunde, E.
1989 Urban Marginality's Perception of Self: Preliminary Note on Ilubinrin Apeja (Lagos) and 35-57th Street, Southside Chicago, in Asiwaju, A.I. and Adeniyi, P.O. (eds.) *Borderlands In Africa: A Multi Disciplinary Comparative Focus on Nigeria and West Africa.* Lagos: University of Lagos Press.

________. 1988 Nigerian Social Problems and Evangelization, *Shalom*, Vol. VI. No. 3.

________. 1983 Kinship Behavior and Patrilineal Ideology: A case study of the Ketu Yoruba, *Journal of Business and Social Studies*, New Series, Vol. 6, No. 1.

________. 1984 Methodologies in Comparative Education: In Search of an Appropriate Model for Developing Countries, *Ilorin Journal of Education*, Vol. 4.

________. 1985 An African Concept of Penance, *Shalom*, Fol. 3.

________. 1986 The Missionary, the Yoruba and the Baconian Idols: The problems of Education for Evangelisation, *INSIGHT, Journal of World Faiths*, New Series, Vol. 13.

________. 1988a The Gẹ̀lẹ̀dẹ́ Masked Dance and Ketu Society: The Role of the Transvestite Masquerade in Placating Powerful Women while Maintaining the Patrilineal Ideology, in S. Kasfir (ed.) *West African Masks and Cultural Systems*. Tervuran: Musee Rajal De L'Afrique Central.

________. 1988b AFRICAN Culture: A Definition? in the *Nigerian Journal of Theology*, Vol. 1, No. 3, Dec. 1986.

________. 1988c Religion and the problem of Order in *Introduction to Sociology* in O. Olusanya and L. Olurode (eds.) Ikeja: John West Publication.

________. 1991 The Status of Women in Ketu Myths and Its Sociological Ramifications, *Journal of Women and Gender Studies*, No. 2, pp. 45-63.

Babatunde, E. D. and Ninalowo B.
1988 Social Justice: A Factor of Effective Mobilization for Self-Reliance and Democratic Culture in *Lectures on Mobilization for Social Justice for 1988/89*, Lagos: Toklast Enterprises.

Babayemi, S. O.
1979 The Fall and Rise of Ọ̀yọ́ Empire, 1760-1905: A Study in the Traditional Culture of an African Polity (Unpub. Ph.D. thesis, University of Birmingham).

Bacon, R. H. 1897 *Benin: The City of Blood*. London: Edward Arnold and Co.

Bamgbose, A. 1966 *A Grammar of Yoruba*. London: C.U.P.

________. 1968 The Form of Yoruba Proverbs, *ODU*, Vol. 4, No. 2.

________. 1971 The Meaning of Olódùmarè: an Etymology of the Name of the Yoruba High God, *African Notes*, VII, 1, pp. 25-52.

Bascom, W. 1942 The Principle of Seniority in the Social Structure of the Yoruba, *Am. Anthr.* 44.

________. 1943 The Relationship of Yoruba Folklore to Divining, *Journal of American Folklore*, LVI, 220, pp. 127-31.

________. 1944 The Sociological Role of the Yoruba Cultgroup, *A.N.A.*, Memoir, No. 63.

________. 1951a Social Status, Wealth and Individual Differences among the Yoruba, *Am. Anthr.*, 53, pp. 490-505.

________. 1951b Yoruba Cooking, *Africa*, Vol. XXI, pp. 125-37.

________. 1951c Yoruba Food, *Africa*, Vol. XXI, pp. 41-53.

________. 1952 The Esusu: A Credit Institution of the Yoruba, *J. Royal Anthr. Inst.*, LXXXII, 1, . 65-9.

________. 1953a Yoruba Acculturation in Buba, Mem. 1 (Inst. Francais d'Afrique Noire, 27, Ifan-Dakar).

________. 1953b African Culture and the Missionary, *Civilisations* Bruxelles, iii, 4.

________. 1955 Organization among the Yoruba, *Am. J. Sociology*, LX, 5.

________. 1956 Yoruba Concepts of the Soul. *Fifth International Congress of Anthropology and Ethnographical Sciences*, Philadelphia. pp. 1-9.

________. 1960 Yoruba Concepts of the Soul in A.F.C. Wallace (ed.), *Selected Papers of the Fifth International Congress of Anthropological and Ethnological Sciences*. Philadelphia: University of Pennsylvania Press.

________. 1969a *The Yoruba of South-Western Nigeria*. New York: Holt Rinehart and Winston.

________. 1969b *Ifá Divination. Communication Between Gods and Men in West Africa*. Bloomington: University of Indiana Press.

________. 1969c The Early Historical Evidence of Yoruba Urbanism. *Social Change and Economic Development in Nigeria* (Ukandi G. Damachi and Hans Dieter Sebel, eds.). New York: Praeger Publications, pp. 11-39.

Bassir, O. 1954 Marriage Rites among the Aku (Yoruba) of Freetown, *Africa*, Vol. XXIV, pp. 251-5.

Bauman, R. 1970 A Review of W. Bascom: *Ifá Divination: Communication between Gods and Men in West Africa* in *R.A.L.*, Vol. 1, No. 2.

Beattie, J. H. M.
1951 Checks on the Abuse of Political Power: A Comparative Study of the Social Factors Acting in Restraint of the Abuse of Such Power by Indigenous Political Authorities in Certain Natives Societies of Africa (Unpub. B. Litt. thesis).

________. 1959 Rituals of Nyoro Kinship, *Africa*, Vol. XXIX, No. 2.

________. 1966a *Other Cultures*. London: Routledge & Kegan Paul

________. 1966b Ritual and Social Change (The Malinowski Memorial Lectures, 1965), *Man* (n.s.) 1(I) pp. 60-74.

Beier, H. U. 1955a The Position of Yoruba Women, *Presence Africaine*, n.s. 1-2, pp. 3946.

________. 1955b The Historical and Psychological Significance of Yoruba Myths, *Odù*, 1, pp. 17-25.

________. 1955c Before Oduduwa, *Odù*, no. 3.

________. 1958a The Egúngún Cult Among the Yoruba, *Presence Africaine*, n.s. 17-18, pp. 33-6.

________. 1958b Gẹ̀lẹ̀dẹ́ Masks, *Odù*, VI, pp. 5-23.

________. 1960 Obatala: Five Myths about the Yoruba Creator God, *Black Orpheus*, 7, pp. 34-5.

Ben-Amos, P.
1973 Symbolism in Olókun Mud Art, *African Arts*, Vol. VI, no. 4, pp. 28- 31, 95.

________. 1976 Men and Animals in Benin Art, *Man* (n.s.) II, pp. 243-52.

________. 1980 *The Art of Benin*. London: Thames and Hudson.

Biobaku, S. O.

________ 1955a *Origins of the Yoruba*. Lagos: Federal Information Service Press.

________. and Beier, H. U.
1955b The Use and INterpretation of Myths, *Odù*, I pp. 12-25.

________. 1957 *The Ègbà and Their Neighbours, 1842-1872*. Oxford: Clarendon Press.

________. 1958 An Historical Sketch of Ègbà Traditional Authorities. *Africa*, XXII, 1, pp. 35-49.

Blair, A. H. 1940 Intelligence Report on Meko, Ilaro. *W. Reg. S.F.*

Bohannan, L. 1952 A Genealogical Charter, *Africa*, XXII, 4, pp. 300-15.

Boston, J. S. 1968 *The Igala Kingdom*. Ibadan: Ibadan University Press.

________. 1977 *Ikenga Figures Among the North-West Igbo and the Igala*. London: Ethnographica Ltd.

Bradbury, R. E.
1957 *The Benin Kingdom and the Edo Speaking Peoples of South-Western Nigeria*. London: O.U.P./I.A.I.

________. 1964 The Historical Uses of Comparative Ethnography with Special Reference to Benin and the Yoruba in J. Vansina, *et. al the Historian in Tropical Africa*. London: O.U.P./I.A.I.

Bradbury, R. E.
1965 Father and Senior Son in Edo Mortuary Ritual in M. Fortes and G. Deiterlen (eds.) *African Systems of Thought*. London: O.U.P.

________. 1967 The Kingdom of Benin in D. Forde and P.M. Kaberry (eds.), *West African Kindgoms in the Nineteenth Century*. London: O.U.P./I.A.I.

________. 1973 *Benin Studies*. London: O.U.P./I.A.I.

Buckley, A. D.
1976 The Secret: An Idea in Yoruba Medicinal Thought in London, J.B. (ed.) *Social Anthro-pology and Medicine*. London: Academic Press.

Burton, R. F. 1863 *Abeokuta and the Cameroons Mountains*. London: Tinsley Brothers.

Butcher Report. *Report of the Committee of Inquiry into the Allegations of Misconduct made against Chieft Salami Agbaje, the Otun Balogun of Ibadan, and Allegations of Inefficiency and Maladministration on the Part of the Ibadan and District Native Authority*. Lagos: Government Printer.

Butt-Thompson, F. W.
1929 *West African Secret Societies*. London: H.F. & G. Whetherby.

Callaway, H. 1978 The Most Essentially Female Function of All: Giving Birth in S. Ardener, *Defining Females*. London: Croom Helm.

________. 1980 Spatial Domains and Women's Mobility in Yorubaland, Nigeria in S. Ardener (ed.) *Women and Space*. London: Croom Helm.

Clark, J. P. 1978 *The Hero as a Villian*. University of Lagos Inaugural Lecture Series, Lagos. University of Lagos Press.

Carroll, K. F. 1956 Yoruba Religious Music, *African Music*, 1, 3, pp. 45-7.

________. 1967 *Yoruba Religious Carving*. London: Geoffrey Chapman.

Clapperton, H.
1829 *Journal of a Second Expedition into the Interior of Africa from the Bight of Benin to Soccatoo*. Philadelphia: Carey, Lea and Carey.

Comhaire-Sulvain, S.
1949 The Status of Women in Lagos, Nigeria, *Pi Lamba Theta Journal*. XXVII, 3, pp. 158-63.

Connah, G. 1965 *The Archaeology of Benin*. Oxford: Clarendon Press.

Cordwell, J. W.
1952 Some Aesthetic Aspects of Yoruba and Benin Cultures (Unpub. Ph.D. thesis, Northwestern University, Evanston, I11).

Courlander, H.
1973 *Tales of Yoruba Gods and Heroes*. Conn.: Fawcett Publications.

Crowther, A. S.
1852 *A Grammar and Vocabulary of the Yoruba Language*. London: Seeleys.

Daramola, O. and Jeje (eds.)
1968 *Awon Asa Ali Orisa Ile Yoruba*. Ibadan: Onibon-Oje.

Dieterlen, G. and Fortes, M. (eds.)
1965 *African Systems of Thought*. London: O.U.P.

Dinesen, I. 1942 *Winter's Tales*. London: Putnam.

Douglas, M. 1966 *Purity and Danger*. London: Routledge & Kegan Paul.

Drewal, H. J. 1974a Efe: Voiced Power and Pagenantry, *African Arts* (2), pp. 26-9, 58-66. 82-3.

________. 1974b Gẹ̀lẹ̀dẹ́ Imagery in D. Fraser (ed.), *African Arts as Philosophy*. New York: Interbook.

________. 1974c Gẹ̀lẹ̀dẹ́ Masquerade: Imagery and Motif, *African Arts* 7(4): pp. 8-19, 62-3, 95-6.

________. 1974d Iyanla: Mask for the Mothers of Western Yorubaland, *Paper Presented at 3rd Triennial Symposium on African Art*.

Durkheim, E.
1947 *The Elementary Forms of the Religious Life*. Glencoe: The Free Press.

________. *The Division of Labor in Society*. Transl. G. Simpson - New York: Free Press.

Eades, J. S. 1980 *The Yoruba Today*. Cambridge: C.U.P.

Egharevba, J. U. 1934 *A Short History of Benin*. Ibadan: Ibadan University Press.

________. 1947 *The Benin Laws and Customs*. Lagos: The Service Press Limited.

________. 1950 *Some Stories of Ancient Benin*. Benin City: Kopin-Dogba Press.

________. 1956 *Bini Titles*. Benin City: Kopin-Dogba Press.

________. 1962 *Marriage of the Princesses of Benin*. Benin: Kopin-Dogha Press.

Eighmy, I. H. 1968 *Problems of Census Interpretation in Developing Countries: The Western Nigeria Case*. Lund: C.W.K. Gleemp Publishers.

Ekeh, P. 1975 Colonialism and the Two Publics in Africa: A Theoretical Statement, in *Comparative Studies in Society and History*, Vol. 17, pp. 91-112.

Ellis, A. B. 1894 *The Yoruba-Speaking Peoples of the Slave Coast of West Africa*. London: Chapman & Hall.

Eisenstadt, S. N.
1954 African Age-Groups: A Comparative Study, *Africa*, XXIV, 2, pp. 100- 4.

Evans-Pritchard and Fortes, (eds.)
1940a Special Character of Bride-Wealth with Special Reference to the Azande. *Man*, XXXIV, 194, p. 172.

________. 1940b *African Political Systems*. London: O.U.P.

Evans-Pritchard, E. E.
1940 *The Nuer*. Oxford: Clarendon Press.

________. 1945 Some Aspects of Marriage and the Family Among the Nuer, *Rhodes- Livingstone Paper*, II.

________. 1965 *The Position of Women in Primitive Societies and Other Essays in Social Anthropology*. London: Faber and Faber.

________. 1969 Zande Notions about Death, Soul and Ghost, *S.N.R.*

________. 1970 A Note of Some Zande Physiological Notions, S.N.R., LI, pp. 162-5.

________. 1974 *Man and Woman Among the Azande*. London: Faber and Faber.

Fadipe, N. A. 1970 *The Sociology of the Yoruba*. Ibadan: U.I.P.

Fagg, B. E. B. 1959 The Nok Culture in Prehistory, *J.H.S.N.*, Vol. 1, No. 4.

________. 1965 Carbon Dates for Nigeria, *Man*, LXV, No. 8.

Fajana, A. 1966 Some Aspects of Yoruba Traditional Education, *Odù*, 3, pp. 16-26.

Faniyi, D. 1975 Ekun Iyawo: A Traditional Yoruba Nuptial Chant in W. Abimbola (ed.) *Yoruba Oral Tradition*. Ibadan: I.U.P.

Farrow, S. S. 1926 *Faith, Fancies and Fetich*. London: Society for Promoting Christian Knowledge.

Ferguson, J. 1970 *The Yorubas of Nigeria*. Bletchley: Open University Press.

Fieldhouse, D. K.
1986 *Black African 1945-80: Economic Decolonization and Arrested Development*. London: Allen D. Unwin.

Finnegan, R. 1977 *Aspects of African Religion*. Milton Keynes: Open University Press.

________. (ed.)
1978 *Oral Poetry*. Thetford: Lowe and Brydone Printers Ltd.

Folayan, K. 1967 Egbado up to 1832: The Birth of a Dilemma. *J.H.N.S.*, IV, No. 1.

Forde, D. 1951 *The Yoruba-Speaking Peoples of South-Western Nigeria. Ethnographic Survey*. London: I.A.I.

________. 1967 *West African Kingdoms in the Nineteenth Century*. London: O.U.P./I.A.I.

Fortes, M. 1959 *Odeipus and Job in West African Religion*. Cambridge: C.U.P.

________. (ed.)
1962a *Marriage in Tribal Soceities* (C.P. Soc. A.) Cambridge: C.U.P.

________. 1962b Ritual and Office in Tribal Society in M. Gluckman (ed.), *Essays on the Rituals of Social Relations*.

________. 1965 Some Reflections on Ancestor Worship in Africa in Fortes, M. and Dieterlen, G. (eds.), *African Systems of Thought*. London: O.U.P.

________. 1976 Introduction' to W. Newell (ed.), *Ancestors*. The Hague: Mouton.

Fox, R. 1967 *Kinship and Marriage*. Harmondsworth: C. Nicholls & Co. Ltd.

Freud, S. 1933 *New Introductory Lectures on Psycho-analysis*. New York: W.W. Norton.

________. 1938 Three Contributions to the Theory of Sex, *The Basic Writings of Sigmund Freud*. New York: The Modern Library.

________. 1949 *An Outline of Psychoanalysis*. New York: W.W. Norton and Co.

________. 1950 *Some Psychological Consequences of the Anatomical Distinction Between the Sexes. Collected Papers*. London: Hogarth Press.

________. 1952 *An Autobiographical Study*. New York: W.W. Norton and Co.

Freund, B. 1978 Oil Boom and Crisis in Contemporary Nigeria, *Review of Political Economy*. 13th May - August 1978.

Frobenius, L. 1913 *The Voice of Africa* (trans. R. Blind). London: Hutchinson & Co.

Garigue, P. 1954 Changing Political Leadership in West Africa, *Africa*, XXIV, 3, pp. 220-32.

Gbadamosi, B. and Beier, U.
1959 *Yoruba Poetry*. Ibadan: Nigerian Printing and Publishing Co.

Gluckman, M.
1950 Kinship and Marriage among the Lozi of Northern Rhodesia and the Zulu of Natal in *African Systems of Kinship and Marriage*.

________. 1955 *Custom and Conflict in Africa*. Oxford: Basil Blackwell.

Goody, E. N. 1962 Conjugal Separation and Divorce among the Gonja of Northern Ghana in Fortes, M. (ed.) *Marriage in Tribal Societies*. Cambridge: C.U.P.

Goody, J. 1956 Comparative Approach to Incest and Adultery, *British Journal of Sociology*, VII, 4.

________. 1965 *Death, Property and the Ancestors*. London: Tavistock Publications.

________. 1961 The Classification of Double Descent, *Current Anthropology*, ii, 1, pp. 3-25.

Griaule, M. 1960 The Idea of Person among the Dogon in Simon and Phoebe Ottenberg (eds.), *Cultures and Societies of Africa*. New York: Random House Inc.

Gutkind, P. C. W. and I. Wallerstein (eds.)
1976 *The Political Economy of Contemporary Africa*, London: Sage Publications.

Hamlyn, P. 1960 *Benin Art*. London: Batchworth Press Ltd.

Harper, P. 1970a The Role of Dance in the Gèlèdé Ceremonies of the Village of Ijio, *Odù*, n.s. 4, pp. 67-94.

________. 1970b A Festival of Nigerian Dances, *African Arts*, Vol. III, pp. 48-53.

Harrell-Bond, B. E.
1972 *Some Factors Influencing Attitudes towards Family Limitation and the Use of Contraceptives among the Professional Group in Sierra Leone.* Leiden: Afrika-Studiecentrum.

Harris, J. S.
1940 The Position of Women in Nigerian Society. *Trans. of New York Adademy of Sciences*, 2, 5.

Harris, G. 1962 Taita Bridewealth and Affinal Relationships in M. Fortes (ed.) *Marriage in Tribal Societies* Cambridge: C.U.P.

Hertz, R. 1910 *Death and the Right Hand* (trans. R. Needham). London: Cohen and West.

Hoch-Smith, J. and Spring, A. (eds.)
1978 *Women in Ritual and Symbolic Roles*. Ncw York: Plenum Press.

Horton, R. 1961 Destiny and the Unconscious in West Africa. *Africa*, Vol. XXXI, no. 2.

________. 1962a The Kalabari World-View: An Outline and Interpretation, *Africa*, XXXII, no. 3.

________. 1962b The High God: A Comment on Fr. OConnells Paper, *Man*, LXII, pp. 137-40.

________. 1966 Conference of the High God in Africa, *Odù*, 2, 2, pp. 87-95.

Idowu, E. W. 1962 *Olódùmarè: God in Yoruba Belief.* London: Green.

Igbafe, P. A. 1970 Tradition and Change in Benin Marriage System, *N.J.E.S.S.*, XII, 1.

________. 1971 The Benin Trials of 1897 and 1899, *Odù*, n.s., no. 5, pp. 68-90.

________. 1979 *Benin Under British Administration*. London: Longman.

Ihonvbero, J. O.
The Oil Industry in Nigeria: An Annotated Bibliography. Montreal: Bibliography Series, Center for Developing Area Studies. McGill University.

Ijimere, O. 1966 *The Imprisonment of Obatala and Other Plays.* London: Heinemann.

Imoagene, S. O.
1969 Kinship and Marital Stability among the Weppa-Wano (Mid-western Nigeria), *J.B.S.S.*, 2, 1, pp. 42-52.

________. 1970 The Marriage System of the Wappa-Wano (Mid-western Nigeria), *A.S.Q.J.*, XXIX, no. 3.

Imokhai, C. 1979 The Missionization of Uzairue: A Study of Missionary Impact on Traditional Marriage (Unpubl. Ph.D. thesis, Columbia University).

Isichei, P.S. 1970 Marriage and Family in Traditional Asaba (Unpub. B. Litt. thesis).

________. 1973 Sex in Traditional Asoba, *Cahiers dEtudes Africaines*, Vol. XIII, 3.

Jahoda, G. 1959 Love, Marriage and Social Change: Letters to the Advice Column of a West African Newspaper, *Africa*, XXIX, no. 1.

James, W. 1978 Matrifocus on African Women in S. Ardener (ed.), Defining Females. London: Croom Helm.

Jeffreys, M. D. W.
1957 Palm-Wine Among the Ibibio, *Nigerian Field*, Vol. XXII, 1.

Johnson, S. 1921 *The History of the Yorubas from the Earliest Times to the Beginning of the British Protectorate.* Lagos: C.M.S. Bookshop.

Jones, R. W. 1946 Orisa-Oko, Yoruba Goddess of the Farm and Agriculture, *Nigeria*, 23, pp. 18-21.

Kalous, M. 1969 Some Hypotheses about the Art of Southern Nigeria, *Afrika und Ubersee*, Band, Lll. 2, March.

Karanja, W. 1980 Lagos Market Women (Unpub. D.Phil thesis, University of Oxford.

Kirk-Greene, A. H. M.
1974 *Mutumin Kirkii: The Concept of the Good Man in Hausa*. Bloomington: Indiana University African Studies Program.

Krapf-Askari, E.
1966a Brass Objects from the Owe Yoruba, Kabba Province, Northern Nigeria, *Odù*, 3, No. 1.

________. 1966b Time and Classifications, *Odù*, n.s. Vol. II, no. 2, pp. 3-18.

________. 1968 *Ogori*: *The Sociology of an Akoko Village*. Unpublished Doctor of Philosophy Thesis, Oxford University Institute of Social Anthropology.

________. 1969 *Yoruba Towns and Cities: An Enquiry into the Nature of Urban Social Phenomena*. Oxford: Clarendon Press.

LaFlesche, F. 1912 Osage Marriage Customs. Am. A., XIV, no. 1, pp. 127-30.

La Fontaine, J. S. (ed.)
1972 *The Interpretation of Ritual. Essays in Honour of A.I. Richards*. London: Tavistock Publications.

La Fontaine, J. S.
1972 The Ritualization of Womens Life Crises in Bugisu in La Fontaine (ed.) *The Interpretation of Ritual*.

Laitin, R. 1986 *Culture and Hegemony*. Chicago: C.U.P.

Lambo, A. T. (ed.)
1961 *First Pan-African Psychiatric Conference*. Abeokuta: Nigeria.

Laroche, C.
1968 Traditional African Religions in C G. Basta (ed.), *Christianity in Tropical Africa*. O.U.P.

Lasebikan, E. L.
1952 The Yoruba in Brazil, *West Africa*, 10 August, p. 843.

Law, R. C. C. 1973a Heritage of Oduduwa: Traditional History and Political Propaganda among the Yoruba, *J. of African History*, XIV, 2, pp. 207-22.

________. 1973b Anthropological Models in Yoruba History, *Africa*, vol. XLIII, no. 1, pp. 18-26.

________. 1977 *The Ọ̀yọ́ Empire*. Oxford: Clarendon Press.

Liell, O., Okedeji, G.. Trout and Vlaches, E.
1965 A Research Design for a Comparative Study of Urbanism and Fertility A Progress Report, *N.J.E.S.S.*, pp. 63-9.

Lienhardt, R. G.
1950 Review of *African Ideas of God: A Symposium* in E.W. Smith (ed.), *Man*, L, pp.164-5.

________. 1951 Some Notions of Witchcraft among the Dinka, *Africa*, Vol. XXI, pp. 303-18.

________. 1961 *Divinity and Experience. The Religion of the Dinka*. Oxford: Clarendon Press.

________. 1980 Self: Public, Private. Some African Representations, *J.A.S.O.*, Vol. XI, no. 2. pp. 69-82.

________. 1981 The Sudan - Aspects of the South: Government Among some of the Nilotic Peoples, 1947-52, *J A.S.O.*, Vol. XII, no. 3, pp. 185-98.

Little, K. 1970 *West African Urbanization: A Study of Voluntary Associations and Social Change*. Cambridge: C . U . P .

________. 1979 Women in African Literature, *West Africa*, nos. 3241-45.

Lloyd, B. B. Divorce Among the Yoruba, *Am. Anthr*, LXX, 1, 67-81.

Lloyd, P. C. 1953 Some Problems of Tenancy in Yorubaland Tenure, *African Studies*, XII, 3, pp. 93-103.

________. 1954 The Traditional Political System of the Yoruba, *South-Western Journal of Anthropology*, X, 4, pp. 366-84.

________. 1955a The Yoruba Lineage, *Africa*, XXV, 3, pp. 235-51.

________. 1955b Yoruba Myths - A Sociologists Inter-pretation *Odù*, 2, pp. 20-28.

________. 1959 Some Notes on Yoruba Rules of Succession and on Family Property, *Journal of African Law*, III, 1, pp. 7-32.

________. 1960 Sacred Kingship and Government among the Yoruba, *Africa*, III, 3, pp. 221-37.

________. 1962 *Yoruba Land Law* . London: O.U.P.

________. 1963 The Status of the Yoruba Wife, *Sudan Society*, II, pp. 35-42.

________. 1966 Agnatic and Cognatic Descent among the Yoruba, *Man*, I, 4, pp. 484- 500.

________. 1971 *The Political Development of Yoruba Kingdoms in the Eighteenth and Nineteenth Centuries*. London: R.A.I.

________. 1974 *Power and Independence: Urban Africans Perception of Social Mobility*. London: Routledge and Kegan Paul.

Lombard, J. 1967 The Kingdom of Dahomey in D. Forde and P. Kaberry (eds.) *West African Kingdoms in the Nineteenth Century*. London; O.U.P./I.A.I.

Lubeck, P. M. 1981/82 Islamic Networks and Urban Capitalism. *Cahiers d'Etudes Africans*. Vol. XXVI.

________. 1985 Islamic Protest Under Semi-Industrial Capitalism: Yan Tatsine Explained. *Africa*, 55(4).

Lucas, O. 1948 *The Religion of the Yorubas*. Lagos: C.M.S.

Mabogunje, A. 1958 The Yoruba Home, *Odù*, .5, pp. 28-35.

Macfie, J. W. S. 1913 A Yoruba Tattooer, *Man*, XIII.

Magubane, B. 1976 The Evolution of the Class Structure in Africa in P.C.W. Gutkind and I. Wallerstein (eds.) *The Political Economy of Contemporary Africa*. London: Sage Publications.

Mauss, M. 1954 *The Gift, Forms and Functions of Exchange in Archaic Societies* (transl. I. Cunninson). London: Cohen and West.

Mayer, P. 1950 Privileged Obstruction of Marriage Rites among the Gusii, *Africa*, XX, 2, pp. 113-25.

________. 1970 The Witches in Marwick, M. (ed.) *Witchcraft and Sorcery*. Harmondsworth: Penguin Books.

Mbiti, J. S. 1969 *African Religions and Philosophy*. London: Morrison and Gibb.

Melzian, H. 1937 *A Concise Dictionary of the Bini Language of Southern Nigeria*. London: Routledge & Kegan Paul.

Meyerowitz, E. L. R.
1944 Ibeji Statuettes from Yoruba Nigeria, *Man*, XLIV, pp. 105-7.

________. 1946 Notes on the King-God Shango and his Temple at Ibadan, Southern Nigeria, *Man*, XLVI, pp. 25-31.

Mill, J. S. 1879 *System of Logic: Ratioinactive and Inductive*, London, Longmans and Green and Co.

Molade, T. 1973 The Concept of Abeku, *African Arts*, VII, 1, pp. 62-4.

________. 1971 Ibeji Custom in Yorubaland, *African Arts*, IV, 3, pp. 14-15.

Momoh, C. S. (ed.)
The Substance of African Philosophy.

Moore, B. 1958 Strategy in Social Science in *Political Power and Social Theory*. Cambridge: Harvard University Press.

Morel, E. D. 1911 *Nigeria: Its Peoples and Its Problems*. London: Smith Elder and Co.

Morton-Williams, P.
1960a The Yoruba Ogbóni Cult in Ọ̀yọ́, *Africa*, XXX, 4, pp. 362-74.

________. 1960b The Yoruba Responses to the Fear of Death, Africa, XXX, pp. 34-40.

________. 1962 The Yoruba Kingdom of Oyoin Forde and Kaberry (eds.) *West African Kingdoms in the Nineteenth Century*. London: O.U.P.

________. 1964 Outline of the Cosmology and Cult Organisation of the Ọ̀yọ́ Yoruba, *Africa*, pp. 243-61.

Nadel, S .F. 1942 *A Black Byzantium*. London: O.U.P.

Newbury, C. 1961 *The Western Slave Coast and its Rulers*. London: O.U.P.

Newell, W. (ed.) *Ancestors*. Mouton: The Hague.

Niven.,C. R. 1937 *A Short History of Nigeria*. London: Longman.

Obayemi, H. A.
1976 The Yoruba and Edo-speaking Peoples and their Neighbours before 1600 in J.F.A. Ajayi and M. Crowder, (eds.), *History of West Africa*, I, (2nd ed.). London: Longman.

Odugbesan, C.
1966 Femininity of Yoruba Religious Art in Douglas and Kaberry (eds.) *Man in Africa*, London: Tavistock Publications.

Ogunmodede, E.
1979 Social Customs: Female Circumcision, *African Currents*, 14, (Spring edition), pp. 30-1.

Oguntuyi, A. Rev. Fr.
1970 *A Short History of Ado Ekiti*, Part II. Ibadan: Bisi Books Co.

Ojo, G. J. A. 1963 The Changing Patterns of Traditional Group Farming in Ekiti, North- eastern Yoruba Country, *N.G.J.*, Vol. VI, 1, pp. 31-8.

________. 1966 *Yoruba Culture*. London: University of Tfe and U.I.P.

Okedeji, O. and Okedeji, F.
1966 Mental Stability and Social Structure in an African City, *N.I.S.E.R.*, n.s., no. 27, pp. 151-63.

Okedeji, F. 1967 Some Social Psychological Aspects of Fertility Among Married Women in an African City, *N.J.E.S.S.*

________. 1970 Review: J.P. Peels *Aladura: A Religious Movement among the Yoruba*, *Am. Anthr.*, LXXII, 3, pp. 649-51.

Olabimtan, A.
1979 African "Juju": Myth or Reality, *Gangan, A Magazine of Ọ̀yọ́ State of Nigeria*, no. 8, pp.4-11.

Olajubu, O. and Ojo, J. R.
1977 Some Aspects of Yoruba Masquerades, *Africa*, XLVII, no. 3, pp. 253- 75.

Olaniyan, R. 1975 Elements of Yoruba Diplomacy in Oral Tradition in W. Abimbola (ed.) *Yoruba Oral Tradition*. Ibadan: I.U.P.

Olayemi, V. 1975 The Supernatural in the Yoruba Folktale in W. Abimbola (ed.) *Yoruba Oral Tradition*.

Olatunbosun, Oke, D.
1972 Language (Choice in the Yoruba-Edo Border Area, *Odù*, 3, No. 1.

Olumide, 1948 *Religion of the Yorubas*. Lagos: C.M.S.

Olusanya, P. O.
1967 The Educational Factor in Human Fertility: A Case Study of the Residents of a Suburban Area of Ibadan, *N.J.E.S.S.*, pp. 351-74.

Omo-Ananigie, P. I.
1946 *A Brief History of Etsakor*. Lagos: Ope-Ifá Press.

Osborne, O. H.
1968 The Egbado of Egbaland (Unpub. Diss., Michigan State University).

Parkinson, J. 1906 The Legend of Oro, *Man*, 6, pp. 103-5.

Parrinder, E. G.
1947 Yoruba-speaking Peoples in Dahomey, *Africa*, XVII, 1.

________. 1949 *West African Religion*. London: S.P.C.K.

________. 1956 *The Story of Ketu*. Ibadand: I.U.P.

Peel, J. D. Y. 1068 *Aladura. A Religious Movement among the Yoruba*. London: O.U.P./I.A.I.

________. 1978a The Christianization of African Society: Some Possible Models in R. Gray et. al. *Christianity in Independent Africa*. London: Rex Collings.

________. 1978b Olaju: A Yoruba Concept of Development, *J.D.S.*, Vol. XIV, no. 2, pp. 39-165.

Perham, M. 1937 *Native Administration in Nigeria*. London: O.U.P.

Peristiany, J. G. (ed.)
1965 *Honour and Shame: The Values of Mediterranean Society*. London: Weidenfeld and Nicolson.

Popper, K. 1960 *The Poverty of Historicism*. London: Routledge and Kegan Paul.

Population Census of the Western Region of Nigeria 1952.
1953 Bulletins 1-8. The Gavernment Statisti-cian, Lagos.

Quinn, N. 1977 Anthropological Studies on Womens Status in J. Siegel *et. al.*, Annual Review of Anthropology, pp. 181-225.

Richards, A. I.
1956 *Chisungu: A Girls Initiation Ceremony Among the Bemba of Northern Rhodesia*. London: Faber and Faber.

Rodney, W. 1972 *How Europe Underdeveloped Africa*, London: Bogle - l'Ouventure.

Rogers, S. C. 1975 Female Forms of Power and the Myth of Male Dominence, *Am. Ethnologist*, II, pp. 727-50.

Ryder, A. F. C.
1961 The Benin Missions, *J.H.S.N.*, Vol. II, no. 2.

________. 1965 A Re-consideration of the Ife-Benin Relationship, *J.A.H.* Vol. VI, no. 1.

________. 1967 The Rise of the Benin Kingdom in R. Oliver (ed.), *The Middle Age of African History*. Oxford: Clarendon Press.

________. 1969 *Benin and the Europeans 1485-1897*. York: Humanities Press.

Sarpong, P. K.
1970 Traditional Beliefs, *Insight*, Vol. V, no. 3.

________. 1971 A Theology of Ancestors, *Insight*, Vol. VI, no. 2.

________. 1977 *Girls Nubility Rites in Ashanti*. Accra/Tema: Ghana Publ. Corp.

Schwab, W. B.
1955a Kinship and Lineage among the Yoruba, *Africa*, XXV, 4, pp. 352-74.

________. 1955b Continuity and Change in the Yoruba Lineage System, *Annals of the New York Academy of Sciences*, XCVI, pp. 590-605.

________. 1958 The Terminology of Kingship and Marriage among the Yoruba, *Africa*, XXVIII, 4, pp. 301-13.

Simpson, M. 1937 An Intelligence Report on the Ọ̀yọ́ Division of the Ọ̀yọ́ Province, Mss. Afr. S.526, Rhodes House.

Siroto, L. 1967 The Twins of Yorubaland (in scripture). *Bulletin of the Field Museum of Natural History* (Chicago), XXXVIII, 7, pp. 4-8.

Smith, R. 1969a *Kingdoms of the Yoruba*. Norwich: Methuen & Co.

________. 1969b To the Palaver Islands: War and Diplomacy on the Lagos Lagoon in 1854-1952, *J.H.S.N.* Vol. V, no. 1.

Sofola, J. A. 1970 Whats in a Name? ... The Sociological Uses of Names and Naming Among the Yoruba and the Ibo Ethnic Groups of Nigeria. Ibadan XXVIII, pp. 43-8.

Soyinka, W. 1976 *Myth, Literature and the African World.* Cambridge: C.U.P.

Sudarkasa, N. 1973 *Where Women Work: A Study of Yoruba Women in the Market Place and in the Home.* Ann Arbor: University of Michigan.

Swanston, H. 1981 Luther and the Structures of Catholicism, *Paper Presented at the 1981 Annual Meeting of the Association of Social Anthropologists.*

Talbot, P. A. 1926 *The Peoples of Southern Nigeria.* London: O.U.P.

________. 1927 *Nigerian Fertility Cults.* London: O.U.P.

The Olive Club, 1979 The Origin of the Benin Monarchy: Myths and Truths, *Royalty Magazine, A Pictorial Souvenir,* Printed on the coronation ceremony of Uku Akpolokpolo Omo n Oba N Edo Oba Eredianwa of Benin.

Thomas, N. W. 1910 The Edo-Speaking Peoples of Nigeria, *J.A.S.*, Vol. X, no. xxxvii, pp. 1-15.

Thompson, R. F. 1970 The Sign of the Divine King ... an Essay on Yoruba Bead-Embroidered Crowns, with Veil or Bird Decorations, *African Arts*, III, 3, pp. 74-9.

________. 1971 Sons of Thunder: Twin Images among the Ọ̀yó and other Yoruba Groups, *African Arts*, IV, 3, pp. 8-13, 77-80.

Turner, V. 1962 Three Symbols of Passage in Ndembu Circumcision Ritual: An Interpretation in *Essays on the Ritual of Social Relations.*

________. 1967 *The Forest of Symbols: Aspects of Ndembu Ritual.* Ithaca: Cornell University Press.

Uchendu, V. 1965 *The Igbo of South-east Nigeria.* New York: Holt, Rinehart and Winston.

van Gennep, A.
1960 *The Rites of Passage*. London: Routledge and Kegan Paul.

Verger, P. 1976 The Yoruba High God: A Review of Sources, *Odù*, 2, 2, pp. 19-40.

Wallerstein, I.
1976 The Three Stages of African Involvement in the World - Economy, P.C.W. Gutkind and I. Wallerstein (eds.) *The Political Economy of Contemporary Africa*. London: Sage Publications.

Ward, E. 1938 *The Yoruba Husband-Wife Code*. Baltimore: Watkins Printing Co.

Ward, I. C. 1952 *Introduction to the Yoruba Language*. Heffer.

Westcott, R. W.
1957 Did the Yoruba Come from Egypt?, *Odù*, 4, pp. 10-15.

Willett, F. 1959 Bronze Figures of Ita Yemoo, Ife, Nigeria, *Man*, LIX, no. 308.

________. 1966 On the Funeral Effigies of Owo and Benin and the Interpretation of the Life-size Bronze Heads from Ife, *Man*, n.s. 1.

________. 1973 The Benin Museum Collection, *African Art*, Vol. VI, no. 4, pp. 8-17, 94.

Welldon, J. C. E.
1892 *The Nicomachean Ethics of Aristotle, with An Analysis and Critical Notes*. London Macmillan.

APPENDIX

Vernacular rendering of verses in Chapter Two

Vernacular to verse of *Iwori Meji*

Vernacular Text 1

Ọ̀rọ̀ kì í gba àárọ̀
Ki a fi alẹ́ so ọ́
A dífá fun òkòkóyẹ̀lẹ̀
Tí, yóò bá ni tún ile yí wò.
Kini yóò bá ni tún ilè yi se?
Òkòkóniyẹ̀lẹ̀,
Ifa yóò ba ni tún Ílè yí se
Nigbàti àwon eniyan ko de'le aiyẹ́
Won o ri ibi gbé
Nitori ogédé omi ni ilé aye,
Ni òrumìlà ba lo si ọdọ Olódùmarè
Olódùmarè wa fun Ọ̀rúnmìlà ni ẹiyẹle mẹrin ati àkùkọ kan
Awọn ni wọn tan erùpẹ̀ inu karahun ìgbín
Ti Olódùmarè fiṣọ ile kalẹ̀ lati ọrun wa
Titi ofi di tigbotiju bayii
Ìwòrì Mejì ni wọ́n si da fun wọ́n ni ọjọ naa
Oun *na* ni adiẹ ma fi'wi tioba ntanlẹ̀ di oni oloni pe:
"Iwori yẹ̀lẹ̀
Iwori yẹ̀lẹ̀yẹ̀lẹ̀"

Vernacular of interview with Asipa Oguntegbe:

Vernacular Text 2

Òrun dara sugbon ki enia fi gbogbo ara duro lojukanna ribiti kodara
Ki eniyan wa larin awon tire lo daraju
Nitorina ni Edùmàrè sẹ fase sii pe ki
Apa ara ẹni ki ole lọsọrun bọ,
Ṣe bi idi rẹ ti wọ́n fi npe yin ni Babatunde niyen.

Vernacular to verse of Ejiogbe:

Vernacular Text 3

Oyinikange,
A dífá fún Òrúnmìlà
Ni ọjọ ti Ifa nlo reefọta ogbó Kan'ri
Ni ọjọ ti Òrúnmìlà nlọ ree ba'ku mu'lẹ̀
Pe kiku o ma báà á pa òun ni Kekere
O lo rè é ba Ọ̀yìnkánge pe kini òun yio se
Ọ̀yìnkánge ni ki o tọ́jú
Ògbógbo orọ́se, òrí,ọṣẹ,
Ki óbu èrùpẹ̀, idu igba òké,
Ki osì tọju gbọngbọn irin,
Ki ofi rúbọ fun íkú
Ogbo Oruu pẹlu ọta inu omi
Òrúnmìlà ni njẹ:
Mo d'ogbogbo orόse
Ng o ku mọ
Mo digba òkè
Mo le gboin
Gbogbo nkan ni ng o mọ̀
Gbogbo nkan ti òrun ati taye ni ng ori
Ng o sì máa pa ẹnu mi mọ
Furu ni mo dakẹ
Mo rìnrìn rìn ng o sọnu
Wọn ni ki wọn o wa ibi wa
Oju mi o ri r'ibi
Òrúnmìlà nlọ lọna
Afẹ́fẹ́ nka aṣọ alaṣọ
Ẹ̀fufu lile nka ẹ̀wù

Vernacular Text 4

Ọmọ ọwọ́ kii ku lọ́jú ọwọ́
Ọmọ ẹsẹ̀ kii ku lójú esẹ̀
Bi ina baku afi eeru boju
Bi Ọ̀gẹ̀dẹ̀ baku áfọmọ ẹ̀ rọ́po
Bi aladin ko si nile ọmọ ni jogun rẹ
Ọmọ ni yio jogún ẹwa lọdọ wa.

Vernacular to verse of *Iyeku Meji*:

Vernacular Text 5

Ẹṣín já ẹṣin a relé olóyè
Jẹbutu awo sọnù awo a re Ìjero
Ìpagbópàdàn ni afii nsawo
A difa fun erinlọjọ ero Apa
Ti nrele Alapa Rawe
Wọ́n ni ẹbọ ẹlẹ́hìntẹ́hìnṣe ni Kiwọ́n ọse
Se bi ẹṣín bájá
Ẹṣin a firù saiye lọ
Òmo eni awọn ina lẹhin ẹni
Ewe na wa di ewe ẹlẹhin fẹhin rere filẹ lọ
Omo eni na lehin ẹni
Nitori b'ẹṣin já a rele oloye
Jẹbuti awo son awo a roke Ijero
Ipagbópàdàan ni afi nsawo
A difa fun enilọjọ ero Apa
Ti nrele Alapa ni Rawe
Wọn ni kiwọn orubọ
Egberindinlogun owo
Iru ẹṣin kan
Ewe Ẹyinlopẹ, ẹyẹlẹ́ merindinlogun ati ikòkò oogun kan.
Kiwon ole bi ọmọ ni ọ̀pọ̀lọpọ̀ ti yio tehin won se
Won gbọ wọn ru
Won si bi ọ̀pọ̀lọpọ̀ ọmọ
Awon ọmọ na sjẹ eniya nlanla
Okan ninu won ni Ògún
Won wa nsope aṣe
Bi ẹṣin bá já
A fi iru saiye lọ
Aṣe ọmọ ẹni ni aifi sẹyin bi iru

Vernacular rendering of verses in Chapter Three

Vernacular Text 6 (pg. 58)

Hunter's salute to the baboon

1 Olojuaride ti i-r' obìnrin ará oko...
Kà-nkà-ka-nkà lori ìgbá, baba ìjímèrè
Bòòkìní ori òkè, er-tewa npa bi oti
Ladoogi ab enubọọbobọọ
Abìpọnlẹnu, abìtìkùninlaya
Os 'ojuliorohòroje' Ko anare
Irinwo l'alo
Egbẹ̀gfà l'abawọ̀gbẹ
O so se
l'oko àná òún ni
Bi bẹ́ẹ̀ ko, òún ì ba je igba síì
Eniti lya rẹ wò, wò, wò, t'o bu sẹkun
O'léwà nio p'ọmọ òún
Abìdíreterete
Elekana iṣo afẹju toto weniyan
Ọlọmunmasunmawo, abiyamọ, tinro 'gi nigbakungba

Song: Oba-n-tu, lalaoko, mo b'obolegan, ti njeun

Chorus: Gudugba onjeun

Praise Song of Orish-nla

Vernacular Text 7 (pg. 60)

2 Òrìshà-nlá a da'mu doju
Ada baba loju ada omo ẹ lẹnu
Odamọ daya
Oyibiri piwada
Ataiye ro bí ọkọ̀
Iwọ l'ọba, iwọ looṣa

Vernacular Text 8 (Pg. 69)

Hunter's salute to Ògún

3 Ki a wa re le Ògún mi
Onija, o le o
Ejemu Oluilu Iworan
A-di-giri-giri-re 'bi-ja
Labalaba kan mi eta o fo rákinrákin
Ògún má ba mija
Ma ba m'sire
Ẹgbẹ ni o ṣe fun mi
O ni o mob 'ọmọde ṣire
Mo r'ẹjẹ l'oju-itò ọmọbìrín yẹ̀lẹ̀yẹ̀lẹ̀
Ògún má ba mi jà
Ma ba m'sire
O mb'ẹyẹle ṣire
Nwon fa a lọrun tu
Ògún ma ba mija
Ma ba m'ṣire
Omb' akọjá ṣire
Nwon bẹ akọja ni ọrì
Ògún ma bamija
Ma ba m'ṣire

Vernacular Text 9 (Pg. 74)

Song in praise of Òrúnmìlà – Ogunde

Abisere
Asanmenmen
Asawosawo-kun-ikaa-meindinlogun
Won sagede f'Òrúnmìlà
L'Ọjọ ti Baba n t'ikoleorun bo nikole aye
Òrúnmìlà de, o de sita àjẹ́
Awon àjẹ́ l'orita awon niyii
Won l'Òrúnmìlà kilofẹṣe
Òrúnmìlà l'oun fẹ l'owo
Òrúnmìlà l'oun fẹ laya
Òrúnmìlà l'oun fẹ bimo
Won n'irọ lo pa, eke lo ṣe
Òrúnmìlà loju yin ni yio ṣe

L'oju onile l'alantakun ntale
Oju Onigbo l'alantakun nta 'gbo
A kii m'ohun t'olukoyin fii ṣafara
A kii m'ohun t'oore fii se ipe rẹ
B'Ọjọ ba yọ gbogbo aye l'aṣẹ rẹ imu
Ogunda ni ki ẹ d'ajé bo mi pitipiti.

INDEX

G

H

I

P

R